WOMEN IN GRAY

~ THE LOCHLAINN SEABROOK COLLECTION ~

Everything You Were Taught About the Civil War is Wrong, Ask a Southerner!
Everything You Were Taught About American Slavery is Wrong, Ask a Southerner!
Confederate Flag Facts: What Every American Should Know About Dixie's Southern Cross
Give This Book to a Yankee! A Southern Guide to the Civil War For Northerners
Honest Jeff and Dishonest Abe: A Southern Children's Guide to the Civil War
Confederacy 101: Amazing Facts You Never Knew About America's Oldest Political Tradition
Slavery 101: Amazing Facts You Never Knew About America's "Peculiar Institution"
The Great Yankee Coverup: What the North Doesn't Want You to Know About Lincoln's War!
Confederate Blood and Treasure: An Interview With Lochlainn Seabrook
Women in Gray: A Tribute to the Ladies Who Supported the Southern Confederacy
A Rebel Born: A Defense of Nathan Bedford Forrest - Confederate General, American Legend (winner of the 2011 Jefferson Davis Historical Gold Medal)
A Rebel Born: The Screenplay
Nathan Bedford Forrest: Southern Hero, American Patriot - Honoring a Confederate Icon and the Old South
The Quotable Nathan Bedford Forrest: Selections From the Writings and Speeches of the Confederacy's Most Brilliant Cavalryman
Give 'Em Hell Boys! The Complete Military Correspondence of Nathan Bedford Forrest
Forrest! 99 Reasons to Love Nathan Bedford Forrest
Saddle, Sword, and Gun: A Biography of Nathan Bedford Forrest For Teens
Nathan Bedford Forrest and the Battle of Fort Pillow: Yankee Myth, Confederate Fact
Nathan Bedford Forrest and the Ku Klux Klan: Yankee Myth, Confederate Fact
Nathan Bedford Forrest and African-Americans: Yankee Myth, Confederate Fact
The Quotable Jefferson Davis: Selections From the Writings and Speeches of the Confederacy's First President
The Quotable Alexander H. Stephens: Selections From the Writings and Speeches of the Confederacy's First Vice President
The Alexander H. Stephens Reader: Excerpts From the Works of a Confederate Founding Father
The Quotable Robert E. Lee: Selections From the Writings and Speeches of the South's Most Beloved Civil War General
The Old Rebel: Robert E. Lee As He Was Seen By His Contemporaries
The Articles of Confederation Explained: A Clause-by-Clause Study of America's First Constitution
The Constitution of the Confederate States of America Explained: A Clause-by-Clause Study of the South's Magna Carta
The Quotable Stonewall Jackson: Selections From the Writings and Speeches of the South's Most Famous General
Abraham Lincoln: The Southern View - Demythologizing America's Sixteenth President
The Unquotable Abraham Lincoln: The President's Quotes They Don't Want You To Know!
Lincolnology: The Real Abraham Lincoln Revealed in His Own Words - A Study of Lincoln's Suppressed, Misinterpreted, and Forgotten Writings and Speeches
The Great Impersonator! 99 Reasons to Dislike Abraham Lincoln
The Quotable Edward A. Pollard: Selections From the Writings of the Confederacy's Greatest Defender
Encyclopedia of the Battle of Franklin - A Comprehensive Guide to the Conflict that Changed the Civil War
Carnton Plantation Ghost Stories: True Tales of the Unexplained from Tennessee's Most Haunted Civil War House!
The McGavocks of Carnton Plantation: A Southern History - Celebrating One of Dixie's Most Noble Confederate Families and Their Tennessee Home
Jesus and the Law of Attraction: The Bible-Based Guide to Creating Perfect Health, Wealth, and Happiness Following Christ's Simple Formula
The Bible and the Law of Attraction: 99 Teachings of Jesus, the Apostles, and the Prophets
Christ Is All and In All: Rediscovering Your Divine Nature and the Kingdom Within
Jesus and the Gospel of Q: Christ's Pre-Christian Teachings As Recorded in the New Testament
Seabrook's Bible Dictionary of Traditional and Mystical Christian Doctrines
The Way of Holiness: The Story of Religion and Myth From the Cave Bear Cult to Christianity
Christmas Before Christianity: How the Birthday of the "Sun" Became the Birthday of the "Son"
Autobiography of a Non-Yogi: A Scientist's Journey From Hinduism to Christianity (with Amitava Dasgupta)
Britannia Rules: Goddess-Worship in Ancient Anglo-Celtic Society - An Academic Look at the United Kingdom's Matricentric Spiritual Past
The Book of Kelle: An Introduction to Goddess-Worship and the Great Celtic Mother-Goddess Kelle, Original Blessed Lady of Ireland
The Goddess Dictionary of Words and Phrases: Introducing a New Core Vocabulary for the Women's Spirituality Movement
Princess Diana: Modern Day Moon-Goddess - A Psychoanalytical and Mythological Look at Diana Spencer's Life, Marriage, and Death (with Dr. Jane Goldberg)
Aphrodite's Trade: The Hidden History of Prostitution Unveiled
UFOs and Aliens: The Complete Guidebook
The Caudills: An Etymological, Ethnological, and Genealogical Study - Exploring the Name and National Origins of a European-American Family
The Blakeneys: An Etymological, Ethnological, and Genealogical Study - Uncovering the Mysterious Origins of the Blakeney Family and Name

Five-Star Books & Gifts From the Heart of the American South

~ SeaRavenPress.com ~

WOMEN IN GRAY

A TRIBUTE TO THE LADIES WHO SUPPORTED THE SOUTHERN CONFEDERACY

Includes Female-Oriented Reminiscences, Stories, Speeches, Reports, Poems, Photos, Illustrations, & Obituaries Regarding the Great War & the Southern Confederacy

ILLUSTRATED BY THE AUTHOR, COLONEL
LOCHLAINN SEABROOK
JEFFERSON DAVIS HISTORICAL GOLD MEDAL WINNER

Sea Raven Press, Nashville, Tennessee, USA

WOMEN IN GRAY

Published by
Sea Raven Press, Cassidy Ravensdale, President
The Literary Wing of the Pro-South Movement
PO Box 1484, Spring Hill, Tennessee 37174-1484 USA
SeaRavenPress.com • searavenpress@gmail.com

Copyright © 2016 Lochlainn Seabrook
in accordance with U.S. and international copyright laws and regulations, as stated
and protected under the Berne Union for the Protection of Literary and Artistic
Property (Berne Convention), and the Universal Copyright Convention (the UCC).
All rights reserved under the Pan-American and International Copyright Conventions.

1st SRP paperback edition, 1st printing October 2016, ISBN: 978-1-943737-35-2
1st SRP hardcover edition, 1st printing October 2016, ISBN: 978-1-943737-36-9

ISBN: 978-1-943737-35-2 (paperback)
Library of Congress Control Number: 2016954331

This work is the copyrighted intellectual property of Lochlainn Seabrook and has been registered with the Copyright Office at the Library of Congress in Washington, D.C., USA. No part of this work (including text, covers, drawings, photos, illustrations, maps, images, diagrams, etc.), in whole or in part, may be used, reproduced, stored in a retrieval system, or transmitted, in any form or by any means now known or hereafter invented, without written permission from the publisher. The sale, duplication, hire, lending, copying, digitalization, or reproduction of this material, in any manner or form whatsoever, is also prohibited, and is a violation of federal, civil, and digital copyright law, which provides severe civil and criminal penalties for any violations.

Women in Gray: A Tribute to the Ladies Who Supported the Southern Confederacy,
by Lochlainn Seabrook. Includes an index, endnotes, and bibliographical references.

Front and back cover design and art, book design, layout, and interior art by Lochlainn Seabrook
All images, graphic design, graphic art, and illustrations copyright © Lochlainn Seabrook
Cover image & design copyright © Lochlainn Seabrook
Cover photo: United Daughters of the Confederacy, Washington, D.C., 1912

The views on the American "Civil War" documented in this book are those of the publisher.

The paper used in this book is acid-free and lignin-free. It has been certified by the Sustainable Forestry Initiative and the Forest Stewardship Council and meets all ANSI standards for archival quality paper.

PRINTED & MANUFACTURED IN OCCUPIED TENNESSEE, FORMER CONFEDERATE STATES OF AMERICA

Dedication

To every female, whatever her age, race, ethnicity, nationality, or religion, who has ever loved the Southern Confederate States of America.

Confederate Southern belles

Epigraph

After the surrender of Vicksburg, when a Yankee officer asked Confederate General Stephen Dill Lee why the Southern people themselves hadn't given up yet, he replied: "Because the women of the South would never agree to it."

A group of UDC members meeting at Nashville, Tennessee, November 11, 1896.

CONTENTS

Notes to the Reader 9
Introduction 14
Abbreviations 17

ALABAMA 21
ARKANSAS 31
CALIFORNIA 42
COLORADO 43
FLORIDA 44
GEORGIA 49
INDIANA 64
IOWA 65
KENTUCKY 67
LOUISIANA 88
MARYLAND 96
MASSACHUSETTS 100
MINNESOTA 102
MISSISSIPPI 105
MISSOURI 125
NEBRASKA 130
NEW MEXICO 131
NEW YORK 132
NORTH CAROLINA 133
OKLAHOMA 149
PENNSYLVANIA 152
SOUTH CAROLINA 153
TENNESSEE 159
TEXAS 233
VIRGINIA 244
WASHINGTON, D.C. 261
WEST VIRGINIA 270
WISCONSIN 273
MISCELLANEOUS 275

Appendix A: The Constitution of the UDC, 1895 308
Appendix B: Excerpts from the 7th Annual Meeting, UDC 312
Appendix C: Modern Female Supporters of the Confederacy ... 323
Appendix D: Contacting the UDC & OCR 324

Notes 325
Bibliography 328
Index 330
Meet the Author 343

NOTES TO THE READER

THE TWO MAIN POLITICAL PARTIES IN 1860

☞ In any study of America's antebellum, bellum, and postbellum periods, it is vitally important to understand that in 1860 the two major political parties—the Democrats and the newly formed Republicans—were the opposite of what they are today. In other words, the Democrats of the mid 19th Century were Conservatives, akin to the Republican Party of today, while the Republicans of the mid 19th Century were Liberals, akin to the Democratic Party of today.

Thus the Confederacy's Democratic president, Jefferson Davis, was a Conservative (with libertarian leanings); the Union's Republican president, Abraham Lincoln, was a Liberal (with socialistic leanings). This is why, in the mid 1800s, the conservative wing of the Democratic Party was known as "the States' Rights Party."[1]

The author's cousin, Confederate Vice President and Democrat Alexander H. Stephens: a Southern Conservative.

Hence, the Democrats of the Civil War period referred to themselves as "conservatives," "confederates," "anti-centralists," or "constitutionalists" (the latter because they favored strict adherence to the original Constitution—which tacitly guaranteed states' rights—as created by the Founding Fathers), while the Republicans called themselves "liberals," "nationalists," "centralists," or "consolidationists" (the latter three because they wanted to nationalize the central government and consolidate political power in Washington, D.C.).[2]

Since this idea is new to most of my readers, let us further demystify it by viewing it from the perspective of the American Revolutionary War. If Davis and his conservative Southern constituents (the Democrats of 1861) had been alive in 1775, they would have sided with George Washington and the American colonists, who sought to secede from the tyrannical government of Great Britain; if Lincoln and his Liberal Northern constituents (the Republicans of 1861) had been alive at that time, they would have sided with King George III and the English monarchy, who sought to maintain the American colonies as possessions of the British Empire. It is due to this very comparison that Southerners often refer to the "Civil War" as the Second American Revolutionary War.

Without a basic understanding of these facts, the American "Civil War" will forever remain incomprehensible.

THE TERM "CIVIL WAR"
☞ As I heartily dislike the phrase "Civil War," its use throughout this book (as well as in my other works) is worthy of an explanation.

Today America's entire literary system refers to the conflict of 1861 using the Northern term the "Civil War," whether we in the South like it or not. Thus, as all book searches by readers, libraries, and retail outlets are now performed online, and as all bookstores categorize works from this period under the heading "Civil War," book publishers and authors who deal with this particular topic have little choice but to use this term themselves. If I were to refuse to use it, as some of my Southern colleagues have suggested, few people would ever find or read my books.

The American "Civil War" was not a true civil war as Webster defines it: "A conflict between opposing groups of citizens of the *same* country." It was a fight between two individual countries; or to be more specific, two separate and constitutionally formed confederacies: the U.S.A. and the C.S.A.

Add to this the fact that scarcely any non-Southerners have ever heard of the names we in the South use for the conflict, such as the "War for Southern Independence"—or my personal preference, "Lincoln's War." It only makes sense then to use the term "Civil War" in most commercial situations, distasteful though it is.

We should also bear in mind that while today educated persons, particularly educated Southerners, all share an abhorrence for the phrase "Civil War," it was not always so. Confederates who lived through and even fought in the conflict regularly used the term throughout the 1860s, and even long after. Among them were Confederate generals such as Nathan Bedford Forrest, Richard Taylor, and Joseph E. Johnston, not to mention the Confederacy's vice president, Alexander H. Stephens.

In 1895 Confederate General James Longstreet wrote about his military experiences in a work subtitled, *Memoirs of the Civil War in America*. Even the Confederacy's highest leader, President Jefferson Davis, used the term "Civil War,"[3] and in one case at least, as late as 1881—the year he wrote his brilliant exposition, *The Rise and Fall of the Confederate Government*.[4] Pro-South authors writing for *Confederate Veteran* magazine often used the phrase well into the early 1900s.[5]

TIME PERIOD
☞ The time period represented in this book: 1860 to 1918.

THE TERM "LADIES"
☞ The word "ladies," used in my subtitle, is unpopular with some today, particularly left-wing feminists, who find it "politically incorrect" and thus "offensive." However, their view—being based on emotion, opinion, and presentism—is unhistorical, and therefore false. Most Victorian women, particularly *Southern* Victorian women, proudly described themselves as "ladies," and the word was often incorporated into the names of various organizations.

STATES REPRESENTED
☞ I have listed my "Women in Gray" by state, and without bias—including toward my home state, Kentucky. Nonetheless, some states have only one individual while others contain many dozens, such as Tennessee and Virginia. This is due not only to the source material that was available to me, but also because the Volunteer State was the founding state of the United Daughters of the Confederacy (originally the Daughters of the Confederacy), while the Dominion State was the founding state of the Sons of Confederate Veterans (originally the United Confederate Veterans).

NAMES AND LOCATIONS

☞ Concerning the names, home cities, and home states of the women included in this book: this information cannot be guaranteed entirely accurate since the original sources themselves are not always accurate, or in some cases are unclear (misspellings and misidentifications, for example, are not uncommon). Thus I list individuals under the state that seems most appropriate—which may differ from the state they were born in, lived in, or died in.

Additionally, some women appear in my Index more than once under different names. This is due to the manner in which they are listed in the original documents. For instance, some women are listed by their maiden name (e.g., Jane Smith) and by their husband's full name (e.g., Mrs. Robert Johnson), and even by their first name and married surname (e.g., Mrs. Jane Johnson), all in the same article.

LEARN MORE

☞ Lincoln's War on the American people and the Constitution can never be fully understood without a thorough knowledge of the South's perspective. As this book is only meant to be a brief introductory guide to these topics, one cannot hope to learn the whole truth about them here. For those who are interested in a more in-depth study, please see my comprehensive histories listed on page 2.

"Away down South in Dixie!"

Keep Your Body, Mind, & Spirit Vibrating at Their Highest Level

YOU CAN DO SO BY READING THE BOOKS OF

SEA RAVEN PRESS

There is nothing that will so perfectly keep your body, mind, and spirit in a healthy condition as to think wisely and positively. Hence you should not only read this book, but also the other books that we offer. They will quicken your physical, mental, and spiritual vibrations, enabling you to maintain a position in society as a healthy erudite person.

KEEP YOURSELF WELL-INFORMED!

The well-informed person is always at the head of the procession, while the ignorant, the lazy, and the unthoughtful hang onto the rear. If you are a Spiritual man or woman, do yourself a great favor: read Sea Raven Press books and stay well posted on the Truth. It is almost criminal for one to remain in ignorance while the opportunity to gain knowledge is open to all at a nominal price.

We invite you to visit our Webstore for a wide selection of wholesome, family-friendly, well-researched, educational books for all ages. You will be glad you did!

Five-Star Books & Gifts From the Heart of the American South

SeaRavenPress.com

INTRODUCTION

"A people which takes no pride in the noble achievements of remote ancestry will never achieve anything worthy to be remembered by remote descendants." — Thomas Babington Macaulay

Contrary to what we have been taught, half of the U.S. and most of Europe sided with the Confederacy during Lincoln's illegal and unnecessary war on traditional America in the years 1861 to 1865. And over half of these supporters were female!

The women who threw their hats in with the Confederate States of America were not rabid radicals who hated the Union and sought to "destroy the U.S.," as our mainstream history books teach. They were everyday females, young, middle aged, and old; they came in every color, white, black, brown, and red, and from every background, from unread to highly educated, from rural to urban, from indigent to wealthy.

They all had one thing in common, however, patriotism: a passionate love for the United States of America and her most sacred document, the U.S. Constitution—*and* a fervent desire to defend both. Thus whether they hailed from the South, the North, the East, or the West, nearly all of America's early female Confederate supporters were Democrats, the Conservative Party of the 1860s (the Republicans at the time were the Liberal Party).

When, after the election of big government Liberal Abraham Lincoln in November 1860, the secession of the Southern states became inevitable, millions of women from around the globe quickly endorsed the Confederate States of America, whose citizens stood squarely for small government, free trade, states' rights, state sovereignty, self-government, traditional family values, conservative politics, rugged individualism, and old-fashioned Christianity. After all, "The Confederate States of America" had been one of the nicknames for the U.S. itself, originating shortly after its inception in 1776, when it was officially known as "The Confederacy"[6] and our first Constitution was called "The Articles of Confederation."[7]

When the misnamed "Civil War" came in April 1861, and with Southern Conservative Jefferson Davis now in the Confederate White House, these same female supporters voluntarily served the CSA in literally every conceivable capacity, from seamstresses and cooks to nurses and spies. Some even pretended to be men in order to sneak into the Confederate military, eager to shoot down Yanks in defense of hearth and home. Thousands opened up their doors to the wounded, from humble cabins to sumptuous plantation houses, transforming homes into bloody field hospitals that often served in this capacity for the entire duration of the War, and even long after.

While their menfolk were away fighting the meddlesome blue-coated invaders, Southern women, often with the financial and spiritual aid of many like-minded women in the American North and in Europe, stoically tended their children, homes, farms, plantations, servants, and businesses. It was a frightening and chaotic period, the work exhausting, tedious, and seemingly thankless at times. But it was all done with the type of dedication, enthusiasm, care, and love that can only spring from the heart of a woman!

After the War Southern men, and especially former Confederate soldiers, had only the highest praise and gratitude for their wives, lovers, mothers, sisters, daughters, grandmothers, and aunts, who had kept the home fires burning for four long, difficult, harrowing years. It is little wonder that President Davis penned the following dedication in his landmark 1881 work, *The Rise and Fall of the Confederate Government*:

> "To the women of the Confederacy, whose pious ministrations to our wounded soldiers soothed the last hours of those who died far from the objects of their tenderest love; whose domestic labors contributed much to supply the wants of our defenders in the field; whose zealous faith in our cause shone a guiding star undimmed by the darkest clouds of war; whose fortitude sustained them under all the privations to which they were subjected; whose annual tribute expresses their enduring love and reverence for our sacred dead; and whose patriotism will teach their children to emulate the deeds of our Revolutionary sires; these pages are dedicated by their countryman, Jefferson Davis."[8]

The book you hold in your hand is a memorial to these very women; the brave, industrious, powerful, resourceful females who risked everything to help Southern men preserve the Constitution and the conservative values upon which America was founded.

I am proud to say that I am related to many of the women in these pages, some closely, some distantly. But I consider all of them "family," true sisters-in-arms, just as I do the thousands of women who are still fighting to maintain true Southern history. For the conflict through which our "Civil War" ladies labored continues into the present day: the archetypal age-old battle between conservatism and liberalism, common sense and emotion, fact and ideology. This book and the women in it represent the former in each case, the traditional American who would rather struggle under freedom than be a slave under government.

Women in Gray is not meant to be all-inclusive. Indeed, no amount of volumes could name, describe, and honor every woman who supported the Confederate States of America, an impossible task for an impossible number of reasons. But I believe that in its brevity my book aptly reflects the countless women who suffered, and even gave their lives, in the fight for personal liberty, constitutional government, and our great Confederate Republic—personally created in 1776 by the Founding Generation at monumental cost.

May the images, words, and memories of our country's magnificent "Women in Gray" inspire this generation, as well as future generations, to continue the arduous but fulfilling work of preserving authentic Confederate, Southern, and American history against the onslaught of the uneducated, the misinformed, and the biased.

Colonel Seabrook, SCV
Nashville, Tennessee, USA
October 2016
Deus Est Lux

ABBREVIATIONS

DAR - "Daughters of the American Revolution," formed October 11, 1890, at Washington, D.C.

NCDC - "National Confederation of Daughters of the Confederacy," a term that dates from the 1890s.

NOUDC - "National Order of the United Daughters of the Confederacy," used in the late 1890s.

NUDC - "National United Daughters of the Confederacy," a title used in the late 1800s.

SCV - "Sons of Confederate Veterans," the modern descendant of the UCV.

UCV - "United Confederate Veterans," organized in Richmond, Virginia, July 1, 1896; it was the forerunner of today's SCV.

UDC - "United Daughters of the Confederacy," which, in 1895, replaced the original title, "Daughters of the Confederacy." The General Organization of the UDC was founded in Nashville, Tennessee, September 10, 1894.

USCV - "United Sons of Confederate Veterans," a title used in the late 1800s and early 1900s.

Our president, Jefferson Davis.

"If ever the world sees a time when women shall come together purely and simply for the benefit and good of mankind, it will be a power such as the world has never known."

Matthew Arnold
1822-1888

The STATES

ALABAMA

Miss Ella Nelson, Confederate Sponsor for Alabama.

Mrs. J. C. Lee of Alabama.

Mrs. Anne J. Hamill of Cullman, Alabama, a descendant of Scottish poet Robert Burns.

Miss Carrie T. Cochran of Eufaula, Alabama, Confederate Representative for her state at the UCV Reunion, Birmingham, Alabama, 1894.

Miss Eliza Laurens Chisolm, Birmingham, Confederate Representative of Columbia in the Tableaux.

Miss Jennie Van Hoose of Alabama, Confederate First Maid of Honor for the Alabama Division at the 1898 Atlanta Reunion.

Miss Sallie Jones of Camden, Alabama, President of the Alabama Division of the UDC.

Miss Josie Oxford of Birmingham, Alabama, Confederate Sponsor for Camp Jeff Davis at the Atlanta Reunion, 1898.

Miss Mary Clare Milner of Alabama, Confederate Sponsor for her state.

Miss Lillian Roden of Birmingham, Alabama, Confederate Sponsor for her state. Her father, B. F. Roden, enlisted in the Confederate military at the age of 17 and was severely wounded at the Battle of Shiloh. Of Miss Lillian it is said: "She is tall and slender, of the distinctly Southern type, olive complexion, and dark-brown eyes and hair."

Miss Idene Key of Birmingham, Alabama, Confederate Sponsor for Camp W. J. Hardee at the UCV's Atlanta Reunion, 1898.

Mrs. Clement Clay Clopton of Alabama, member of the UDC, 1896.

Mrs. Sophia Bibb of Alabama, President of the Ladies Memorial Association of Montgomery, organized April 16, 1866.

Miss Kittiebelle Stirling of Mobile, Alabama, "the popular and gifted" piano accompanist who performed at numerous Confederate Veterans' meetings throughout the South. Her "family gave eleven members to the cause of the Confederacy, five of whom came from Pennsylvania to engage in the services of the Confederate States — a most remarkable record."

Mrs. E. Musgrove, President of the Jasper, Alabama, Chapter, UDC.

Long wave our flag!

Miss Claude V. Coleman of Huntsville, Alabama, Confederate Sponsor for the Alabama Division.

Miss Maribel Williams, Confederate Chief Maid of Honor from Mobile, Alabama.

Miss Mary Kirkpatrick of Montgomery, Alabama, Confederate Sponsor for the Army of Tennessee Dept.

Miss R. M. Pollard of Montgomery, Alabama, Confederate Maid of Honor for the Army of Tennessee Dept.

The celebrated deaf and blind author and lecturer Helen Keller of Tuscumbia, Alabama, daughter and granddaughter of Confederate officers.

Miss Ethel Tillman Heard of Auburn, Alabama, Confederate Sponsor for the South, New Orleans Reunion.

Miss Marjorie Catchings of Birmingham, Alabama, Confederate Sponsor 4th Division, UCV, New Orleans Reunion.

Dr. Lafayette Guild and his wife Pattie Guild of Alabama.

From *Confederate Veteran*, 1898

D r. Lafayette Guild was a native of Tuscaloosa, Ala., and a nephew of the late Judge Jo C. Guild, of Nashville, Tenn. When the great war broke out he was a surgeon in the U.S. Army and on duty in California. He resigned and went on to Richmond, Va., with Gen. A. S. Johnston, and became a surgeon in the Army of Northern Virginia. When Gen. Lee took command of the army he telegraphed: "Send me Dr. Lafayette Guild." He appointed him on his staff, and made him medical director of the Army of Northern Virginia.

Gen. Lee was very fond of and confidential with Dr. Guild. His report to Gen. Lee of the battle of Gettysburg is a part of the commander's official report in the "War Records." After the war Dr. Guild commenced the practise of medicine in Mobile, Ala, in partnership with a brother of Admiral Raphael Semmes. He died, however, soon after going to Mobile.

[The following story, from the same article, is by Dr. Guild's wife, Pattie Guild, a loyal Confederate woman. — Colonel Lochlainn Seabrook]

JOURNEY TO AND FROM APPOMATTOX, BY PATTIE GUILD
The dear old army had passed away from me for ever, and I had been through the Confederacy. It was the last week of the war. Gen. Lee's army was camped near Petersburg, and I had been there all winter, at Mrs. Richard Kidder Meade's, to be near my husband, who was medical director of the Army of Northern Virginia and on Gen. Lee's staff. Agnes Lee had been on a visit at Mrs. Meade's, but left Saturday morning for Richmond. Sunday morning I was dressing for church, when my ambulance drove up to Mrs. Meade's door, and old Wilson, my faithful old soldier driver who had always driven my ambulance, gave me a note from my husband saying: "The enemy are entering Richmond. I do not wish to leave you within their lines. Wilson will know where to take you." I immediately put some necessary articles in a small trunk and had it put in the ambulance, got in, and Wilson drove off.

All that day and all that night we drove and drove. I do not remember eating, but I do know I slept. Once in the night I awoke and heard sounds of sorrow, and was told that they were from Mrs. A. P. Hill's ambulance, and that [Confederate] Gen. [Ambrose Powell] Hill had been killed just before our army left Petersburg.

Well, we went on and on. Occasionally I saw my husband, and other officers would ride up and say: "Mrs. Guild, we have no command; we will rally around your ambulance." Our poor soldiers would come to me and ask for food, and know I had none to give; but each day my husband, I suppose, would manage to get me something to eat, for I was never hungry.

Often on that march my husband or some other officer would ride up hurriedly and speak to old Wilson, and he would whip up the mules, and we would rush across fields in any direction. It would be because the enemy had cut our lines. Finally Col. Baldwin, of Gen.

Lee's staff, came to me and gave me fifty dollars in greenbacks—the first, I believe, I ever had. He said he did not know what would happen, and I might need it; but I was so young and thoughtless in those days I did not dream of danger or surrender. I was even happy on that dreadful march; everything was so strange. I was the only lady. My husband would often ride up to my ambulance and cheer me in every way he could.

At last, one evening at sunset, my ambulance stopped, Wilson saying he had orders to halt. By and by several officers came up, and soon the baggage-wagons. My husband ordered his servant, Nathan, whom he had brought from the old plantation, and who had been with him through the war, to get out his best clothes. He and other officers dressed themselves in their best. I asked Dr. Guild why it was, and he replied that they might be captured, and wanted to make a good appearance. Then my husband went with me to a house near by, where I refreshed myself. Returning to the ambulance, I found all the officers lying around on the ground with their military cloaks thrown over their faces, asleep in the moonlight. It was a strange sight. I got in my ambulance, and was soon asleep myself.

When I awoke it was daylight, and we were moving. Soon my husband came to me and said there might be a fight there, but that I was in no danger, and must not be frightened. He took me out of the ambulance and put me in a gully, barricaded it with wagons, and told old Wilson to keep the ambulance ready, so he could put me in it, and where to take me if certain things happened; but just then an officer rode up and said there was a house a mile off, and my husband put me in the ambulance and took me there. It was the home of Gen. Morton, and he made me welcome, and took me to a room on the first floor, where my husband bade me good-by and returned to Gen. Lee.

He had hardly left me, when a body of our men and a party of the enemy met in a skirmish right in front of my room. When it was over I laid my hat, watch, and chain off, and went to bathe my face, just as my door was burst open and a Dutch soldier, with pistol in his hand, came in, cursing the Rebels. I said not a word, but quietly left the room. I found the whole house filled with soldiers. I saw an officer, and told him what had happened, and he instantly went with me. I found my watch and chain gone, but was too glad to escape with that to murmur.

I heard that Gen. John Gibbon, who used to be a dear old army friend, was near, and I asked if I could send him a note. Immediately a man was sent with my little penciled note to Gen. Gibbon, and quickly a reply came, saying he would come to me; and he came even while I was reading his note, the same kind old friend. He put a safe guard around the house; but, notwithstanding that, the next morning a negro soldier came to my room, but, as they had always been my slaves, I did not feel afraid of him. I ordered him out, and he went. Our little Indian boy, Joe, whom we had since he was seven years old (then twelve), was with me. Then my husband came and told me of the surrender, and he broke completely down when he spoke of Gen. Lee.

Well, we left Appomattox Court-House. My ambulance followed Gen. Lee's, which was empty, he riding with his staff and those of the army who went with him to Richmond. I shall never forget how, as Gen. Lee rode away from Appomattox the Union soldiers cheered and cheered him. He was grander to me on that sad march back to Richmond than he ever was after one of his great victories. Often on that march he would come to my ambulance early in the morning with a cup of coffee, depriving himself for the only woman who was on that sorrowful, hopeless march. We would all, from the highest officer to the humblest soldier, have given him our last drop of water or food, we loved him so; and on that march, when we would camp near a house, they would prepare their best for Gen. Lee; but he would sleep in his tent or on the ground with his staff, and say that I must go and have what was prepared for him. How provoked they must have felt to see a forlorn little woman, instead of Gen. Lee!

When we reached Richmond we all separated. I never saw Gen. Lee again, but my husband went back to Richmond to see him; and now I feel sure they are not very far apart in heaven. And for me,

> Would those hours could come again, with their thorns and flowers!
> I would give the hopes of years for those bygone hours.[9]

ARKANSAS

Miss Grace Lumpkin, "who made an effective plea at Little Rock, Arkansas, for a reunion at Macon, Georgia."

Miss Rose Bennett, Sponsor for the Arkansas Division, Richmond Reunion.

Miss Varina Cook of Arkansas, daughter of General V. Y. Cook and Sponsor of the Trans-Mississippi Dept.

Miss Eula Spivey, Confederate Sponsor for the USCV of Arkansas.

Mrs. Homer F. Sloan, President of the Arkansas Division, UDC, Sloan, Arkansas.

Miss L. Byrd Mock, Confederate Sponsor for the Arkansas Division.

Miss Lillie McGee of Van Buren, Arkansas, Confederate Representative for her state in the UCV Reunion at Birmingham, Alabama, 1894.

The *St. Mary*, Confederate Navy.

Miss Caroline Peyton Peay of Arkansas, Confederate Maid of Honor for her state at the 1898 Atlanta Reunion.

Miss Mimi Polk Horner, Confederate Maid of Honor for Arkansas.

Mrs. James Russell Miller (née Geraldine Hill) of Little Rock, Arkansas, Chaperon for her state's Sponsor and Maids of Honor. The wife of Capt. J. R. Miller of Memphis, Tennessee, of her it is said: "She is a typical Southern woman and one prominent socially by reason of her wit, beauty, and wealth."

Miss Hedwig Penzel of Little Rock, Arkansas, is a Confederate Sponsor for her state and the daughter of a Confederate soldier, Charles F. Penzel.

Miss Lillian C. Reeves of Camden, Arkansas, described as "slight and graceful in figure, with brown hair and dark eyes." She was a Confederate Maid of Honor for the First Brigade, Arkansas Division, UCV.

Mrs. C. A. Forney of Arkansas, President of the Arkansas Division of the UDC.

Mrs. Charles T. Arnett of Arkansas, President of the Winnie Davis Chapter, No. 122, UDC, Mammoth Spring, Arkansas, chartered July 5, 1897, with "about 30 members."

Mrs. J. L. Cravens of Arkansas, President of the UDC Chapter at Fayetteville.

Miss Sue Knox of Arkansas, Confederate Maid of Honor for her state, and student at Belmont College, Nashville, Tennessee.

Miss Margaret T. Toland of Arkansas, Confederate Sponsor for her state.

Mrs. May Stark Fowler (née Stark) of Little Rock, Arkansas, a member of the Little Rock Chapter, UDC, and a Sponsor for numerous Confederate Veterans' reunions.

Miss Edith Kidder of Little Rock, Arkansas, Confederate Chief Maid of Honor, Arkansas Division UCV, New Orleans.

Confederate Gen. Clement Anselm Evans spoke at the UCV Reunion at Camden, Arkansas, in 1909. Accompanying him here are, from L-R: Miss Ann Chester Watts of Camden, Confederate Maid of Honor; Miss Margaret Virginia Ramsey of Camden, Confederate Sponsor; Miss Martha Virginia Marks of Thornton, Arkansas, Confederate Maid of Honor.

The Arlington Hotel, Hot Springs, Arkansas, meeting place of the United Daughters of the Confederacy in 1898.

A group of Daughters at Hot Springs, Arkansas, for the Annual Session of the State Division, October 28-30, 1903.

From *Confederate Veteran*, 1912

ARKANSAS MONUMENT TO CONFEDERATE WOMEN

In sympathy with the general movement inaugurated by the general federation, U.C.V., for the erection of monuments throughout the South to the women of the Confederacy, who bore so noble and heroic a part in the War of the States, 1861-1865, the Arkansas State Convention, U.C.V., several years ago selected a committee to raise the necessary funds to erect one in Arkansas. The committee tried by various methods to accomplish this, and met with partial success. They finally had a bill passed by the last legislature appropriating $10,000 for the purpose and the appointment of a committee with authority to select a design, construct a pedestal, and erect it on the grounds of the new State Capitol.

The committee advertised for designs to be submitted on a certain day. In response twenty-eight designs were submitted, and many of the sculptors or their representatives were present to exhibit their models or sketches. They were admitted one at a time to the committee room, and the committee heard each upon the merits of his design. The committee selected the one designed by J. Shweizer, and the contract was awarded the McNeel Marble Company, of Marietta, Ga. It is a group of four life-size figures in bronze resting upon a base of Winnsboro blue granite, standing nearly fifteen feet above ground. It represents a woman of the Confederacy sitting in a chair bidding good-by to her young son who is going to war. A daughter, somewhat younger, appears in grief with her head resting on her mother's shoulder, and a boy four or five years old, too young to realize anything but the glamour of war, is beating a toy drum at the side of his mother, who has already sacrificed her husband on the altar of his country. There is no suggestion of the tumult of war in the structure. It is feminine and speaks silently but eloquently of the grief and self-sacrifice of the women of that period in giving up their husbands, sons, and brothers for the cause of the South.

Mr. J. Kellogg concludes a description: "In every line there are tenderness and expression. There is nothing in the group that should not be there, and anything else added would mar its beauty."

The monument is to be completed and erected within this year, and it will probably be unveiled with appropriate ceremonies either late in the fall or early next spring.[10]

Miss Alma Greer of Texarkana, Arkansas, Confederate Sponsor for the Arkansas Division.

This proposed design for a "Confederate Women's Statue" was the cause of some controversy when it was first revealed in the early 1900s. Some thought it was too militaristic; some that it was not feminine enough. The engraved words under the feet of the "Amazon" read: "Uphold Our State Rights."

CALIFORNIA

Mrs. Samuel Cary Dunlap of Los Angeles, California, President of the California Division, UDC.

Miss Nannie Harl of Colusa, California, Confederate Maid of Honor for the Los Angeles Camp No. 770, UCV.

Mrs. Albert Sidney Johnston of California, wife of the famous Confederate general.

Mrs. Sidney Van Wyck, of California, President of the San Francisco Chapter, UDC.

COLORADO

Mrs. Margaret "Maggie" Howell Davis Hayes: born in Washington, D.C., she died in Colorado Springs, Colorado, in 1909, where she and her family lived for many years. She was the only surviving child of President Jefferson Davis.

FLORIDA

Miss Cora Mallory of Florida, Confederate Sponsor for the South at the Macon Reunion.

Miss Clara Chipley, Confederate Sponsor for Florida.

Miss Elizabeth Pasco of Monticello, Florida, Confederate Representative for her state in the UCV Reunion at Birmingham, Alabama, 1894.

Mrs. John W. Tench of Gainesville, Florida, president of the E. Kirby Smith Chapter, UDC, organized on February 3, 1898.

A group of Florida girls with the Third National Confederate Flag (left) and the First National Confederate Flag (upper center) on George Washington's Birthday.

Mrs. Roselle Clifton Cooley, President of the Florida Division, UDC.

From *Confederate Veteran*, 1912

FLORIDA MONUMENT TO CONFEDERATE WOMEN

A published sketch of a monument in process of construction contains the following description: "The monument will be placed on a mound 40 x 40 feet. The granite base will be 28 x 28 feet in dimensions, and at each corner three pillars will be placed to support the dome. On a pedestal at the base and surrounded by the pillars there will be a figure in bronze of a woman teaching children the true story of the Civil War. On the dome another figure of a woman, thirteen feet one inch in height, will represent a Confederate woman clasping a half-furled battle flag. Granite steps will make the approaches from the four sides of the monument. The pillars of the memorial will be sixteen inches in diameter, and the interior of the dome is to be of polished marble, with a great electric globe in the center. The figure just beneath will be on a pedestal four by four by about six feet. Florida's tribute to the women of the Confederacy will be the inscription."[11]

Mrs. Ellen Adair Beatty, nicknamed "Florida White."

By Col. Lochlainn Seabrook, from *Confederate Veteran*, 1894

Born Ellen Adair, one of the seven daughters of Kentucky Governor John Adair, she later married the wealthy Florida lawyer Joseph Monroe White, then becoming known by the nickname "Florida White." After the death of her husband she married Dr. Beatty, on whose large estate she lived during Lincoln's War, and whose 200 black servants she lovingly taught to read and write. Though Mrs. Beatty is largely unknown today, this strongly Confederate woman was a celebrity in her own day. The toast of Victorian American society, she was famous enough for the Pope of Rome to give her the gift of a "magnificent diamond cross," which she donated to the building of a Southern Presbyterian Church in Washington, D.C. One female author

> reports an entertainment during John Quincy Adams's administration, in which she refers to Mrs. White as follows:
>
> > "There was also the wealthy and magnificent Florida belle, Mrs. White, with a numerous train of admirers, a

dozen orange blossoms in her hair, the wild light of the gazelle in her dark eyes, and her bust cased in glittering silver, languishing through the crowd, who retired to the right and left to permit her to pass. If met, said an admirer, walking through an orange grove in Florida, or beside a limpid lake amid the eternal spring, she would instantly become an object of worship."

At another time, during Andrew Jackson's administration:

"The lady usually called Mrs. 'Florida' White, because her husband, Col. White, represented Florida, was celebrated for her magnificent beauty and intellectual accomplishments throughout the Gulf States."

Her part in the war is not given in this appropriate place, but no woman in our favored Southland was more loyal and zealous from first to last. She and Mrs. James K. Polk were devoted friends. The latter was pleased to recall in the later years of their lives the eminence of her Presbyterian sister when both were in the prime of young womanhood and conspicuous at Washington.[12]

GEORGIA

Mrs. Walter D. Lamar of Macon, Georgia, President of the Georgia Chapter, UDC, 1912.

Mrs. Mildred Lewis Rutherford of Athens, Georgia, pro-South author and Historian General, UDC, 1911.

Miss Julia F. Ridley, UCV Sponsor for Georgia.

"Baby" May Miller of Milledgeville, Georgia.

Bottom right: Mrs. Levisa Leek McClain (née Dunn) of Dalton, Georgia. Standing: her son, Confederate veteran John D. Dowling of the Georgia Volunteers; her daughter is on the bottom left. During Lincoln's War Union troops frequently camped in the McClain's yard, some resorting to stealing the family's property. One Yankee officer, looking over her lovely home and land, said: "I will lay my land grant here when the South is confiscated." To this Mrs. McClain replied: "You may lay it between here and Atlanta only six feet long and three feet wide."

Mrs. Walter D. Lamar, President Georgia Division, UDC, and friends.

Miss Bessie Brown, Confederate Sponsor at Macon, Georgia.

Mrs. Caroline Mitchell of Lafayette, Georgia.

Miss Regina E. Rambo of Marietta, Georgia, Confederate Sponsor for Georgia.

Miss Blanche Nisbet of Georgia, granddaughter of Captain John McIntosh Kell, an officer on the Confederate cruiser the *Alabama*.

Mrs. Lulu Bringhurst Epperson of Atlanta, Georgia, who, in March 1897, vigorously protested the declaration of a Chicago woman that it is "time to call off Dixie!" Miss Lulu's brother Robert Bringhurst died at the Battle of Franklin II.

Mrs. Mary de Verdery Akin of Georgia was the mother of 13 children and the wife of Colonel Warren Akin, a member of the Confederate Congress and "a close and trusted friend" of President Jefferson Davis.

The "Atlanta Special."

Miss Ella M. Powell of Atlanta, Georgia, was one of the South's most ardent workers in the effort to preserve our wonderful Confederate heritage.

Mrs. Eva Motes of Atlanta, Georgia, Confederate Maid of Honor to Miss Josie Oxford at the Atlanta Reunion, 1898.

Mrs. L. H. Raines of Georgia, first Vice President of the UDC.

Miss Etta Hardeman of Gainesville, Georgia, and the flag she gave to the Georgia Cavalry, UCV.

Miss Sarah Lee Evans of Atlanta, Georgia, a member of the Children of the Confederacy and the daughter of a Confederate General.

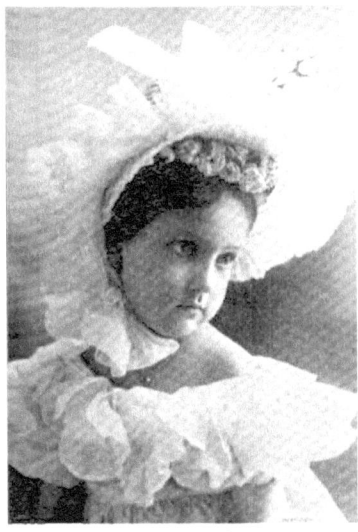

Passie May Ottley of Atlanta, Georgia.

Miss Annie McDougald of Georgia, Confederate Representative of her state in the UCV Reunion at Birmingham, Alabama, 1894.

Miss C. Helen Plane, President of the Atlanta, Georgia, Chapter, UDC.

The Confederate steamer the *Gaines*.

Mrs. Hallie A. Rounsaville of Rome, Georgia, President of the Georgia Division of the UDC.

Mrs. John K. Ottley, Vice President of the Georgia Division of the UDC.

Confederate General Joseph Wheeler of Augusta, Georgia, and his family, comprised of five strong pro-South, pro-Confederate women. Bottom row, L-R: Annie Early; General Wheeler; Mrs. Ella Wheeler; Joseph Wheeler Jr. Top row, L-R: Julia Knox; Lucy L. ("Birdie"); Thomas Harrison; Carrie Peyton.

Mrs. Kate Percy Chestney of Macon, Georgia, Secretary of the Sidney Lanier Chapter, UDC.

Georgia and Jessie Miller, the daughters of Louise Miller (née Marmelstein) of Savannah, Georgia. The wife of Jefferson Davis Miller, Louise's father was Capt. A. F. Marmelstein, signal officer for the Confederate raider, CSS *Alabama*.

Mrs. Robert Carter (née Evelyn Nelson) of Georgia, was one of the "leading spirits" in promoting hospital work among the Confederate sick and wounded soldiers of her state during the War.

Miss Hallie Ellis of Atlanta, Georgia, Confederate Sponsor for the Georgia Division, Reunion, 1908.

Miss Louise A. Williams of Augusta, Georgia, talented "interpreter of negro stories." She often performed at Confederate soldiers' homes.

Mrs. John Milledge of Georgia.

From *Confederate Veteran*, 1895

WORK OF A SOUTHERN WOMAN
[Here we give a brief and overdue account of the] wife of Col. John Milledge, of Georgia, through whose administration [a] handsome monument . . . was erected in Atlanta.

Mrs. Milledge [née Fanny Conway Robinson] was President of the Ladies' Memorial Association for about eleven years, . . . [after which she was] transferred to her reward April 25, 1895. The *Veteran* then failed of proper notice.

There was no other service to her so agreeable and so sacred as to honor Confederate dead; and she was blessed with the sight of the magnificent structure, that she did so much to secure, at its formal dedication in 1894.

While the enterprising press of Atlanta gave in connection with the occasion pictures of many of her lady associates, no presentation of her picture was ever given to the public before this; and it seems fitting in this enduring form to portray the gentle, genial features, and so to supply them to those who will cherish her noble deeds throughout our beloved Southland, to all the other states of the Union, and to devoted Confederates abroad.

There was never, perhaps, in the history of Georgia so much honor given by the press to any woman.

Mrs. Milledge was a native of Richmond, Va.; and was in fair young womanhood when the great struggle of the South for separate independence was made. In a letter to Mr. J. D. Carter, who carried to her mementoes from the grave of Jefferson Davis, while expressing her gratitude, she wrote:

> "In my girlhood I lived in Richmond, and was present at the inauguration of President Davis there. I met him in his own home, and worshipped God, Sunday after Sunday, very near to him. I always admired him greatly, and most in his days of adversity, after failure blasted all of our prospects.
>
> ". . . We have thousands of names of men, who died in the hospitals here in Atlanta and were buried in Oakland; yet the graves of only about nine hundred can be identified. There was no money to keep even the wooden headboards in place for years, until recently, when our City Council appropriated $200 a year for ten years, for the Confederate cemetery. That, with the proceeds of the veterans' fair, enabled us to supply marble headstones.
>
> ". . . I deserve no credit for what I have done. I was in Richmond, when Gen. Lee surrendered, and heard the wail that went up from the cots of the poor fellows maimed for life; and have ever felt that the least we can do is not to forget them."

In his address at the dedication of the monument, Hon. H. H. Carlton said:

> "When but a girl, with the warm heart of youth, which went out in immeasurable sympathy and never-tiring devotion to our southern heroes, living in close proximity to the battle fields of Virginia, where she, daily and almost hourly, witnessed the trials and tribulations, the sickness and sufferings of the Confederate soldiers, she made a silent and solemn vow, that so long as she lived and so far as she could

contribute, these brave men should never be disowned, dishonored or forgotten. Ah, how true and how faithful she has been to that vow, not only in giving her best energies to her noble work, but evidencing in the highest degree her never-ending love and devotion to the Confederate soldier by giving her heart and her hand to as gallant and knightly an ex-Confederate soldier as ever bore arms or drew the sword of combat, the splendid Marshal of this day."

The funeral of Mrs. Milledge was, perhaps, the most noted occasion in the records of the state to her many honored women. The Governor, the Judges of Supreme Court and statehouse officers were honorary pall-bearers. The military of the city attended as a special escort. At a meeting of the Confederate Veteran Association for the formal reception of the portrait of Mrs. Milledge impressive services were held. Col. Albert Cox, Judge R. L. Rogers, Gen. C. A. Evans, Dr. J. Wm. Jones, and others made interesting speeches. An Atlanta friend, who has been from the first an earnest advocate of the Veteran, writes:

"While the beautiful tribute was being paid to her by the orator of the day, every one felt it would be the last time on earth that she would take part in such a scene; and our fears were realized, because the day before the anniversary of that day, she went to sleep. . . . In 1884, when she was elected president of the Ladies' Memorial Association, there was not a dollar in the treasury, and the wooden headboards which had been put up about fifteen years before were rotting down. These head boards simply marked the graves that could be located of the thousands who were buried in the Oakland Cemetery. There was a second class, whose names and commands were known; but there were no headboards to them. Then there was a third class composed of men who had been killed around Atlanta just before its evacuation and who had been buried, a number, perhaps, in one grave. After the war the bones of these men had been disinterred and placed in three blocks along with the others. Of them there was no record of name or command.

"Mrs. Milledge immediately went to work; and through her leadership and by her magnificent management, without raising a dollar by direct contribution from anybody, except such little money as was taken in by boxes at the gates on Memorial Day, she raised enough to erect marble headstones at every spot where wooden ones had been before, and two slabs with the names and commands of the others, whose graves could not be located; and then she addressed herself to the building of a monument to the unknown dead, and the Lion was selected upon her approval of the suggestion of Mr. Brady, the sculptor.

"In fact, while she was the leader and manager, she always had the support of the officers and members of the Association in all she undertook. When the Lion was finished, and she unveiled it with scarcely strength enough to pull the cord, just as the slanting rays of the setting sun brought out the beautiful white figure of the Lion, I know that she felt that her work was done."

A note from her husband states:

"She was a Virginian by birth, her name was Fanny Conway Robinson, the daughter of Edwin Robinson, of Richmond. I first met her in winter quarters at Frederick Hall, in Virginia, in the early winter of 1863. She was the adopted daughter of her cousin, John Thompson Brown, who was in command of the artillery corps at that point, in which artillery corps I commanded a battery. We were married on the eleventh day of July, 1865; and she was a confirmed invalid for twenty-nine years of her married life, but with an energy and will power that enabled her to do wonders."[13]

Georgia Confederate Soldiers' Home.

The "Lion of the South," a memorial to the unknown Confederate dead, erected by the "Atlanta Ladies."

Miss Loulie M. Gordon of Atlanta, Georgia.

From *Confederate Veteran*, 1894

MRS. LOULIE M. GORDON, ATLANTA, GA

Mrs. Gordon is the youngest daughter of a Confederate major, the wife of the youngest captain in the Confederate army, and sister-in-law of one of the most celebrated of Confederate generals. Her husband, Walter S. Gordon, raised and commanded a company at fifteen. He was afterwards on the staff of Gen. Clement A. Evans, who was ardently devoted to him and testifies to his "absolute fearlessness, originality, and clear-headedness." The proud wife and daughter of these worthy men says she belongs with the Confederates. While she is happy in her Atlanta home with their two young daughters, Lute and Linda, thirteen and eight, the mother is so full of life and hope that she has become very prominent, especially in literary circles.

Although mentioned occasionally as a "society woman," she takes her religion to a reception just as she wears it in her daily life. She is of sterling Scotch Irish and Welsh ancestry: the McClendon[s] and Blakes, Virginians and South Carolinans. She is of revolutionary stock. Her grandfather was with Andrew Jackson, and she is an ardent member of the Ladies' Hermitage Association. Her father, Maj. John Jackson McClendon, held his rank in both the Thirty-fourth and Forty-second

Georgia Regiments. She is related to [Edmund] Kirby Smith, and farther back to Thomas Jefferson and President [John] Tyler. This fair lady is a Trustee of the Georgia Baptist Orphans' Home. She is Second Vice President of the International League of Press Clubs, and a member of the Liberty Bell Executive Committee. She is Representative at Large and is one of the Executive Committee of the Woman's Department at the coming Cotton States and International Exposition. "She does not want to vote and cannot make a speech," but is thoroughly womanly in all things.

    The incentive to give this brief sketch is to show what one woman has done recently for the South. As a modest writer for the press she joined the Woman's Press Club, which has done much in developing the literary talent of Southern girls. She was sent to the Convention of Press Clubs at St. Paul last year, and she soon became impressed that that great company of editors knew almost nothing of the South, and she went about bringing them to Dixie. In the name of the Georgia Woman's Press Club she invited them to hold their next meeting in Atlanta. Mr. Murat Halstead gallantly represented her cause on the floor of the Convention. [Georgia] Governor [William J.] Northen and representatives of the daily press telegraphed approval. Well, they went to Atlanta and "were conquered." Mrs. Gordon urges the formation of Press Clubs South, and that they be well represented in the League at Philadelphia next spring. She is confident that these organizations can be made very helpful to literary talent in the South, especially among women.[14]

INDIANA

Little Miss Ruth Owen of Evansville, Indiana, who won a $100 prize for selling the most subscriptions to *Confederate Veteran* magazine. Ruth is the "lovely, patriotic daughter" of former Confederate Lieutenant Frank A. Owen.

Mrs. Modena White of Evansville, Indiana. The first meeting of the Fitzhugh Lee Chapter, UDC, was held in her home.

IOWA

Miss Belle Richardson of Iowa.

From *Confederate Veteran*, 1895

AS SHE DOES TO OTHERS

Miss Belle Richardson is entitled to a secure place in the heart of every true American, whether of Union or Confederate sympathies. Her home is Davenport, Iowa, where her father, Hon. J. J. Richardson, a leading citizen, and a member of the National Democratic Executive Committee resides. Near by is Rock Island, the site of the noted Federal prison, where so many Confederate soldiers were confined, and near which many lie buried in unmarked graves. In the same enclosure are the graves of the Union dead, under the watchful care and guardianship of the National Government.

When the day for decorating the graves of the Federal dead is celebrated, and with tender care and affectionate memories the friends and relatives of the sleeping soldiers are strewing their silent beds with flowers, without ostentation, but with noble, womanly impulse, Miss Richardson, with her own fair hands, places fragrant flowers upon the graves of the unknown and neglected Confederate dead. Such an act, unseen by those who might feel grateful for the remembrance, arising from no impulse save that of womanly love for the friendless and the helpless, is indeed a glorious tribute to the womanhood of Iowa, and a blessing to her country.

Versatile and attractive is Miss Richardson. She is a brunette of beautiful and graceful figure, cordial in her manner. Loyal in her convictions and generous in her impulses, she has an enduring place in the hearts of all her friends.[15]

Confederate President Jefferson Davis (center top) and some of Dixie's finest "Civil War" generals. Every true daughter of the South knows these men by sight.

KENTUCKY

Miss Elizabeth Stovall of Kentucky.

Miss Rebecca Dickenson of Kentucky.

Mrs. Anna E. McFall, historian of the Mayfield, Kentucky, Chapter, UDC.

Miss Pattie McDaniel of Kentucky.

Miss Jovita Boyd, Confederate Sponsor for Kentucky at Houston, Texas.

Elizabeth Shelby Gilbert Burnett of Kentucky, a "grand, stately lady of the Old South," was a charter member of the Albert Sidney Johnston Chapter, UDC.

Mrs. Theodore R. Froudle, Confederate Matron of Honor, Kentucky Division.

Mrs. Phil Pointer Lippman of Owensboro, Kentucky, "one of the most attractive sponsors that Kentucky ever sent to a Confederate Reunion."

Miss Elenora Graves of Lexington, Kentucky, Confederate Representative for her state in the UCV Reunion at Birmingham, Alabama, 1894.

Mrs. Jeannette Robinson Murphy of Louisville, Kentucky, a professional singer specializing in modern renderings of black Southern folk songs.

"A little Kentucky girl," Janie Graham from Hopkinsville.

Mrs. Elise B. Bragg of Elizabethtown, Kentucky, wife of Confederate General Braxton Bragg.

Miss Anna B. Johnson of Kentucky, Confederate Maid of Honor for her state at the 1898 Atlanta Reunion, UCV. She is the daughter of Col. Thomas Johnson, who represented Kentucky (in connection with the Hon. Thomas D. Monroe) in the Confederate Provisional Congress at Richmond, Virginia, in 1861.

Miss Mary S. Semple of Kentucky, Confederate Sponsor for her state in the great UCV Reunion at Atlanta in 1898.

Mrs. Ben Hardin Helm, President of the Ben Hardin Helm Chapter, UDC, of Elizabethtown, Kentucky, organized July 16, 1897.

Miss Holly Witherspoon of Winchester, Kentucky, Confederate Maid of Honor for her state. Of her it is said: "Miss Witherspoon is a perfect blonde, rather above medium height, with a wealth of golden hair and large, expressive blue eyes, that show the character of one of Winchester's loveliest and most attractive girls."

Miss Julia Hughes Spurr of Kentucky, Confederate Maid of Honor for her state. She is described as being "of slender, graceful figure, a brunette, a typical daughter of Kentucky."

Mrs. H. W. Bruce of Louisville, Kentucky, an "ardent Confederate"; she served as Treasurer of the Confederate Memorial Association and President of the Albert Sidney Johnston Chapter, UDC.

Mrs. James B. Camp of Louisville, Kentucky, State President of the UDC.

Miss Nannie Barbee of Danville, Kentucky, "delightfully" entertained members of the UDC at the Atlanta Meeting in 1908.

Mrs. Henrietta Morgan Duke of Lexington, Kentucky, sister of Confederate Gen. John Hunt Morgan and wife of Confederate Gen. Basil Wilson Duke. She was known as one of the "most valued coworkers" at the Confederate Museum at Richmond, Virginia, and the donator of the beautiful "Morgan Collection." Of her it is written that she "exemplified in the highest degree the best type of the Southern gentlewoman, and who was ever loyal to the cause so gallantly defended by her husband and brother."

Mrs. M. B. Pilcher of Bardstown, Kentucky, later removed to Nashville, Tennessee, where she became President of the state's UDC Division, as well as Regent for the Tennessee Room at the Confederate Museum at Richmond, Virginia. Her husband was Confederate Capt. M. B. Pilcher.

Confederate General Thomas Jonathan "Stonewall" Jackson of Virginia.

Miss Ellanetta Harrison of Somerset, Kentucky, Confederate Maid of Honor, Kentucky Division.

Mrs. Mary E. Scott of Versailles, Kentucky.

From *Confederate Veteran*, 1898

OBITUARY: MARY E. SCOTT

A long, useful, and beautiful life, replete with loving devotion to friends and family, recently closed when Mrs. Mary E. Scott passed away at her home in Versailles, Ky., August 3, 1898, in her eighty-third year.

Her memory will be kept first in the hearts of the Confederates whom she served and helped so faithfully during the war. Her home was headquarters for the Confederate army while in that neighborhood. She was mother, nurse, and friend to those who were far from home, and she clothed and fed hundreds of her "boys," as she called them. Repeatedly she was arrested and threatened with imprisonment, but she was never discouraged, and worked on, undaunted, fearing nothing, for the sake of the cause which came next to her religion. It was interesting in after years to hear her relate her many escapes and experiences, and the tears would fill her eyes as she told of her fondest hopes, buried forever with the fall of the Confederacy. Though very modest, she was a woman of the finest information, a delightful companion, generous to a fault, and her friendship was as true as steel.[16]

Mrs. Jennie Catherwood Bean of Winchester, Kentucky.

From *Confederate Veteran*, 1895

WHAT A KENTUCKY WOMAN HAS DONE

The *Veteran* presents the picture and sketch of Mrs. Jennie Catherwood Bean, "Our Lady" of the Clark County Kentucky Confederate Veteran Association. She was born in Lexington fifty-six years ago, and soon after moved to Winchester, where she has ever since resided. Her father, John Catherwood, was for many years clerk of the Clark County Court, and was one of its best citizens—a true Southerner in every sense of the word; he reared his children, boys and girls, in the pure Jacksonian school.

The war was no dream, but a true reality to her. She ardently believed in the sacred principles her father and friends fought for. She is a worshiper of the memories of our cause, of the valor of our brave soldiers and heroic leaders. To her loyalty to the living, we owe the organization of Clark County Veteran Association.

In 1871, grieved to see the graves of the seven brave comrades in the silent city so neglected, with that loving devotion that ever characterizes her, she prepared the garlands, and with a few school children as her companions, in the softened glow of a May evening, knelt at each grave, and lovingly and tenderly covered them with beautiful flowers. Every year since, through sunshine and rain, she goes on "Memorial Day" with evergreen garlands and beautiful flowers to decorate every grave. And now her loving hands twine cypress, cedar, and flowers for thirty-two instead of seven. For years, with untiring zeal and devotion, she called upon the Confederates of the county to organize for such purposes, and she worked and toiled alone. Her efforts have been crowned with success in having the Clark County Confederate Veteran Association fully organized. She has also organized an association of their sons and daughters. She has a complete list of the Confederate dead buried in the Winchester Cemetery, and is perhaps the only person who knows where every brave fellow rests. She knew personally nearly every one, always attends the burial of a comrade, and marks the grave with a card and the colors.

She once said the only epitaph she desired was, "She never forgot the Confederate soldier on tented field, behind prison bars, nor under the sod."[17]

James W. Joplin (seated left center) of Elizabethtown, Kentucky, with his family. Six of his sons were Confederate soldiers.

Mrs. Susan Preston Hepburn of Kentucky.

From *Confederate Veteran*, 1898

SKETCH BY MAJOR J. STODDARD JOHNSTON

Among the many noble women in the South whose names are dear to the Confederate veteran none is held in more affectionate remembrance than Mrs. Susan Preston Hepburn. It was not her privilege to be an active participant in the actual scenes of war, as her residence was within the Federal lines; but, having in the Confederate service a brother and many relatives and friends, her sympathy in the cause was ardent and her efforts to relieve the suffering of the Confederate soldiers in the local hospitals and Northern prisons were active and efficient. Without ostentation she joined quietly with other noble women of similar feeling in the work of visiting the sick, burying the dead, and marking their graves, and in sending relief under the Federal regulations to the prisoners at Camp Chase, Camp Douglas, and Johnson's Island, who were beyond the ministrations of their friends within the Southern lines.

The relief sent by the noble women of Kentucky was not limited to the soldiers of that state, but embraced the unfortunate prisoners of the whole South. Clothing, food, and delicacies for the sick, books, magazines, and everything which could contribute to their bodily, mental, or spiritual comfort were raised by organizations covering the whole state, and sent continuously during the war to relieve the wants of the suffering. And thus, while the women of the South were ministering to the wants of the soldiers in the field, the women of Kentucky were alleviating the necessities of their imprisoned fathers, husbands, and sons.

When the war was over, and the necessity for such exertions was no longer required, Mrs. Hepburn continued her good work in a field where relief was quite as essential. Many helpless orphans were to be cared for and the infirm, maimed, and needy veterans to be looked after. One of her first works in this direction was to aid in the establishment of a Masonic widows' and orphans' home, the first of the kind in the United States, to the successful foundation of which she contributed by her unremitting labors more, perhaps, than any other individual. This great charity, while not limited by any sectional line, was instrumental in relieving many of those left dependent by the war.

But concurrently with this work she, in conjunction with other good women, formed associations for the relief of surviving Confederates and was active in promoting the permanent organization of the Confederate Association of Louisville, through which the necessities of the sick and dependent veterans have been provided for. In her labors she was untiring. Her influence over the Confederate veterans able to contribute by their means or personal exertions was such that they responded with alacrity to her every suggestion, while the Southern women recognized in her a worthy leader, under whom they labored with equal alacrity.

Possessed of a superior faculty for organization and the gift of a conciliating diplomacy, she united elements too often rendered ineffective by dissension and jealousy into a harmonious cooperation. Thus, by inaugurating fêtes, excursions, lectures, and by direct application to those able to contribute, she provided means to meet all the necessities and relieve all requiring help who would apply or could be found by vigilant search, until it can be said that no one ever saw an ex-Confederate begging his bread in her vicinity.

The great work by which Mrs. Hepburn's good name will be perpetuated, and that which engaged her ardent efforts during the last decade of her life, is the handsome Confederate monument which was conceived by her and erected chiefly through her exertions. For this purpose she organized the Woman's Confederate Monument Association, and was made its President. It is doubtful if a movement for this purpose could have been successful if projected by the Confederate soldiers themselves, as from the relation of Kentucky to the war it might have engendered feelings which would have endangered its success. But the devotion of this good woman was so pure, the spirit of her conception was so noble, and her devotion so elevated that she not only enlisted the earnest cooperation of the Confederates, but elicited the fullest sympathy and hearty good will of the Federal soldiers themselves.

A noble granite shaft of sixty feet or more in height occupies a circle on one of the handsomest streets of Louisville, surmounted by a life size Confederate private in bronze and flanked on either side by a bronze cavalryman and artilleryman—all of the most artistic execution. It bears the simple inscription "Confederate Dead" on one side, and on the opposite side one to the effect that it was erected by the Confederate women of Kentucky. It was dedicated with appropriate ceremonies July 30, 1895.

The successful execution of this work crowned the labors of Mrs. Hepburn's life. She had raised the money, $12,000, to pay for it before it was erected, lacking a small sum, which was raised afterward. Her last efforts were directed toward securing a fund for its proper enclosure, and in this she had succeeded a short time before her death.

The infirmities of age and ill health were no barriers to her efforts, but her extraordinary will seemed to sustain her and prolong her life until her aim was completed. Then, rejoicing in the consummation of her labors, she calmly passed from earth. But the monument will not be complete until it bears an appropriate tablet with her name, making it, in fact, to future generations, as it is to the present, a lasting testimonial to her own memory.

Mrs. Susan P. Hepburn was born near Louisville, Ky., July 17, 1819; and died in that city October 5, 1897. She was the daughter and youngest child of Maj. William Preston and Caroline Hancock, his wife, both of Botetourt County, Va., who early settled in Kentucky. Her only brother was Maj.-Gen. William Preston, of the Confederate army, prominent in civil life as a member of the state constitutional convention of 1849, Representative and Senator, Member of Congress, and Minister to Spain under President [James] Buchanan's administration. He was a lieutenant-colonel in the Mexican war, and won distinction in the Confederate war on many fields, but particularly in the battles of Murfreesboro and Chickamauga.

Confederate monument, Louisville, Kentucky.

The eldest of Mrs. Hepburn's four sisters [Henrietta Preston] was the first wife of Gen. Albert Sidney Johnston. In 1841 she [Susan] married Howard Christy, of St. Louis, who died in 1853; and in 1860 she married Hiatt P. Hepburn, a distinguished lawyer of San Francisco. In 1864 she was again widowed, and for the remainder of her life devoted herself to good works. As a young woman, possessed of a superior mind and cultured education, she was conspicuous for her intellectual attainments, her great beauty, and her lovely character. Having had before age had encroached on her vigor her full share of sorrow, she seemed to find relief in taking up the burdens of others. Not blessed with children of her own, she became a mother to the motherless, and never turned a deaf ear to a suffering cry.

When the resources of a once ample fortune restricted her own bounties she inspired others by an unselfish devotion to charity, and became alms-gatherer in its cause and the faithful trustee of the contributions of others, as well as of herself. Her life was sunshine to the afflicted and an inspiration to the many able and willing to do good and yet needing a leader and exemplar, and in her death her memory is embalmed in the gratitude of many whom she succored and in the love and admiration of all who knew her.[18]

Mrs. Kate Moss Vanmeter of Kentucky.

From *Confederate Veteran*, 1912

OBITUARY: MRS. KATE MOSS VANMETER

Mrs. Kate (Moss) Vanmeter, wife of Capt. Charles J. Vanmeter, Chancellor of the Western Kentucky State Normal School, died peacefully after a lingering illness at her home, near Bowling Green, Ky., May 16, in her seventy-sixth year. Mrs. Vanmeter was [from] one of Kentucky's most prominent families. Her four brothers were all faithful and gallant Confederate soldiers. One of them, Col. J. W. Moss, who commanded the 2nd Kentucky Regiment, was mortally wounded at Jonesboro, Tenn., in 1864. Another brother, Maj. Thomas E. Moss, formerly Attorney-General of Kentucky, died in the Philippine Islands about two years ago. She had survived all her immediate family except one sister, Miss Joe Moss, whose home has for years been at the Vanmeter residence. Her venerable husband, Capt. Charles J. Vanmeter, who survives her, though bowed down with grief, and now in his eighty seventh year, entered the quartermaster's service in the Confederate States army in 1861 and so continued until 1865.

Mrs. Vanmeter united with the Presbyterian Church in early life, and was constant in her attendance at worship as long as her health permitted. She retained throughout her simple faith in the Lord and lived a consistent and active Christian, dispensing charity in an unostentatious way, with an eye single to the glory of the Master whom she loved.

As a wife she was truly and devotedly a helpmeet. With her broad-minded, public-spirited, and greatly esteemed husband she was active in educational work, and she cooperated with him in his contributions to the many causes of education and charity.

Mrs. Vanmeter was a woman of great force of character and strong convictions and unflinching courage. What endeared her most, perhaps, to old Confederates and Southern sympathizers was her undying loyalty to the cause of her own Southland—a cause that will never be lost as long as men love liberty and valor lasts. She was a moving spirit and an enthusiastic worker in the Daughters of the Confederacy. She never failed to be present and to take an active part in the decoration of Confederate graves in Fairview Cemetery.

Her last letter, written on her sick bed a day or two before her death, was to the President of the local Chapter, U.D.C., reminding her to make arrangements for the decoration exercises on June 3.

In the death of Mrs. Kate Moss Vanmeter the Confederacy has lost one of its most active and loyal Daughters and its old veterans one of their best friends. The memory of her Christian character—her loyal heart and her good deeds—is deeply enshrined in the hearts of all who knew her. (From sketch by Maj. W. O. Obenchain, Bowling Green.)[19]

Mrs. Caroline Meriwether Goodlett of Todd County, Kentucky, co-founder and first President of what is now the United Daughters of the Confederacy.

From *Confederate Veteran*, 1894

THE PRESIDENT OF THE N.C.D.C.

Mrs. Caroline Meriwether Goodlett, the recently elected President of the National Confederation of Daughters of the Confederacy, is a native of Kentucky and lived until after the war at Woodstock, the old Meriwether homestead, Todd County. Mrs. Goodlett commenced her work for the Confederate soldiers in the recruiting camps of the army. She spent her entire income, amounting to thousands of dollars, to help supply the wants of the Confederates, caring for those in prison as well as those in the ranks. She also did much in making up clothing, etc. She has ever worked for the Confederate soldiers whenever her services have been needed, and has esteemed opportunities for doing so. She is the wife of Col. Michael Campbell Goodlett, a Confederate soldier who was on [Missouri] Gov. [Hancock Lee] Jackson's staff. Col. Goodlett prepared the Ordinance of Secession that took the State of Missouri out of the Union.

Mrs. Goodlett was one of the charter members of the Monumental Association, through whose efforts was erected the handsome monument over the fallen heroes, who lie buried in Mt. Olivet Cemetery, Nashville, Tenn. After the erection of this monument the association went into a permanent organization as an auxiliary to the Confederate Soldiers' Home, and that auxiliary was largely instrumental in securing from the State four hundred and seventy-five acres of the Hermitage farm owned by the State for a Soldiers' Home, and in making the appropriation to improve the property.

Mrs. Goodlett has from the first been President of the State Association of Daughters of the Confederacy, an Auxiliary to the Home. She has worked for many of the charities of her city. She was for a number of years a member of the Board of Managers of the Protestant Orphan Asylum and Mission Home. She is Vice President of the Humane Society of Nashville, a member of the National Prison Association, and for years an active member of the National Conference of Charities and Corrections, and one of the Board of Associated Charities of the State.

Mrs. Goodlett also organized the Ladies Auxiliary of the Masonic Widows' and Orphans' Home, which helped to build and furnish the magnificent home situated in the suburbs of Nashville; and was president of the organization until its home was erected and furnished.[20]

Miss Emily Mason of Kentucky.

From *Confederate Veteran*, 1909

OBITUARY: MISS EMILY MASON

Death loves a shining mark, and yet at times he will leave the most brilliant untouched for years, that, like tall church spires, they may point a guiding finger heavenward.

Miss Emily Mason was born in Kentucky, but of Virginia ancestry, and lived in the latter State till her fifteenth year, when her family moved to Washington. She met and knew all the Presidents from [James] Monroe to [Theodore] Roosevelt, and she spent a part of her girlhood as the guest of her brother [Stevens T. Mason], the Governor of Michigan. During the Civil War she was much engaged in hospital work, being at the head of the Georgia division in Wynder Hospital with eight hundred men under her care. The orphans of some of these men she took under her own protection. After Lee's surrender she had thirty of these depending upon her, all of whom she placed so well that they became self-supporting or, marrying well, became the heads of prosperous families.

In the death of Miss Mason, on February 16, 1909, one of the most notable figures of Washington society has passed away. Tall, erect, with her abundant white hair worn in the fashion of fifty years ago, she attracted all attention at once, and her sparkling black eyes and vivacious manner held entranced all who were so fortunate as to be thrown with her.

She was ninety-three years old, yet "time could not wither nor custom state her infinite variety." By the right divine of intellect, courtesy, and the marvelous charm of her brilliant conversational gift she held a social sway that was never questioned. Her afternoon teas were veritable salons, and she their heart and the center of attraction. Like Madam De Staël, she was the empress of intellect, and like her too she wore her crown with modesty. She was the honored guest wherever she appeared, and to the end of her life men burned incense at her shrine.

Miss Mason wrote only one book, but was a constant contributor to the best magazines. She was a fine linguist, having crossed the ocean fifty times, and spent many years at foreign courts. She was introduced at the court of Alfonso [XIII, King] of Spain, was a close friend of the Empress Eugénie, and was presented at the Austrian court and received on the most intimate terms by the Royal Duke and Duchess. Her court dress of scarlet velvet and gold embroidery was given by her to the Catholic Church and cut up into vestments.

Her funeral was conducted by the highest Church dignities, and was notable for the marvelous profusion of flowers, the gifts of statesmen, public organizations, and of the friends who were so tender and loving.[21]

From the *Chicago Tribune*, October 9, 1902

WOMEN REFUSE TO TAKE DOWN CONFEDERATE FLAG
Emblem is Chief Decoration in U.D.C. Convention at Cincinnati, and Efforts to Dislodge it are Failures.

Excited Daughters of the Confederacy formed a compact blockade in Carnegie Hall, Newport, Kentucky, today and successfully resisted the efforts of janitor William Boyd to tear down an immense confederate flag which occupied the most conspicuous place over the stage. The daughters had been requested to remove the flag from the place of honor, but refused. The janitor then was ordered to tear it down, but the southern women blocked the aisles and nothing short of armed violence could have secured for him a right of way to the flag. The directors were unable to decide on further proceedings to remove the flag and it remained. American flags had conspicuous positions at either end of the stage.[22]

LOUISIANA

Mrs. William B. Mumford (née Baumlin) of New Orleans, Louisiana, whose husband was illegally executed by Union Gen. Benjamin F. Butler for removing a U.S. flag that had been unlawfully hoisted above the city's mint by Federal troops. The heinous crime has gone down in history as a symbol of the North's unwarranted disrespect, viciousness, and cruelty toward the South.

Mrs. Julia Ann White of Clinton, Louisiana. Her father and two brothers fought for the Confederacy. She helped organize a UDC chapter, of which she was elected president.

Miss Ida H. Vinson of Shreveport, Louisiana, Confederate Representative for her state in the UCV Reunion at Birmingham, Alabama, 1894.

Miss Mary Gilmore of Louisiana, Confederate Maid of Honor for her state division, UCV, at the Atlanta Reunion, 1898.

Miss Odile M. Hood of Louisiana, Confederate Sponsor for the Louisiana Division, UCV, Atlanta Reunion, 1898.

Miss Annie Tucker Stubbs of Louisiana, Confederate Maid of Honor for her state at the Atlanta Reunion, 1898.

Miss Elizabeth Q. Walshe, Confederate Sponsor, UCV, Camp No. 1, Louisiana Division, at the Atlanta Reunion, 1898.

Miss A. C. Childress of New Orleans, Louisiana, official stenographer and typewriter of the UCV.

Mrs. J. M. Ferguson, the great-grandniece of Patrick Henry and the Recording Secretary for the New Orleans Chapter, No. 72, UDC.

Miss Edna Sidonie De La Houssaque, Confederate Sponsor for Camp No. 2, Army of Tennessee Association, New Orleans.

Mrs. Victoria Mermillod Jones of New Orleans, Louisiana, Confederate Chaperon for the South at the Tulsa Reunion, September 1918.

Miss Birdie Scott, Confederate Maid of Honor for Louisiana.

WHITE AND BLACK SLAVES
FROM NEW ORLEANS.
Photographed by Kimball, 477 Broadway, N. Y.
Entered according to act of Congress, in the year 1863, by P. Bacon, in the Clerk's Office of the United States, for the Southern District of New York.

REBECCA, CHARLEY & ROSA,
Slave Children from New Orleans.

White and black Southern slaves, more properly known as "servants" in Dixie, helped prolong the War and buoy Southern spirits, working closely with conservative Confederate women of all colors in a patriotic effort to vanquish the liberal North.

Mrs. Katie Walker Behan of New Orleans, Louisiana.

From *Confederate Veteran*, 1918

OBITUARY: KATIE WALKER BEHAN

Mrs. Behan was a prominent philanthropist, patriot, and leader in New Orleans in all movements for the betterment of her fellow men and was known for her rare ability, devotion, and self-sacrifice in the interest of the history and social ideals of the Old South and reverence for our heroic dead. She was President of the Confederated Southern Memorial Association from her election at Louisville. Ky., in 1900, serving for eighteen years with ability and success.

She was also President of the Ladies' Confederate Memorial Association of New Orleans, having been annually elected its President for seventeen years, President of the Ursuline Alumnae, President of the House of the Good Shepherd, Chairman of Branch No. 8, Red Cross Society, a Daughter of the Confederacy, a member of the Louisiana Branch of the King's Daughters and Sons, of the Sunshine Society, and the Era Club (suffrage); she was the official representative of the C.S.M.A. on the board of directors of the *Confederate Veteran* and Regent for Louisiana of the Confederate Museum, Richmond, Va., adding many valuable historical relics to the State collection.

. . . No woman has ever held the hearts of the women of New Orleans and the South more truly than did Mrs. Behan, and none has ever left a sweeter or more gracious memory. One of her strongest characteristics was her loyalty and devotion to the memory of Jefferson Davis. Through her efforts and those of the Confederated Southern Memorial Association a handsome sum was secured for the monument in Richmond, Va., to his memory.

She served as a member of the monument committee until its completion; then she gave her attention to the erection of a monument to his memory in New Orleans, where his death occurred. She was President of the Jefferson Davis Monument Association of New Orleans, and in 1906 a handsome monument in bronze and stone was erected on the widest avenue in the country, known as the Jefferson Davis Parkway, which was so named by the efforts of Mrs. Behan and her associates.

After the unveiling of this monument the surplus sum in the treasury was forwarded to the Jefferson Davis Home Association of Kentucky for the memorial at Fairview. Through her efforts the legislature of Louisiana passed an act making June 3, the birthday of President Davis and our Confederate Memorial Day, a legal holiday; and again, several years later, when Calcasieu Parish was divided by the legislature, the memory of Jefferson Davis, Beauregard, and Allen was perpetuated. The name of Jefferson Davis was restored to Cabin John Bridge at Washington by the order of President [Theodore] Roosevelt, who gave the honor of this restoration to Mrs. Behan.[23]

A POEM TO CONFEDERATE HERO SAM DAVIS
by Ella Wheeler Wilcox, in the *New Orleans Picayune*

Sam Davis

When the Lord calls up earth's heroes to stand before his face,
O, many a name unknown to fame shall ring from that high place!
And out of a grave in the Southland, at the just God's call and beck,
Shall one man rise with fearless eyes and a rope about his neck.

For men have swung from gallows whose souls were white as snow.
Not how they die nor where, but why, is what God's records show.
And on that mighty ledger is writ Sam Davis' name.
For honor's sake he would not make a compromise with shame.

The great world lay before him, For he was in his youth.
With love of life young hearts are rife. But better he loved truth.
He fought for his convictions; and when he stood at bay,
He would not flinch or stir one inch from honor's narrow way.

They offered life and freedom if he would speak the word.
In silent pride he gazed aside as one who had not heard.
They argued, pleaded, threatened—it was but wasted breath.
"Let come what must, I keep my trust," he said, and laughed at death.

He would not sell his manhood to purchase a priceless hope.
Where kings cast down a name and crown he dignified a rope.
Ah, grave! where was your triumph? Ah, death! where was your sting?
He showed you how a man could bow to doom and stay a king.

And God, who loves the loyal because they are like him,
I doubt not yet that soul shall set among his cherubim.
O Southland, fling your laurels! And add your wreath, O North!
Let glory claim the hero's name and tell the world his worth.[24]

The interior of Confederate Memorial Hall, New Orleans, 1898.

Robert E. Lee, Jr. and Elizabeth "Bessie" W. Washington, 1907. Mr. Lee was presented to the UCV Convention, Nashville Reunion, 1897.

MARYLAND

Miss Lula Montague of Baltimore, Maryland, Confederate Representative for her state in the UCV Reunion at Birmingham, Alabama, 1894.

Miss Louise Harrison Beall of Maryland, Confederate First Maid of Honor for her state at the 1898 Atlanta Reunion. Her father was H. D. Beall, who served under Confederate Generals J. E. B. Stuart and Thomas Lafayette Rosser.

Mrs. Owen Norris of the Maryland Daughters.

Mrs. F. G. Odenheimer, President of the Maryland Division, UDC.

Hetty Cary of Baltimore, Maryland, considered by many to be "the most beautiful woman in the Southland" at the time. A strong supporter of the Confederacy, along with her sister Jennie and her cousin Constance Cary Harrison, she sewed the first set of Confederate flags in 1861. She later married Confederate General John Pegram. (Image courtesy Teresa Roane)

Rose O'Neill Greenhow of Montgomery County, Maryland, with her daughter "Little" Rose at the Old Capitol Prison, Washington, D.C., around 1862. Mrs. Greenhow will live forever in the memories of traditional Southerners as a true Confederate heroine, one who risked her life spying for the Confederate States. Captured, she spent time in a Northern prison (seen here), after which she was deported to the South. Returning from a trip to England in 1864, her ship ran aground off North Carolina. Tragically, the small boat she attempted to take ashore sank in the waves and she drowned. She recorded her memoirs in the delightfully pro-South book, *My Imprisonment and the First Year of Abolition Rule at Washington*.

The Confederate Monument at Baltimore, Maryland: *Gloria Victis* ("Conquered Yet Victorious").

MASSACHUSETTS

Mrs. Rebecca Elwell Maxwell of Boston, Massachusetts.

From *Confederate Veteran*, 1907

OBITUARY: REBECCA ELWELL MAXWELL

It is with deep regret that the *Veteran* records the death of Mrs. Rebecca E. Maxwell on the 15th of January at the home of her daughter, Mrs. W. J. Cook, in Jacksonville, Fla. She was in her eighty-eighth year. From the beginning Mrs. Maxwell had been an interested subscriber to the *Veteran* for herself and others, and her kind thought in contributing thus toward its maintenance was indicative of her character of helpfulness.

Mrs. Maxwell was an honorary life member of the Martha Reid Chapter, U.D.C., of Jacksonville, and was always interested in the objects of the Chapter, doing her share in its many good works. She was referred to as the mother of the Chapter, having proposed its name and being its oldest member.

Prior to her marriage she was Miss Elwell, of Boston, Mass. Coming South in her early womanhood to visit relatives in Leon County, Fla., she met Col. C. William McWhir Maxwell, and in marrying him she became an adopted daughter of the South, and there were none by birth who were more devoted to or espoused its sacred cause more ardently. She possessed a wonderfully retentive memory, and was probably better posted than any native in the history of the old aristocratic South. Mrs. Maxwell is survived by two sons (Capt. D. Elwell Maxwell and Clarence W. Maxwell) and two daughters (Mrs. W. J. Cook and Mrs. Jennie Farrell, of Jacksonville).[25]

MINNESOTA

Mrs. Joseph Johnson.

From *Confederate Veteran*, 1909

CONFEDERATE DAUGHTERS IN MINNESOTA
An Address by Mrs. Joseph Johnson of St. Louis, Missouri

We have been brave enough to invade the "North Star State," the home of the Moccasin flower, and where, I am told, Minnesotans never sing "There is a better land." We come not to arouse antagonistic feelings, but to tell you of our grand and glorious work.

During my two years' residence in the "Twin Cities" I have often been asked: "What is the object and origin of your association, now known as the United Daughters of the Confederacy?" I was very much amused when on one occasion some one remarked to me: "Why, I never heard of the Daughters of the Confederacy. What are you—a lot of organized anarchists?" I hope the good people of Minneapolis and St. Paul don't think we look like a lot of anarchists, and with your kind indulgence I will give you a brief history of our work, which, I feel sure, will meet with the approbation of every intelligent man and woman, whether of the North or of the South.

This organization is composed of between 45,000 and 50,000 women, and we are a distinct class, inasmuch as we are working for and giving our time, money, and talents to a cause with no thought of future remuneration whatever. We have Chapters in all the Southern States, including Maryland, West Virginia, and Missouri. We have Chapters also in Washington, California, District of Columbia, Illinois, Indiana, Indian Territory, Montana, Nebraska, New York, Ohio, Oregon, Utah, New Mexico, Minnesota, and Mexico.

The first Southern body of women to call themselves "Daughters of the Confederacy" originated in my own grand old State, "Imperial Missouri," in the year 1890. "A meeting of St. Louis women was called for, and a society was organized with a membership of one hundred and sixteen." Their first work of importance was the Confederate Home at Higginsville, Mo., built by the united efforts of the women of Missouri in 1893, and standing to-day, supported by the State, as a beautiful monument to their untiring energy.

The Daughters of the Confederacy are banded together for mutually preserving to posterity facts, loyal deeds, and valorous acts, embodied in or intimately associated with their individual lives and daily experiences, as well as to perpetuate through all generations the names of those illustrious families participating in the great cause. Its membership includes not only those original daughters, but the daughters of their daughters unto our generation, thus perpetuating this glorious organization for all time.

The motto of our national organization is the beautiful words: "Love makes memory eternal." The objects of our association are historical, educational, memorial, benevolent, and social; to collect and preserve the material for an impartial history of the War between the States, and to teach the coming generations that Jefferson Davis, Robert E. Lee, and Stonewall Jackson were not traitors to their country, but high-minded Christian gentlemen, statesmen, soldiers, and patriots. In our great loyalty to and appreciation of our organization we must not forget these eminent Southern generals and the brave soldiers who fought so valiantly in defending what they believed to be their perfectly justifiable rights. Their names, now reverenced by all, will be perpetuated through all coming generations for the hardships endured and sacrifices made. Their careers elicit the admiration of the world, coequal with that extended to the names of Napoleon, Wellington, and Cromwell. In 1889 at the Piedmont Exposition, held at Atlanta, Ga., attended by the masses, the enthusiasm which greeted our beloved and only President of the Confederacy, Jefferson Davis, will long be remembered by those present.

The Southerner's valor and patriotism is known the world over, and who ever knew a Southern woman to falter where love and duty called her? Southern women are noted for their affability and refinement, and in no quarter of the United States is more hospitality shown than in the South.

We love, honor, and cherish the memories of those who wore the gray. Such a heritage I am proud to own. We come not to fight the war over again, as a few of our Northern friends think, but to heal the wounds; for we are a united country, and the stars and stripes are dear to the heart of every true Daughter of the Confederacy.

. . . Situated as you are, many miles from Mason and Dixon's famous line, I realize that the work will be hard and some times may become irksome, yet greater will be your reward and you stand as a living monument to the heroic lives that were sacrificed in 1861 to 1865.

I must also impress upon the Executive Board the necessity of working together in harmony, remembering the beautiful motto of our country, "United we stand, divided we fall," and ever bearing in mind the object to which we are striving; and while this is also a social organization, my great desire is for this Chapter to be known as one of the most energetic Chapters in the U.D.C.

At your annual election of officers bury all personal animosity, if any should ever exist, and put into office those women whom you know to be thoroughly capable and who will perform accurately the duties of said office, for without such the Chapter is powerless.

I cannot refrain from saying that this Chapter will always occupy a sacred place in the memory of my home Chapter—the St. Louis. She will watch with pride and interest your future progress, and through her worthy and charming President, Mrs. W. L. Kline, she desires me to extend to the Robert E. Lee Chapter of Minneapolis her cordial greetings.[26]

MISSISSIPPI

Mrs. S. E. F. Rose (née Laura Martin), of Mississippi, pro-South author.

Miss McIntosh of Meridian, Mississippi, Confederate Sponsor for her state.

Miss Lucy White Hayes, Sponsor for the Trans-Mississippi Department, Richmond Division.

The Confederate First Couple: Mrs. Varina Howell Davis of Natchez, Mississippi, with her husband President Jefferson Davis.

Mrs. Fanny Sillers Saunders of Port Gibson, Mississippi, an officer in the J. Harvey Mathis Chapter, UDC.

Mrs. Saunders (above) and her husband [Confederate] Colonel W. J. Saunders were described as "kind, generous, and cheerful, and much courted; neither would have wounded, by word or deed, a fellow-being; both were tender, affectionate, consistent, and natural."[27]

Miss Etta Mitchell of Mississippi, Confederate Representative for her state in the UCV Reunion at Birmingham, Alabama, 1894.

Another image of the Confederate First Lady, Varina Howell Davis of Natchez, Mississippi.

Mrs. E. C. Pendleton (née Jones) of Columbus, Mississippi, pro-South writer and Representative for her state at the opening of the Confederate Museum, February 22, 1896. She was also the Vice Regency of the Confederate Memorial Literary Society.

Mrs. Will S. Green (née Morgan) of Hinds County, Mississippi, sister of Confederate Major William H. Morgan. At the start of the Great War she made socks for our Confederate boys.

Miss Minnie Clopton of Aberdeen, Mississippi, Confederate Sponsor for the Mississippi Division at Richmond.

Mrs. E. D. Wright of Vicksburg, Mississippi.

From *Confederate Veteran*, 1895

Mrs. E. D. Wright (above) served as President of the Vicksburg Confederate Monument Association for over a quarter century, and often took part in handling the sacred dust personally. As President of the Confederate Cemetery Association, she supplemented the four years' work as President of the Confederate Aid Association, to which she had given such marvelous efficiency during the war.[28]

A Confederate Battle Flag from a Mississippi unit—like its brave soldiers, war-torn and battle-scarred.

Miss Estelle Coleman, President of the Daughters of Confederate Veterans, Vicksburg, Mississippi, 1895.

Jefferson Davis and his family (three generations), with his wife Varina Howell Davis on the right, c. 1885.

From *Confederate Veteran*, 1893

OUR SOUTHERN WOMEN IN WAR TIMES
Vivid reminiscences by Mrs. (Varina Howell) Jefferson Davis

The women of the South did not shrink from the prospect of great and painful economies; they also appreciated that their own patriotic duty was, as cheerfully as possible, to bid farewell to the men of their family who must go to the front, perhaps never to return. Sometimes hope buoyed them up, and they looked on the sunny side and believed that their dear ones would be spared because their cause was righteous. They did shrink, however, affrighted from the prospect of being left alone with a multitude of ignorant [that is, illiterate] negroes who might be instigated to rebellion [by Yanks and scallywags], without physicians to attend their children or priests to bury them if they died. These horrors oppressed them.

Many a woman, buckling on her husband's sword, asked him to show her how to load and shoot a pistol, adding, "not that I am afraid of anything, but in case of need." Her next problem was how to handle that pistol, which was an object of almost as great dread as would be the foe it was to repel.

GOOD CONDUCT OF THE NEGROES

All Southern women acknowledge with pride the good conduct of the rank and file of negroes on the breaking out of the war. They generally remained true to the families left in their charge, and protected the women and children to the best of their ability. In short, their course was a powerful testimonial to the life-long kind and just exercise of their masters' power over them.

Black Confederate soldiers on picket duty in the swamps of Louisiana, just two of the estimated 1 million African-Americans who served in some capacity in the Confederate military.

However, the crops failed frequently. The negroes grew to partake more or less of the excitement which pervaded the whole country, and this interfered with the needful routine of their labor. Then again, the work horses were levied upon for the use of the Government. Thus were the means of cultivation narrowed. The fallow land grew impassable with weeds, the fences and levees fell, the fields which had waved with corn and cotton blooms became a tangle of vines and bushes, "unprofitably gay with the blue flowers of the destructive morning glory, the execrated tie-vine."

Moreover, all large balances of cash lay out of reach, invested, so that there was little wherewith to buy from the neighboring towns or cities; and as the prosperity of these centers was dependent upon the grain and cotton sent in from the plantations, want came upon all.

The very poor suffered in the absence of their breadwinners. Necessarily those better provided for gave of their surplus, and when they became sorely pressed themselves they shared whatever could be spared by their families; as the poorer classes expressed it, they "had a divide."

The harbors were closed by the [naval] blockade. No supplies of clothing could be imported. The time came when the stock of cloth, shoes, medicines, machinery—indeed, of almost everything necessary to civilized people—was nearly exhausted. The South had proved agriculture to be the most profitable employment, and had never fostered manufactures; besides, her operative classes were not suited to the care of machinery. Now the people found themselves confronted with new problems which they must learn to solve. All these needs must be supplied by the women.

The store each family possessed themselves, of quinine, and such other drugs as were needful for the diseases of a warm climate, was gradually relinquished for the use of the soldiers. Replenishment was impossible. Quinine had been proclaimed by the [Yankee] blockaders "contraband of war."

The women turned, undaunted, to the indigenous *materia medica*. Decoctions of willow bark, of dewberry root, orange flowers and leaves, red pepper tea and other "tisanes" took the place of the drugs.

One heart-broken woman wrote to her husband: "Twenty grains of quinine would have saved our two children. They were too nauseated to drink the bitter willow tea, and they are now at rest, and I have no one to work for but you. Do not think of coming [home]. I am well and strong, and am not dismayed. I think day and night of your sorrow. I have their little graves near me."

The sheep were sheared; the wool was cleansed, carded and spun in the house. Small looms were set up and the warp adjusted under the eye of the practical weaver—this being the mistress, generally. All the clothes for the plantation, as well as some cloth to exchange for other commodities, was woven for the winter use. In winter the cotton clothes were made for summer. Pretty homespun checks, brown, black, blue, or red and white, were manufactured for the ladies' and children's frocks. The ladies spun the wool and knitted the stockings and socks their children and husbands wore, also many for the soldiers.

When the longing for the silk stockings, habitually used, pressed upon refined women, the old pieces of black silk were picked to a "'frazzle" and spun to make stockings and gloves for themselves and their daughters. Said one, putting out her nattily clad slender little feet: "I could not bear to wear coarse stockings, my husband takes such pride in my small feet."

Towels and sheets were spun from the house linen which had

been cut into bandages, or scraped into lint for the surgeons in the field. One handsome young woman, the daughter of an ex-Minister to Spain, rises before me out of the haze of bygone years, stepping lightly to and fro winding bandages on the spindle of her wheel and talking pleasantly to her visitors, while her patriotic mother sat by cutting up the table linen which she had treasured for forty years. The daughter showed great callous knots on her shapely hands made by scraping lint, and mentioned them with an expression of gratitude to God that she could procure material for so much work.

A general officer's wife called to see the wife of the President [Davis] and brought her, as the most acceptable present, a paper pattern of a glove like those she herself wore, beautifully embroidered and exactly fitted to her delicate hands. This paper pattern is still extant, and very precious to the recipient. It was very useful in providing the President's whole family with presentable gloves made from the sleeves and breast of an old Confederate uniform and the cast-off black cloth garments of the gentlemen of the family.

Ladies plaited exquisite straw hats and bonnets, and learned every brand except that of Leghorn [a straw hat made of bleached wheat]. The birds of the country furnished feathers for their adornment.

INGENIOUS LUXURIES

When new companies or battalions organized, for which flags were needed, the sisters and sweethearts of the men sacrificed their best silk frocks to make the flags. With cunning embroidery they emblazoned them in such royal style that they are wondrously beautiful even in this day of the Renaissance. Is it astonishing that our men wrapped these flags about their bodies and like the stern Scotch father who gave another and another son "for Eachim," died one after the other to preserve them from capture?

The snippings left by the army tailors, pieces of gray and black cloth five or six inches across, were pieced together and then cut into jackets for the soldiers' children. Very acceptable these "Joseph's coats" proved to those who could boast no better covering.

Such rags as could be utilized in no other way were wound in balls and woven into carpets, which did duty in place of those long since cut up for horse and saddle blankets, and these home-made carpets were contributed later as the need of them arose.

Bits of the clippings of the best gown were sewed neatly over the worn-out house slippers of the women, and they straightway became dandy little congeners of the gown, and were dainty to look upon, as well as objects of pride to their owners.

Flannel was very scarce, and cost $15 or $20 a yard; but underwear was knitted of homespun wool, and was quite as comfortable as the woven. Dyes were made of the juice of plants. The raw silk wound from cocoons was dyed and twisted into very smooth thread. The finest and most even flax thread, nearly as strong as wire and quite as smooth and fine as sewing silk, was made in Virginia, and even now there is none so good in the market.

HOW WE LIGHTED OUR HOUSES
Lampwicks were plaited by hand and the oil was fried out of refuse pork. Sometimes wild myrtle berries were stewed until they yielded a pale green wax, which made beautiful and aromatic candles. The oil of peanuts served also for illuminating purposes. When none of these were to be had the resinous pine—"fat pine"—was cut into splinters and burned one at a time, while the overworked women sat around the flickering light and sewed until late in the night.

I once saw five soldiers' wives making clothes by this light, and while they worked they talked over the chances of their "men" coming home alive. "I don't expect mine," said one, "but God knows I do not want to complain. Since my baby died he hasn't any occasion to come." By "occasion" she meant inducement.

During all these laborious occupations the children had to be clothed, generally without the assistance of a sewing machine; they must be watched, fed, taught and disciplined. Night schools were established in the basements of the churches, where the ragged children were taught by the young ladies.

Great barrels of soap were made of the refuse of the hogs killed for family and plantation use. Was toilet soap required the need was supplied each time that a home-cured ham was boiled for family use, and the old-fashioned sweet flowers and herbs of the garden furnished the perfume.

The principal food in every house was pork or corned beef. The meat was cured under the supervision of the ladies of the family, and hams, sausages and "spareribs" were prepared in the most dainty manner. Pork, sugar, sorghum molasses, corn-meal, fowls, eggs, butter—everything produced on the plantation—were exchanged with grocers for other commodities. Any surplus of cotton, buttons, and such like drapers' stores, were exchanged in the same way.

A few sauces were invented to add zest to our poor fare, and some of these have been accepted by the world of gourmets. Wine was made of elderberries, bitter oranges, or wild cherries. Hundreds of gallons of blackberry brandy were manufactured and sent to the hospitals for the soldiers.

COFFEE AND TEA

In order that the wounded might have tea and coffee, "substitutes" were made for home use of sassafras leaves, balm, or sage, and even orange leaves, were steeped in hot water sweetened with sorghum molasses. For coffee parched sweet potato shavings, parched corn or wheat, and parched carrots, were used.

All the coffee, tea, white or brown sugar, and every other scarce luxury, was sent to the soldiers. "Real coffee and sure enough tea" were for the sick and wounded, not for people in health.

The strong tension upon the nerves of the women was not relieved by pleasant new books or magazines. The newspapers were annals of ardent endeavor, some triumphs, but also of sorrow, wounds and death.

All work and no play began to tell upon our nervously organized women. Some of them turned for relief when any of the soldiers were home for reunions, called, from the absence of any refreshments save cold water, "starvation parties." To these came the young officers, who danced as gaily as though there were no serried ranks of the enemy confronting them to do battle to the death, perhaps, on the morrow. There were charades, private theatricals and tableaux. One lovely young woman, who has since bloomed into an authoress of much renown, personated a marble Niobe embracing her stricken children, and the sculptors of antiquity have left us no more beautiful statue.

OUR HOSPITAL NURSES
The hospital nurses were largely women, and mostly ladies. What they did is recorded in the "Book of Life," but mortal pen would fail to depict their loving service amidst the horrors of military hospitals near the battlefields. The food was generally prepared by private families; delicate breads, strong broths, or ounces of the precious "real tea and coffee" were daily taken in baskets, and the soothing voices of the nurses could be heard whispering hopes of victory and home, or murmuring comforting texts from the Scriptures, while the sufferers were fed or cooling lotions poured upon the dressing of their wounds. I wish it were possible to give the names of these devoted women who administered to the wounded, soothed the dying, and received the little tokens and messages for their absent families. The list would be too long here, but their names are household words in every Southern home—and "when shall their glory fade?"

HOW DEFEAT WAS BORNE
How can justice be rendered to the wives of the common soldiers? On those women fell the burden of deprivation unheard of. In silence they sowed and reaped the land, clothed and tended their children, buried them when they sank under want and exposure, or themselves laid down in solitude and died.

It was the exception when the men in the field knew the trials to which their wives were subjected. The women were vocal in hope, silent in despair. The wives of the common soldiers labored and sorrowed without the expectation of earthly honor or eclat. For if the men of their household perished in battle it was only "collective glory" acquired for the army, for their cause, not for themselves; a nameless grave their share.

When the last sad days of the struggle drew nigh and every heart was cast down, the women were the most cheerful. When the young and old non-combatants were summoned to man the trenches there were no tears and repinings. Such preparations as were practicable for the comfort of the aged or infirm citizen guards were quietly made, and the men were dispatched with as much cheer as trembling lips could summon.

At last, when Gen. Lee's half-starved army must be withdrawn from before the overwhelming force of the enemy, he sent an officer to inform Mr. Davis of the fact. The message was delivered in St. Paul's Church during morning service, where the President had gone to pray for his people. The congregation divined the purport of the dispatch, and though they expected, as the outcome of it, that their homes would be burned and the city laid waste, there was no panic, no plea for protection. The women gathered about Mr. Davis and said: "Leave us to our fate if you can save the country. Perhaps some time you may win Richmond back; but if not, we know you have done your best, and you must not grieve over us." In this spirit our women met defeat, starvation, labor, humiliation, and all the heart-rending conditions of "reconstruction."

The placid, gray-haired matrons of to-day have covered with decorous pride the scars of that dread struggle, but they are no less veteran conquerors in a mortal conflict in which every noble aspiration and human effort was called forth, and answered with a cheerful *ad sum* ["I am present"].[29]

Mrs. James M. Duncan, Jr. of Yazoo City, Mississippi.

From *Confederate Veteran*, 1898

Mrs. James M. Duncan, Jr., of Yazoo City, Miss., Corresponding Secretary of the National Order of the United Daughters of the Confederacy, elected in their late convention, is a daughter of "historic Vicksburg." She is the presiding officer of the Mississippi Division, U.D.C., and bears the distinction of being the most youthful of all the State Presidents. Mrs. Duncan was born after the famous siege.

In the Baltimore convention Mississippi was conspicuous in her plea to the National Order for cooperation and assistance to purchase "Beauvoir," the home of the Confederate President, Jefferson Davis. In voicing the sentiment for her constituents, the Baltimore Sun said: "Mrs. Duncan made a brilliant and eloquent appeal for 'Beauvoir.'"[30]

Miss Annie Grant Cage of Mississippi.

From *Confederate Veteran*, 1898

The U.D.C. of Mississippi, in state convention at Columbus April 26, made a wise choice in the election as State Vice-President of Miss Annie Grant Cage, who is also President of the chapter of U.D.C. at Jackson. Miss Cage is represented as the highest type of young Southern Christian womanhood. She is enthusiastic and patriotic, and is from good Southern stock. On the maternal side she hails from the Grants of Virginia; on the paternal side she is a granddaughter of Col. Edward Cage, at whose hospitable home, near Clarksville, the poor received the same courtesy as the guest of the house. All the men of her family were Southern soldiers. The regiment commanded by her eldest brother was among the most daring and efficient in the Trans-Mississippi Department, and turned the tide of victory in our favor at Springfield, Mo.[31]

Mrs. E. S. Eggleston of Vicksburg, Mississippi.

From *Confederate Veteran*, 1895

OBITUARY: MRS. E. S. EGGLESTON

Mrs. E. S. Eggleston died at her home in Vicksburg, Miss., March 9th, 1895. She was a woman exalted in all virtues, a mother having honored children unto the third generation surviving her, whose example among good men and women tells us how pure and strong was the nurture that gave them character. Her home was a very temple of hospitality. In society, she was a charm; lofty in principles, though modest in dispensing charities, like the wide spreading Magnolia in the May of its blooming, ever emitting exhilarating perfume to the refreshing of all life about it. As a "Mother of the Confederacy," she not only gave sons and grandsons to the service, but the Confederate Army when it came into her loving presence. A soldier in gray, regardless of rank, was welcome to her last crumb. It is said that when mule meat and parched corn were luxuries in camp, Mrs. Eggleston never closed the doors of her dining room, keeping it supplied as abundantly as possible, and invited every passing soldier to break bread at her table.

Whatever Mrs. Eggleston espoused as good to be done was caught up in fervid patriotism by men and women who deemed it a privilege to follow her as a leader. She was a zealous student in literature, and a devout Christian for more than half a century. She had passed her eightieth year, and her mental faculties were strong and true to the last. Mrs. Eggleston gave to the Confederacy that love which knoweth no bounds. In the morning of its birth, she stood out in the sunlight and caught it to her motherly bosom in reverential affection; in the zenith of its glory, she watched it with anxious pride; when reverses came, she always pointed to the anchor of hope, and bade the boys take courage, in its distress, no effort at amelioration in her power was too great a sacrifice, and when the climax was reached, she was of those who accepted the situation as unalterable, and went about making conditions better, never yielding to despair. In 1866, she became President of the Vicksburg Confederate Cemetery Association, organized to secure a lot, to place the remains of every dead Confederate of that section in it, also to procure their names, and mark their graves. One list contains the names of about 1,800—from Missouri, Arkansas, Texas, Louisiana, Tennessee, and Kentucky. In the midst of their abiding place, there was erected by this noble old lady and her compatriots, in May, 1892, a beautiful monument to the memory of these noble soldiers, and no spot in our cemetery is held in higher reverence.

Mrs. Eggleston's funeral was conducted from Christ Church, Rev. Drs. Sansom and Logan officiating. The services were touchingly impressive, the congregation large, and nearest the family in front, there assembled every ex-Confederate able to attend, and many good friends who wore the blue.[32]

Mrs. Ella K. Newsom of Brandon, Mississippi, known as the "Florence Nightingale of the South."

From *Confederate Veteran*, 1898

MRS. E. K. NEWSOM: THE FLORENCE NIGHTINGALE OF THE SOUTHERN ARMY

Professor J. Fraise Richard, Washington, D. C., a Union veteran, writes:

"For more than two years I have been a careful and interested reader of the *Confederate Veteran*, and have, as a Northern man and ex-Union soldier, been deeply concerned to see all the incidents and events of the great war carefully and impartially presented. I am free to confess that no paper or magazine is a more welcome visitor to my table than the *Veteran*. I appreciate and endorse the earnest appeals made in behalf of its extension and enlarged usefulness. I sincerely wish it could be extensively read throughout our Northern states.

"In all that this valuable periodical has contained I have seen no record of the philanthropic and angelic ministrations of a most useful class of beings: the army nurses. Perhaps this is not strange. Commanding officers, in their official reports, were concerned in narrating the movements in battle that resulted in the defeat of the enemy, and hence had little time for and less knowledge of the sacrifices and endurances of those who cared for the maimed and suffering soldiers. But the ministrations of these angels of mercy were none the less meritorious.

"To the honor of one of these I desire to contribute, in recalling the deeds and sacrifices of Mrs. Ella K. Newsom, the handsome, wealthy, and accomplished young widow who at the outbreak of the war placed upon the altar of the Confederacy her wealth, her time, and all her consecrated womanly powers.

"Mrs. Newsom is the daughter of Rev. T. S. N. King (deceased), a Baptist minister of prominence in North Carolina, Tennessee, and Arkansas. She is a native of Brandon, Miss., but in her childhood her parents removed to the wilds of Arkansas, where, amid the adversities of pioneer life, she was thoroughly trained in horsemanship, and became fully qualified for the ordeals through which she passed in the service of the Confederacy. She became acquainted with Dr. Frank Newsom, an educated and accomplished physician of her section, who had removed from Tennessee. This acquaintanceship culminated in matrimony. Within two years he died, leaving her a young widow at the opening of the war with ample fortune. Her only relief from her loss of companionship was in consecration to labor in the busy scenes and thrilling events of the time. She concluded to devote all to the cause of her beloved Southland, utterly oblivious to personal comfort, and hence entered the hospital service.

"Mrs. Newsom's experiences were identified mainly with the Army of Tennessee, in the hospitals of Bowling Green, Nashville, Memphis, Chattanooga, Corinth, Marietta, Atlanta, and other points. When the war began she was residing at Winchester, Tenn., supervising the education of her younger sisters. These sisters returning to the parental roof in Arkansas, she collected suitable hospital supplies, and, taking a number of her own servants, went to Memphis, where her career began.

"In various capacities Mrs. Newsom labored until December, 1861, when, taking her own servants and a car-load of supplies, at her own expense, she repaired to Bowling Green, Ky., to alleviate the almost inexpressible sufferings of the Confederate sick. The scenes of destitution at that place beggar description. Want of organization, lack of suitable buildings, scarcity of supplies, and exceeding cold weather produced untold suffering. With tireless energy she consecrated her efforts to this distressing condition, often laboring from four o'clock in the morning until twelve o'clock at night.

"It is impossible to chronicle here her devotion and sacrifices to the soldiers as they moved to Nashville, to Corinth, to Chattanooga, to Atlanta, and other points. In all these movements, even to the capture of President Davis, she remained devoted to the cause she had espoused. Letters, seen by the writer, from [Confederate] Gen. [William Joseph] Hardee and other prominent officers speak fully of the value of her services. One prominent officer averred that her presence in the army was, like that of Queen Louise, of Prussia, equal to that of an army corps.

"Before me lie two letters, from which I quote a paragraph or two. The first was written from Murfreesboro, Tenn., by Gen. Joseph B. Palmer. He says: 'I was in command of a regiment at Bowling Green, Ky., and witnessed her appearance there as the friend of the Confederate soldier, and saw her readiness to devote her handsome estate, together with all the energies of her splendid mind, heart, and the labor of her own hands, to do all that was possible to aid her struggling land, and to provide for the sick, disabled, and suffering members of all grades in the Southern army. Later during the war she became chief matron of the Hospital Department in that part of the army commanded by Gens. Bragg, Johnston, and others, and so remained until the close of our memorable and heroic Confederate struggle. To this hospital service she gave order and system, value and efficiency, much above and beyond any similar effort in that direction ever before made anywhere or by anyone. This may, indeed, be said with emphasis, when the limited means at her command and the general embarrassments of the well remembered situation are all properly considered.'

"Ex-Gov. Albert S. Marks, in a letter written at Nashville, October 29, 1885, called her the 'Florence Nightingale of the Confederate Army,' and says: 'When the Confederate soldiers needed her she was by their side, and her sacrifices for them is one of the memorable events of the war.'

"I need not say here that Mrs. Newsom was well known to the leading officers of the Western army. That fact is patent to all. In the two portraits herewith presented they will recognize two significant pictures: one the ministering angel of 1861-65; the other, the lady in the year 1898, with impaired vision and hearing, but possessed of all the graces and accomplishments which only time and the severe experiences and conflicts of real life can bestow upon people. The second picture represents Mrs. Ella K. Trader, widow of Col. W. H. Trader, a Confederate officer, whom she married in 1867, and who died in 1885, leaving her to struggle with life's buffetings and disappointments as best she could. Through the aid of friends she secured a clerical position under the U. S. Government, and is now an employee in the Pension Office.

"I close this article with a paragraph taken from a tribute I published in the *American Tribune*, of Indianapolis, in the winter of 1895:

'Could the stately pines and the redolent magnolias of the sunny Southland reveal the many sacrifices made by the maimed and dying beneath their refreshing foliage; could the twinkling stars that looked down with silent grief upon the heroic scenes witnessed upon numerous battle-fields unfold their heart-breaking records; could the hospital tents and hurried ambulances give up the secrets of intense suffering and unutterable woe which they only possess; could the briny tears of joy and satisfaction that chased one another down the checks of some darling boy, lately given up to war by a devoted and affectionate mother—express the message of gratitude experienced on account of loving and timely ministrations in suffering; could the ominous look, the suppressed whisper, the affectionate farewell messages of the dying, and the untold evidences of sincerest appreciation and gratitude voice forth their real and full significance—yea, could all these multiform witnesses of humane and almost godlike ministrations on the battle-field, on the march, in the hospital, in the camp, everywhere, join their testimonies in one mighty chorus of gratitude—they would proclaim, in notes quite divine, the untiring, the unselfish, the incessant, and the inexpressible services of the army nurse; and most prominent among these would stand the name of our subject, Mrs. Ella K. Newsom, the Florence Nightingale of the South.'"[33]

MISSOURI

Mrs. John W. Black of Kansas City, Missouri, member of the Robert E. Lee Chapter, UDC.

Miss Lida Kelley, UCV Sponsor for Missouri.

Miss Gladys Shelby of Missouri, granddaughter of Confederate General Joseph Orville Shelby.

Miss Emory Todhunter, Confederate Sponsor for Missouri.

Miss Anna Maud McGowan of Nevada, Missouri, Confederate Sponsor for her state at the 1898 Atlanta Reunion. Her father R. J. McGowan rode with [Confederate General John H.] Morgan's famous cavalry and "was with Jefferson Davis and his family during their flight from Richmond and to within a few hours of their capture." Miss Anna is described as "one of the most intelligent and beautiful Daughters in Missouri."

Miss Helen Chestnut, Confederate Maid of Honor for St. Joseph, Missouri.

Mrs. Annie Patee, President of the Sterling Price Chapter, No. 401, UDC, St. Joseph, Missouri.

Miss Corinne Landis of St. Joseph, Missouri, Confederate State Sponsor.

Mrs. M. A. E. McLure of St. Louis, Missouri.

From *Confederate Veteran*, 1895

FAITHFUL WOMEN OF MISSOURI

All honor to the heroism of Southern women, who would not surrender their principles for ease to retain their own property and live at home during the great war. A batch of official papers has just been perused, showing the severity of Federal authority in Missouri. One of these [anti-South propagandist] documents is from the war department at Washington, under date April 24, 1863. It is in reply to [Union] Lieut. Col. F. A. Dick, Provost Marshall of St. Louis, in which he suggested sending through the lines to be exchanged such women, and adds:

> "They are determined rebels whose purposes no length of imprisonment will change. . . . Several Rebel mails have been taken in the last few weeks, and I find that a large number of women have been actively concerned both in secret correspondence and collecting and distributing Rebel letters. I have for some time been thinking of arresting them, but the embarrassment is in knowing what to do with them. Many of them are wives and daughters of officers in the Rebel service.

These women are wealthy and wield a great influence. They are avowed and abusive enemies of the government; they incite our young men to join the rebellion. . . . These disloyal women, too, seek every opportunity to keep disloyalty alive among the Rebel prisoners."

One of the most prominent persons now living whose devotion to the South is illustrated in this above, is Mrs. M. A. E. McLure of St. Louis. Every Confederate in Missouri doubtless knows of this noble woman's beneficence to the Confederate Home at Higginsville, and in other like worthy objects. The *Veteran* anticipates some interesting data about her ere long. The excellent likeness is the engraving herein, which will delight her friends. Mrs. McLure was the wife of Mr. Wm. R. McLure, who with twenty-three others, was sent South from St. Louis, May 12, 1863.

The *Veteran* has been favored with copies of various official orders made by her son, Lewis S. McLure, when he was a boy of fourteen. At that age he was imprisoned and tried by a Military Commission, but the court found him not guilty of the charges upon which he was arraigned.[34]

Miss Grace McCulloch, Confederate Sponsor for Camp Sterling Price, USCV, St. Louis, Missouri.

Mrs. Hester H. Barnhart, State Chaperon for the Missouri Reunion.

Col. Minor Meriwether.

From *Confederate Veteran*, 1894

Mrs. Minor Meriwether [née Elizabeth Avery], President of the Southern Woman's Historical Association, St. Louis, made emphatic reply to the criticisms of that Association for commending Rev. Dr. Cave's address at Richmond when the Confederate monument to private soldiers was dedicated. In its account of it the *St. Louis Republic* quotes [her]:

> "I had an interview with [Union General Ulysses S.] Gen. Grant in Memphis, Tenn., in 1862, and he said to me that the war had no reference to slavery. It was to keep and save the Union. The freedom of the negro was the one and only good result of the war. Therefore the North seeks to cover and keep out of sight the awful horror of its wicked war of conquest under that one accidental good. . . . The North lost by the war 279,376 men. The South lost 133,821, making in all 413,197 men killed in wicked battles, or by disease that was the direct outcome of the war. . . . The object of the Southern Woman's Historical Society," she said, "is to keep the truth before the public, and correct the errors that are made with regard to the causes of the war. And another object of our society is to teach our children the truth regarding that series of battles. We don't want to have them taught in the schools that their parents and grandparents were rebels. We want them to understand the situation as we understand it, and as it really was."[35]

NEBRASKA

Miss Grace Lennon Conklin of Omaha, Nebraska, founder of the Omaha Chapter, UDC, and its first President.

Confederate President Jefferson Davis and his cabinet.

NEW MEXICO

Miss Laura Lester of Deming, New Mexico, Confederate Sponsor for the Pacific Division in the Reunion at New Orleans.

NEW YORK

Mrs. L. Z. Duke, a native Kentuckian, was living in New York City at the time of her death, where she was active in the New York Chapter, UDC.

Confederate mountain howitzers.

NORTH CAROLINA

Mrs. Alice Caldwell Ray of Asheville, North Carolina, known by her friends and admirers as "a grand woman of the old Confederacy."

Miss Stella M. Thomson of Fayetteville, North Carolina.

Miss Nesfield Cotchet of Wilmington, North Carolina.

Miss Martha W. Philips of Tarboro, North Carolina.

Mrs. T. W. Thrash, President of the William Dorsey Pender Chapter, UDC, Tarboro, North Carolina, and granddaughter of Confederate Col. Elisha Cromwell, holding a facsimile of the first official flag of the CSA, the seven-star First National Confederate Flag.

Miss Penelope B. Myers of Washington, North Carolina, Confederate Sponsor for her state at the 1898 Atlanta Reunion.

Miss Fannie Burwell of Charlotte, North Carolina, Confederate Sponsor for the Mecklenburg Camp.

Miss Blanche Alpen Thornton, State Confederate Sponsor for the Confederate Veterans Reunion, Winston-Salem, North Carolina, 1912.

Miss Bessie B. Henderson of Salisbury, North Carolina. After the UCV Reunion at Birmingham, Alabama, she said: "I have just returned from my charming visit to Birmingham, and have exactly one dollar left. I most fittingly devote that to *Confederate Veteran* magazine."

Miss Lydia L. Nash of Charlotte, North Carolina.

Miss Gladys Gorman of North Carolina, Maid of Honor at the state's Confederate Veterans Reunion, Winston-Salem, 1912.

Miss Lily Hoke of North Carolina, daughter of Confederate General Robert Frederick Hoke.

Miss Jennie Mitchel Rankin of Salisbury, North Carolina.

Miss Convére Springs Jones of Charlotte, North Carolina.

Miss Kate Theodosia Cantwell of Wilmington, North Carolina, Confederate Representative for her state in the UCV Reunion at Birmingham, Alabama, 1894.

Miss Feriba Grier, Confederate Maid of Honor, of Charlotte, North Carolina.

Miss Margie Overman of Salisbury, North Carolina.

Left, Miss Kate Torrance of Charlotte, North Carolina.

Miss Sadie W. Baruch, Confederate Maid of Honor, of Charlotte, North Carolina.

Miss Josie Craige of Salisbury, North Carolina.

Miss Grace Rankin of North Carolina, Confederate Sponsor of the Fourth Brigade.

Miss Emily A. Long of Enfield, North Carolina.

Miss Daisy M. Sawyer of North Carolina, Confederate Sponsor of the Zebulon Vance Camp.

Miss Annie Blount De Rosset of Wilmington, North Carolina.

Mrs. John P. Allison of Concord, North Carolina, President of the Dodson Ramseur Chapter, UDC.

Miss Sarah Keenan of Wilmington, North Carolina.

Miss Bessie Whitaker of Enfield, North Carolina.

Miss Eliza M. Bellamy of Wilmington, North Carolina.

Emma and Elizabeth Woodward of North Carolina.

Miss Daisy Sims of Charlotte, North Carolina, daughter of J. M. Sims, Fourth (Bethel) North Carolina Regiment.

Miss Willie Emily Ray of North Carolina, Confederate Maid of Honor for her state at the Nashville Reunion.

Miss Elizabeth Christopher Hindsdale of North Carolina, Confederate Maid of Honor for her state at the Nashville Reunion.

Miss Ellen Underwood of Fayetteville, North Carolina.

Miss Kate H. Broadfoot of Fayetteville, North Carolina.

Elizabeth College, Charlotte, North Carolina, 1898. A "high-grade school for young ladies" that supported the Confederacy.

Another image of Mrs. T. W. Thrash, President of the North Carolina Division, UDC, 1918.

Miss Elise Emerson, of Wilmington, North Carolina, the nine year old granddaughter of Confederate Lieut.-Col. Murdoch Parsley. Note that her dress is covered with small Confederate flags.

Miss Olivia B. Saunders of North Carolina, Confederate Maid of Honor for her state in the great UCV Reunion at Atlanta, Georgia, in 1898.

Mrs. Thomas B. Beall, President of the Rowan Chapter, UDC, Salisbury, North Carolina.

Left, Miss Eugenia Roberts of Gatesville, North Carolina, Confederate State Sponsor; right, Miss Lizzie Mitchell of Aulander, North Carolina, Chief Maid of Honor for her state.

Mrs. Elizabeth Reed Watt of North Carolina, organizer of the Children of the Confederacy.

From *Confederate Veteran*, 1912

Mrs. Elizabeth Reed Watt, daughter of William Gibbons Reed, of Savannah, Ga., an officer in the Confederate army, with Mrs. Stonewall Jackson organized Julia Jackson Chapter, Children of the Confederacy, and was its first leader under her. Mrs. Watt served as State Registrar of the North Carolina Division, U.D.C., and for three years was a member of the Committee on Education of the general organization. She served as Regent of the Thomas Polk Chapter, D.A.R., of North Carolina, as State President for the North Carolina National Society U.S. Daughters of 1812, and was the North Carolina member for the Jackson Highway Committee.[36]

Mrs. Armand J. De Rosset of Wilmington, North Carolina.

From *Confederate Veteran*, 1895

PATRIOTIC MRS. ARMAND J. DE ROSSET

This noble character deserves prominent record for her services to the South. She was President of the "Soldiers' Aid Society," of Wilmington, N.C, from the beginning, to the end of the war.

Endowed with administrative ability, which called forth the remark, "she ought to have been a General," gifted with unusual largeness of heart and breadth of sympathy, she was a leader of society, yet ever alive to the wants and sufferings of the poor and needy. Under her direction the Soldiers' Aid Society was early organized, and for four years did its work of beneficence with unabated energy.

The North Carolina coast was especially inviting to the attacks of the enemy, and Mrs. De Rosset's household was removed to the interior of the State. Her beautiful home in Wilmington was despoiled largely of its belongings; servants and children were taken away, but she soon returned to Wilmington, where her devoted husband was detained by the requirements of business, and she devoted herself to the work of helping and comforting the soldiers.

Six of her own sons and three sons-in-law wore the grey. The first work was to make clothing for the men. Many a poor fellow was soon without a change of clothing. Large supplies were made and kept on hand. Haversacks were home-made. Canteens were covered. Cartridges for rifles, and powder bags for the great columbiads [cannon] were made by hundreds. Canvas bags, to be filled with sand and used on the fortifications, were largely used at Fort Fisher—and much more was in requisition. The ladies would daily gather at the City Hall and ply their busy needles or machines, with never a sigh of weariness.

When troops were being massed in Virginia, Wilmington, being the principal port of entry for the Confederacy, was naturally an advantageous point for obtaining supplies through the [naval] blockade, and Mrs. De Rosset, ever watching the opportunity to secure them, had a large room in her dwelling fitted up as a store room. Many a veteran in these intervening years has blessed the memory of Mrs. De Rosset and her faithful aids for the comfort and refreshment so lavishly bestowed upon him. Feasts without price were constantly spread at the depot. Nor were their spiritual needs neglected. Bibles, prayer books and hymn books were distributed. Men still live who treasure their war Bible among their most valued possessions.

Mrs. De Rosset's ability to cope with and overcome difficulties to get all she needed for the men, was the constant wonder of those who daily assisted in her labors. An incident of her surpassing executive power is worthy of record. After the first attack on Fort Fisher, the garrison, under the command of the gallant officers, Whiting and Lamb, was in great peril and in need of reinforcements, which came in Hoke's Division of several thousand men—Clingman's, Kirkland's, Colquitt's and Hagood's Brigades—and with some of the North Carolina Junior Reserves. The wires brought the news that in a few hours they would arrive, hungry and footsore. Mrs. De Rosset was asked if they could feed them. The ready reply was flashed back: "Of course we can," and she proved equal to the task. Through her energies and resources, and her able corps of assistants, she redeemed her pledge. Alas! all efforts to relieve the garrison failed, and many heroic lives were sacrificed. The Fort fell, Whiting and Lamb were both seriously wounded and carried off to prison, and our last available port was in possession of the enemy.

The harrowing scenes of hospital life followed, and here, as elsewhere, Mrs. De Rosset's labors were abundant. The sick were ministered to by tender hands, the wounded carefully nursed, and the dead decently buried. The moving spirit in all these works of beneficence was the Soldiers' Aid Society, directed by Mrs. De Rosset.

When all was over, Mrs. De Rosset was the first to urge the organization of the Ladies' Memorial Association, for perpetuating the remembrance of the brave soldiers who died for our cause. Though persistently refusing to accept office, she remained a faithful member of the Association as long as she lived.

A sketch of Mrs. De Rosset's work during the Confederacy would not be complete without some recognition of the valuable assistance given her by all of her colleagues, and especially by the Vice-President, Mrs. Alfred Martin. That she was looked up to as their leader does not in the least degree detract from the value of their services, for without strong hands and willing hearts the head would be of little avail, and she never failed to give their due meed of appreciation to all who helped in her work. From her own countrywomen such devotion was to be expected, but the German women of the city entered into the work, giving their means as well as their time, ever zealously to the call of the President. Were it not open to a charge of invidiousness, a few names might be singled out as specially helpful and interested in serving the country of their adoption, with the unwearied fidelity of true-hearted women of every land.

Her labors ended, Mrs. De Rosset has for years rested peacefully under the shade of the Oakdale trees, waiting her joyful resurrection. The Daughters of the South could have no better, purer model, should their beloved country ever call on them as it did on her, in time of great need.

Of her own sons, one noble boy of seventeen sleeps in Oakdale Cemetery, with "Only a Private" inscribed on a stone marking his resting place.

Her oldest son, Col. Wm. L. De Rosset, of the gallant Third North Carolina Infantry, was wounded nigh unto death at Sharpsburg. He had succeeded his brother-in-law, Col. Gaston Meares, in the command of his regiment, that noble officer having fallen at Malvern Hill.

Her second son, Dr. M. John De Rosset, Assistant Surgeon at Bellevue Hospital, New York, with most flattering offers of promotion in a New York regiment, resigned his commission, came South, and was commissioned Assistant Surgeon, with orders to report to Jackson. With that command he shared the perils of the famous Valley Campaign of 1862. Later he was one of the surgeons in charge of the hospital in the Baptist College, Richmond.

Another son, Capt. A. L. De Rosset, of the Third North Carolina Infantry, was several times disabled by slight wounds, and at Averysboro was left for dead on the field, and owes his recovery to the skill and care of a Federal surgeon, into whose hands he fell.

Louis H. De Rosset, being physically incapacitated for active duty, was detailed in the ordinance and quartermaster's departments, and was sent to Nassau on business connected with the latter.

Thomas C. De Rosset, the youngest of the six, a boy at school, enlisted before the call for the Junior Reserves, and was detailed for duty under Major M. R. Taylor, at the Fayettville arsenal. He died in 1878 from sun stroke when in command of the Whiting Rifles, attending the memorial services at Oakdale Cemetery.[37]

A mountain team in Asheville, North Carolina.

OKLAHOMA

Miss Lassie Tanner of Oklahoma.

Miss Bessie Brewster of Muskogee, Oklahoma, Confederate Sponsor for the Indian Territory Division at the McAlester Reunion, 1907.

Miss Ora Selma Maxey, Confederate Maid of Honor for the Oklahoma Territory.

Miss Lucille B. Casler, Confederate Maid of Honor for the Oklahoma Territory.

Miss Leoma Cobb of Oklahoma, Confederate Sponsor for her state.

Miss Mary Virginia Casler, Oklahoma Representative at the Birmingham Reunion, UCV, 1894.

From L-R: Confederate Sponsor Mrs. A. L. Bond; Confederate Maid of Honor Miss Nellie Sentell; Brig. Gen. Sam Porter; and Confederate Maid of Honor Miss Fannie Busby, Third Brigade, Oklahoma Division, UCV.

From *Confederate Veteran*, 1912

RESOLUTION AGAINST FALSE HISTORY

The Oklahoma Division of the United Daughters of the Confederacy condemns the *Gordy Elementary History of the United States*, the *Gordy History of the United States for Grammar Schools*, and the *James and Sanford American History for High Schools*, recently adopted by the State Board of Education for use in the public schools in that State for the next five years. Said books are strongly partisan and sectional. They contain inflammatory illustrations and quotations, and practically all of their references are strongly partisan for the North. The entire spirit of these books is such that it will prejudice the child's mind against the South.

A committee of three was appointed to act with a committee from the Veterans and the Sons and instructed to present resolutions embodying the above to the State Board of Education, together with a list of books that are fair to the South, and demand of the Board that they supplant these books with some text that deals fairly with the South.

The committee for the Daughters is composed of Mrs. W. R. Clement, Oklahoma City; Mrs. T. C. Harril, Wagoner; Mrs. G. A. Brown, Mangum.

The Sons' committee to cooperate in this matter is composed of Reuben M. Roddie, Ada; Rev. Percy Knickerbocker, Tulsa; I. H. Payne, Oklahoma City.

The Division officers, U.D.C., are: President, Mrs. T. D. Davis; Vice Presidents, Mrs. W. B. Crump, Mrs. J. H. Copass, Mrs. G. H. Hancock; Recording Secretary, Mrs. B. L. Jones; Treasurer, Mrs. M. C. Farmer; Corresponding Secretary, Mrs. Arthur Walcott; Registrar, Mrs. Kelly; Historian, Mrs. G. A. Brown; Recorder of Crosses, Mrs. William Beal; Custodian of Flags, Mrs. Ellis; Auxiliary Director, Mrs. Durham. Mrs. W. R. Clement was made Honorary President, sharing that honor with Mrs. W. T. Culbertson.[38]

PENNSYLVANIA

Mrs. Turner Ashby Blythe, of Philadelphia, Pennsylvania, President of the Gen. Dabney H. Maury Chapter, UDC.

SOUTH CAROLINA

Miss Margaret Waring, Confederate Sponsor for South Carolina.

Miss Della Hayne of South Carolina, Confederate Representative for her state in the UCV Reunion at Birmingham, Alabama, 1894.

Miss Mary Pagan Davidson of South Carolina, Confederate Sponsor for the Walker Gatson Camp of Chester, South Carolina, at the Atlanta Reunion, 1898.

Miss Hallie Hunt Austin of Greenville, South, Carolina, Confederate Sponsor for her State Division.

Miss Emmie Sweet James of South Carolina, Confederate Sponsor for her state at the Atlanta Reunion in 1898.

Miss Mary Armistead Jones of Raleigh, North Carolina, Confederate State Sponsor for the SCV.

13-star Confederate First National Flag.

Miss Marguerite Sloan of South Carolina, Confederate Maid of Honor for her state at the Atlanta Reunion, 1898. She is the daughter of Col. J. B. E. Sloan of the Fourth South Carolina Volunteer Infantry. Of her it is said: "She is pretty and piquant, spirited and kind."

Confederate Gen. Stephen Dill Lee of Charleston, South Carolina, a cousin of Gen. Robert E. Lee and the author. This monument of Gen. S. D. Lee was unveiled in the National Park at Vicksburg, Mississippi, June 11, 1909. "Not a cloud lowers around his name. He was brave, since he fought without malice; his courtesy had the charm of chivalry. He was generous to the opinion of others. His tongue did not falter in his praise when merited even by a foe. He will take his place in the biography of Americans as the type of the true citizen and noble soldier, the ardent Confederate, the affectionate husband and father, and the humble Christian gentleman."

Mrs. Mary Amarintha Snowden of Charleston, South Carolina.

AN AUTHENTIC CONFEDERATE WOMAN
A true Daughter of the Confederacy, in 1866 Mrs. Snowden raised the money to purchase 800 marble headstones for the Confederate dead at Magnolia Cemetery, along with a bronze statue of a Confederate soldier on a marble column, which was placed in the center of the graves. In 1867 she began plans for a home for mothers, widows, and daughters of Confederate soldiers, the only one of its kind in the South. Though the public had doubts that such a novel institution could ever be built, Mrs. Snowden mortgaged her own home to help pay the costs, which inspired a landslide of donations and subscriptions. The building was finished, and "hundreds of impoverished daughters of South Carolina" were eventually educated there. — Colonel Lochlainn Seabrook.[39]

The South Carolina "Woman's Monument."

Membership certificate to Summerville, South Carolina, Chapter, UDC, organized by 32 ladies on December 10, 1897.

Original sheet music with lyrics of "Dixie's Land" (better known today as "Dixieland"), composed by Daniel Decatur Emmett of Mount Vernon, Ohio, in 1859.

TENNESSEE

Mrs. Josephine E. Ellis (née Towson) of Hartsville, Tennessee, an "ardent Confederate daughter."

Mrs. Mae Belle Gregory Brackin of Nashville, Tennessee.

Mrs. Owen Walker of Franklin, Tennessee.

Mrs. Virginia Bell Armstrong (née Matthews) of Nashville, Tennessee. Her father Robert Matthews was known to be Andrew Jackson's "closest personal friend."

Mrs. John C. Brown of Tennessee, second President of the UDC.

Miss Carrie Jennings, Confederate Sponsor for Tennessee.

Mrs. Alexander B. White of Paris, Tennessee, President, UDC, 1912.

Miss Omagh Armstrong of Nashville, Tennessee, composer of Confederate music.

Miss Loulie Compton of Nashville, Tennessee. Her childhood home was on land over which the Battle of Nashville was fought, the famous Shy's Hill being originally known as Compton's Hill, after her family name.

Mrs. W. B. Romine of Pulaski, Tennessee, addressed a meeting of the UCV at her hometown in 1907.

Miss Mary Cox, daughter of Tennessee Governor John Isaac Cox, gave a pro-South address at the "Silver Service" for an armored cruiser named the *Tennessee*, at Hampton Roads, Virginia, on December 15, 1906.

Mrs. Annie Caldwell Black, beloved member of the Lewisburg, Tennessee, Chapter, UDC. "She was sweet and gracious in social life, a source of comfort to those in need of sympathy. To know her intimately was to be strengthened for better service to Christ and to the world. Her presence was like blessed sunshine. She was a true type of Southern womanhood."

Mrs. M. E. Cummings of Memphis, Tennessee; during Lincoln's War she turned her home into a field hospital.

Mrs. Caroline P. Davis of Wilson County, Tennessee, wife of Confederate officer John R. Davis, who organized the Fourth Tennessee Battalion and fought at such battles as Murfreesboro and Perryville. An impeccable and devout Christian, Mrs. Davis' motto was: "Never let the sun go down on a duty unaccomplished."

Virginia Dyer of Nashville, Tennessee, was one of the most brilliant women and most respected educators in the South. A noble descendant of Confederate families, through her teachings and speeches the noted orator helped rebuild Dixie after the scourge of Yankee "Reconstruction."

Mrs. Mary E. Dudley of Nashville, Tennessee, was "ardently for the South in the sixties . . . and was a prominent member and official in the Woman's Auxiliary to the Confederate Soldiers' Home and of the United Daughters of the Confederacy." Her husband, Major R. H. Dudley, was a Confederate officer and a former mayor of Nashville.

Mrs. Mary Eloise Wormeley of Memphis, Tennessee, helped organize the "Southern Mothers," a group that sewed Confederate uniforms and treated the sick and wounded during Lincoln's War. She was the Honorary Vice President of the Ladies' Confederate Memorial Association and a member of the Sarah Law Chapter, UDC. She helped arrange the unveiling of Forrest's monument in Memphis in May 1905. She was described by her friends as "patriotic and philanthropic, but first and always a Christian."

Miss Meta Orr Jackson of Tennessee, Confederate Representative of her state in the UCV Reunion at Birmingham, Alabama, 1894.

Mrs. Adelaide E. Lyon (née Deaderick) of Tennessee (seated center), with her five children on her 85th birthday. She was the niece of Confederate General Alfred E. Jackson.

Miss Fannie Baird of Columbia, Tennessee, married Confederate Captain John M. Hickey of Howard County, Missouri.

Miss Annie Vinson of Gallatin, Tennessee, sang the song "Ben Bolt" at an 1894 reunion of Confederate soldiers "with a pathetic tenderness which will long be remembered."

Mrs. Alice Smith Baker of Tennessee was a member of the Tyree Bell Chapter, UDC, at Fresno, California.

Miss Adele McMurray of Nashville, Tennessee, Confederate Representative for her state in the UCV Reunion at Birmingham, Alabama, 1894.

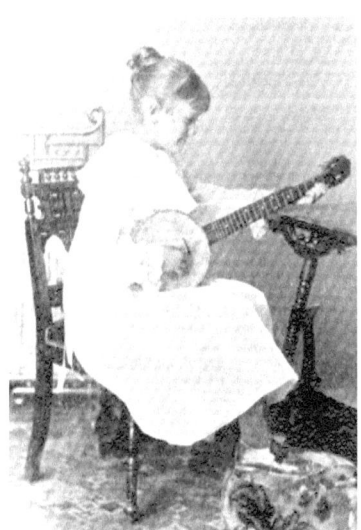

Little Emmie Tyler, daughter of Judge C. W. Tyler of Clarksville, Tennessee, a member of the design committee of the Confederate Monument Association.

Miss Sarah A. Foster of Tennessee represented the Indian Territory (now Oklahoma) at an 1894 reunion of Confederate soldiers.

The daughters of Confederate soldier and Henry County Sheriff Felix G. Trousdale of Paris, Tennessee.

Mrs. L. W. Clark, President of the Ladies' Monumental Association of Clarksville, Tennessee.

Miss Kate Thompson Crawford of Tennessee, Confederate Maid of Honor for her state at the 1898 Atlanta Reunion. Of her it is said: "She is of engaging manner, striking beauty, sunny disposition, and great goodness of heart."

Southern heroine "Old Mrs. Thedford" (née Debbie Simmons), of Bradley Creek, Tennessee. She was known as "The Mother of Chickamauga" for turning her home into a hospital during that famous battle in order to care for the Confederate wounded.

Mrs. John P. Hickman of Nashville, Tennessee, Secretary of the Nashville Chapter, UDC.

Mrs. Carey A. Folk of Brownsville, Tennessee, President of the Forrest Chapter, UDC.

Miss Sue Johnston, Confederate Sponsor for Tennessee at the Atlanta Reunion, 1898.

Mrs. E. A. Clark, President of Chapter No. 5, UDC, Jackson, Tennessee. The wife of Confederate Major E. A. Clark of the Fifty-First Tennessee Regiment, she is "an enthusiastic Daughter of the Confederacy" and describes herself as "unreconstructed."

Miss White May of Nashville, Tennessee. She is the niece of Col. John Overton, whose home Confederate Gen. John Bell Hood used for his headquarters during the Battle of Nashville. Throughout the War Miss May tended Confederate soldiers "whether in garrison, in the field, or languishing in a Northern prison." Of her it is said: "She lived and died a true Confederate."

Miss Harriet Marshall of Tennessee, beloved by all, sadly died in her twenties. Of New England parents, she was always an ardent supporter of the South and of the Confederacy, and wished to be buried in Dixie. At her funeral in Nashville "the aisles were filled with friends, rich and poor, white and black."

Miss Mary Adean Wilkes of Tennessee, Confederate Sponsor for her state.

Mrs. Harriet Angeline Spinks Thornton (née Crawford) of Nashville, Tennessee. An "ardent supporter of the Confederate Cause," during the War "she worked day and night making uniforms for the Confederate soldiers." She turned 100 years of age on October 15, 1917.

Mrs. Grace Meredith Newbill of Pulaski, Tennessee, served as historian of her city's UDC Chapter, as state historian, and later as Historian General of the UDC.

Miss Nellie Ely of Tennessee, Confederate Maid of Honor for her state.

Mrs. Tennie Pinkerton Dozier of Franklin, Tennessee, served as historian of the Tennessee Division, UDC and as President of the Tennessee Historical Society.

Mrs. Sarah E. Brewer of Tennessee donated $500 ($15,000 in today's currency) for the Jefferson Davis monument.

Camille Fitzpatrick of Gallatin, Tennessee, the 13 year old winner of the UDC's "Jefferson Davis Competition" in 1909 for "the best paper on the life and character of Jefferson Davis."

Mrs. Mary Isabella Pitman of Arlington, Tennessee. Two of her sons served in the Confederate army. She was known as a "remarkable woman, noted for her calmness, patience, and charity."

Mrs. T. J. Latham, President of the Tennessee Division, UDC.

Mrs. Fannie Van Dyke Ochs (née Van Dyke) of Chattanooga, Tennessee. "Of quick wit and engaging manners, she pleases on first acquaintance. As that acquaintance ripens and the rich qualities of her intellect and her heart are seen the feeling deepens into admiration and love."

Miss Rose Deering, Confederate Maid of Honor, Third Brigade Tennessee Division UCV, Shelbyville, Tennessee.

Mrs. R. O. Winstead of Tennessee, sister of hero-martyr Sam Davis.

Mrs. Annie B. McKinney of Knoxville, Tennessee, a pro-South author, originally from Vicksburg, Mississippi.

Bronze tablet on the Sam Davis Monument, 1909.

Elizabeth Davis, the grandniece of Sam Davis; she unveiled the Sam Davis Monument in 1909.

Mrs. Harriet Leonora Whiteside of Chattanooga, Tennessee, "one of the most noted women the South has ever known." Highly educated, respected, well-bred, talented, and graceful, her house was confiscated by the Yanks, rendering the widow and her eight children homeless. Using an empty train car for shelter, they were taken to Nashville and onto Louisville, where her family was illegally imprisoned. On release she was permitted to go to Springfield, Ohio, at which place she rented a temporary home. Lincoln had just been assassinated and the South-hating citizens in the town did not appreciate Mrs. Whiteside's presence. When she refused to drape her home in black mourning crepe, an angry mob gathered outside threatening to burn it down. She survived this danger, as well as many others, and was able to return to Chattanooga in the fall of 1865, where she passed away at age 78 in 1903. She was a most remarkable Southern woman and a Confederate through and through.

Nathan Bedford Forrest, III, of Memphis, Tennessee, in 1909. In 1942, during World War II, he was killed in action at Kiel, Germany.

Miss Ann Marie Zollicoffer of Tennessee.

From *Confederate Veteran*, 1903

FROM THE OBITUARY OF MISS A. M. ZOLLICOFFER

Miss Zollicoffer resembled her father [Confederate General Felix Kirk Zollicoffer] in face and form. She was fearless in temperament, upright in character, and unswervingly faithful in her affections. In manner like her father also, she combined rare dignity with a most winning gentleness of demeanor.

Aside from the pursuit of art, her life was devoted to making those around her happy. Her influence on others was altogether ennobling. She inspired with the highest aspirations those she loved, and called out the best that was in the nature of each. The world is better that she lived. Having pointed the way to right living and reared a stainless standard for those who are left behind, she passed into the spirit world on October 3, 1902, at the home of her sister, Mrs. R. H. Sanson, in Knoxville, Tenn.

The surviving sisters are Mrs. Virginia Wilson, of Nashville; Mrs. J. M. Metcalfe (Felicia), of Fayetteville, who is President of the Zollicoffer-Fulton Chapter of U.D.C. at that place; Mrs. J. B. Bond (Octavia), of Maury County, Tenn.; and Mrs. R. H. Sanson (Louisa), President of the Knoxville Chapter U.D.C. Mrs. Nat Gaither (Mary Dorothea), of Hopkinsville, Ky., died many years ago, leaving one son, Felix Zollicoffer Gaither, who now lives in Fort Worth, Tex.[40]

A view of the Tennessee State Library, with paintings of Confederate Generals Robert E. Lee and Nathan Bedford Forrest hanging on the right.

Miss Nellie Duncan of Tennessee, Confederate Sponsor for Camp at Talbott, Tennessee, Dallas Reunion.

Miss Mary Taylor Haley of Columbia, Tennessee, Confederate Sponsor for the Leonidas Polk Bivouac and the William Henry Trousdale Camp.

Mrs. Florence Phillips Hatcher of Columbia, Tennessee.

From *Confederate Veteran*, 1903

MRS. FLORENCE HATCHER

Mrs. Florence (E. H.) Hatcher, of Columbia, Tenn., is a daughter of the late Charles W. Phillips, who was a devoted Confederate. He raised and equipped the "Phillips Rangers," and served under [Confederate General William] Wirt Adams. Mrs. Hatcher has ever been an ardent Daughter of the Confederacy. She is a charter member of the Maury Chapter, Columbia, Tenn., and was for three years its President. She has also been Treasurer of the Tennessee Division, U.D.C. She raised the largest sum yet secured from one source ($125) for the Sam Davis Monument.[41]

Mrs. Perry Cantrell of Tennessee.

Mrs. Perry Cantrell (above right) planted a tree at the spot where Confederate General Albert Sidney Johnston was mortally wounded during the Battle of Shiloh, Tennessee, April 6-7, 1862. The tree (a replacement of the original) is shown here as it looked many years later. It was said that Mrs. Cantrell (née Nancy Cunningham) and her family "were ever true to the Cause espoused" by the South.[42] — Colonel Lochlainn Seabrook.

Charter members of the Shiloh, Tennessee, Chapter, UDC, 1912. Officers on bottom row, L-R: Mrs. D. A. Welch, Treasurer; Mrs. L. V. Sevier, Recording Secretary; Mrs. J. W. Irwin, President; Mrs. D. J. Hughes, Second Vice President; Mrs. H. E. Woodside, Corresponding Secretary.

Miss Ethel Moore of Pulaski, Tennessee.

From *Confederate Veteran*, 1898

REUNION OF TENNESSEANS
Address of Welcome by Miss Ethel Moore

Confederate Veterans: In the name of the John H. Wooldridge Bivouac, I welcome you to Pulaski. To you and to us this has become historic ground, the scene of a tragedy at once sorrowful and dear to us: the cruel death of one of your comrades [Sam Davis], who met it like a hero.

In the eyes of Southern people all Confederate veterans are heroes. It is you who preserve the traditions and memories of the old-time South—the sunny South, with its beautiful lands and its happy people; the South of chivalrous men and gentle women; the South that will go down in history as the land of plenty and the home of heroes. This beautiful, plentiful, happy South engendered a spirit of chivalry and gallantry for which its men were noted far and near, and as gallant gentlemen we welcome you to Pulaski.

The hearts of the young people of this generation swell with pride over the praises of Confederate veterans, which so many have sung. We are proud of you; we are proud of our inheritance. We are proud of you because you fought for the Confederacy and because you fought like the heroes you were; for we know that you but followed the dictates of a conscience created by a true construction of the Declaration of Independence and the Constitution of the United States. You violated no law, and your foes stood aghast at the undaunted courage with which you contended for your rights; for, brave as some of them were, they could but doff the hat to the "Johnny Reb," who showed them how a gentleman could fight. It was the same spirit which led Gen. Wheeler on to astound the Spaniards with his distinguished bravery that you and he displayed when you fought so desperately for a sacred cause.

Put away by loving hands and preserved with tenderness ever since, we find sometimes an old gray coat. Its very raggedness brings tears of pride to our eyes and makes it far dearer than any coat of mail would be. It tells silent stories of hardships that were heroically endured, of heartaches that were never given utterance to, and of bravery that made the heart of many a loved one swell with pride. There are marks of bullets in some of these old coats that speak of the shedding of noble blood and of countless tears. And we cherish the old hats and caps that you wore. Mere wrecks they are, but they serve to remind us that the crown never became too tattered nor the brim too torn to be lifted to a woman.

And you have not forgotten how to pay reverence and devotion to your women. There needed only to be bestowed the title "Daughter of the Confederacy" upon a young woman to endear her to every man who fought or shed blood for the cause; and last month, when Confederate veterans throughout the whole Southland with beautiful sentiment paid touching tribute to the memory of [Varina Anne] Winnie Davis, it was but proof to all Southern women that in your hearts are monuments to them that speak out at times more effectively than the tallest shaft of marble would.

It has been said of you that you never forget. You do not forget your heroes, and it is very fitting that while here you should do special honor to the memory of Sam Davis. It is very right, too, that you should pay reverence and devotion to the times which brought you so closely together, and it is our dearest wish that only the pleasantest memories of those times be revived during your stay here, and that you may always retain pleasant associations with Pulaski, one of them being that your presence was a delight to all the members of the Wooldridge Bivouac, in whose name I again bid you welcome, welcome, welcome to Pulaski.[43]

"Women of the Confederacy," by sculptor Belle Kinney of Nashville, Tennessee.

Miss Belle Kinney, Confederate artist from Nashville, Tennessee.

Mrs. Susan Winter Lyon of Nashville, Tennessee. Her father was a half-cousin of Confederate Admiral Raphael Semmes, and one of her brothers joined Gen. Forrest's cavalry at age 16. Her husband, Dr. A. A. Lyon, worked in the medical dept. of the Confederate army. Miss Susan was described as "intensely Confederate in every respect, and as long as she lived refused to be entirely reconstructed."

Mrs. W. H. Sebring of Memphis, Tennessee.

From *Confederate Veteran*, 1896

THRILLING EXPERIENCES NEAR MEMPHIS IN 1862
By Mrs. W. H. Sebring, Memphis, Tenn.

After Memphis fell and the Federals took possession, mother and family moved out to a country home three miles east of Memphis. We had a variety of fine fruits and the Yankee soldiers soon found it near enough to forage. They made frequent visits to the place and would always get fruits, fresh milk, etc., when they asked for it. However, they preferred a less courteous way and helped themselves.

One night a party of marauders came into our yard after having plundered every kitchen and poultry yard in the neighborhood. An invalid brother and an adopted brother were aroused by voices near their window. They sprang out of bed, and saw several soldiers in the yard. Brother took a pistol, the other a very fine shotgun, went out and asked what was wanted. They immediately attacked Charley, my own brother and Joe Elliott, who had the gun. One stout fellow struck Joe and felled him to the ground. Charley quickly fired at Joe's assailant, who fell dead. His comrades started to run. Sister Mary, who was aroused by the boys' running out the hall, arose and followed them. Just as Charley was in the act of firing at another, she threw herself between them; the pistol snapped and the man's life was thus saved. I ran into the yard and demanded from them the gun they had taken from Joe. They were so frightened (six in number), one deliberately walked over to where their dead comrade lay, took the gun from under him and handed it to me. I ran into the house and gave Charley the gun. Charley had pulled Joe into the hall, he being stunned from the blow. The marauding party left their dead comrade in the yard all night.

The next morning, about 8 o'clock, they returned, some forty or fifty in number, and surrounded the house. Sister Mary had the buggy ready to go and reported the event of the night and had the dead man removed. She went into the garden for fruit to take to a sick friend. Mother had sent Charley off very early to a neighbor's, fearing the Yankees would return. I was standing in the hall arranging some letters to be sent off South, when Joe, from the gallery, saw glistening bayonets in the hands of men double-quicking up the avenue. He ran in to report it and to hide the gun. He crossed the hall just as they got opposite the hall door. Seeing him they cried out, "There goes the rebel!" and with the vilest curses cried: "Shoot him! shoot him!" Two of them rushed by me, one pulled Joe out, and the other leveled his gun and fired. Just as he did, I threw the gun up and the ball went through the ceiling.

He then, with the glare of a demon, placed the gun against my temple and with a vile oath said he would blow out my rebel brains—I was not the least frightened then, though I shudder now at the thought. I said, "All you are fit for is to frighten children." The other demon pulled Joe out and was beating him with his gun when Sister Mary ran in and threw herself over Joe to protect him. A negro girl took up a chair and said, "You strike Marse Joe again and I'll break dis chair over yo head." That enraged the brute who had pinioned me and he let go to strike the "damned nigger."

Mary and I got Joe into a corner to ward off their blows; seeing one [Union] man with the badge of an officer, she said; "You are an officer. Can you not protect this boy; he has done nothing to you." Two or three were pounding him over our shoulders until he was covered in blood, as was our clothing. The man replied: "I'm no officer, and if I were I would not stop them." I said, "Oh, Mary, don't ask anything of him. Look at him! Don't you see he was born a brute?" He cursed us.

They went through the house, turned every bed and piece of

furniture into heaps in the middle of the floor, threw everything out of the kitchen and turned the stove upside down. My dear, sweet, gentle mother did all in her power to appease their wrath, but she got only the vilest of curses for it. An Irish girl, who had been [working for us] as housekeeper and maid, took up a turkey they had left the night before, tied with the cord and tassel off one of their hats, threw it into the wagon when they put their dead comrade in, and said: "There, take all your dead. We want none of them."

They left and took Joe with them, telling us we would never see him again. Sister Mary and I followed them. When we got to the pickets those demons who had Joe said, "Don't let those women pass," and they would not. We drove around to another road and passed, following closely after them. Joe turned to look after us, when they told him we saved him once, but we could not now; that they would hang him as soon as they reached camp, and would come back, tie us in the house and burn us up.

When we reached the camp the whole regiment crowded around us, cursing and hallooing, "Why didn't you hang them in their own yard?—they have fine trees there!" We went at once to the young man in command; the Colonel (Blood) had absented himself, fortunately for us. The [Yankee] officer in command (I regret I have forgotten his name) ordered the men back to their camps. They retreated a few steps, then turned and came around, using the vilest of curses. The officer told us to go at once to [Union] Gen. Smith, which we did. They, knowing they had been beyond the Federal lines, marauding against orders, followed us to Gen. Smith's headquarters, bringing Joe.

Gen. Smith asked, "Whom have you there?" They said, "A guerrilla." "Where did you find him?" They hesitated, and Gen. Smith asked Joe. He told all and said, "We shot one last night." Gen. Smith said, "It's a pity you did not shoot all six." He punished the leader with ball and chain and sixty days hard labor in the fort.

We went home, but for many days after received messages from them saying they would yet carry out their threats. The neighborhood was all excitement. Gen. Sherman issued orders that no one should pass the lines that day, Saturday. Every neighbor called for guards. We did not, but were prepared to escape should they come and fire the house.

We sent mother off to a safe distance. Sister Mary and I kept watch all the night through. At the dawn of day the [Union] soldiers came upon the gallery and rapped at the door—they had guarded our near neighbors. One said, "Do not be afraid, ladies. We honor you for your brave and lady-like manner of yesterday. We are not all such hardened wretches as those who came here yesterday. Rest assured they will be afraid to come again."

Mrs. Sebring had beautiful testimonials by the Missouri Confederates of their appreciation of her friendly services, and quotes from one of the officers in a letter of Nov. 3, 1862, as they were leaving Holly Springs. She already had a letter from [Confederate] Gen. Sterling Price that she recalls with patriotic pride.[44]

Miss Mary L. Morris.

From *Confederate Veteran*, 1896

In a seminary of this city [Nashville] a few years ago, a little girl [Mary L. Morris, above] came to her history teacher one morning and told her she didn't intend to study Mr. [Thomas Wentworth] Higginson's *History* any more, that she had burnt her book up, for "it made the Yankees win all the battles." The other little girls in the class who were daughters of old soldiers burned their books, too, and there was no history class. Frank Cheatham Bivouac heard of it and passed resolutions of approval, and the newspapers throughout the South noticed it in the most complimentary manner. From Arkansas came a most flattering paper, signed with 500 names, telling these little girls that, innocently, they dared to take the first step toward writing a history that would do justice to the South.[45]

Mrs. Caroline "Carrie" E. McGavock (née Winder), of Franklin, Tennessee, was, with her husband Col. John W. McGavock, owner of famous historic Carnton Plantation. Her family was deeply involved with the UDC, which to this day serves as the trustee of the McGavock Confederate Cemetery, located behind the main house on what was once Carnton property.

CARRIE McGAVOCK: "THE GOOD SAMARITAN OF WILLIAMSON COUNTY"

During the 2nd Battle of Franklin, November 30, 1864 (and for many months afterward), the McGavock family, owners of the town's famous Carnton Plantation, turned their home into a hospital for the Confederate wounded. As several bedrooms were converted to surgeries, the family all crowded into the master bedroom for the duration. It is said that the amputated arms and legs of our brave "men in gray" were tossed out of the Mansion's upper windows, making gruesome piles that completely covered the windows on the first floor.

One of the principle assistants to the doctors was the mistress of the house, Mrs. Caroline "Carrie" E. McGavock, whose role in aiding the Confederacy through this difficult period is highlighted in the following description. — Colonel Lochlainn Seabrook.

From Lochlainn Seabrook's *The McGavocks of Carnton Plantation*, 2011

Confederate Captain William D. Gale, who was present at Carnton at the time (and who, in a few short weeks, would act as assistant adjutant general of Stewart's Corps at the Battle of Nashville), penned one of the most memorable accounts of the conditions at the plantation on Wednesday November 30, and on Thursday December 1. In it he included a description of Mrs. McGavock's sterling humanitarianism. Her house, Carnton Mansion, Gale wrote,

> "was in the rear of our line. The house is one of the large old-fashioned houses of the better class in Tennessee, two stories high, with many rooms. . . . This was taken as a hospital, and the wounded, in their hundreds, were brought to it during the battle, and all the night after. Every room was filled, every bed had two poor, bleeding fellows, every spare space, niche, and corner under the stairs, in the hall, everywhere—but one room for her family.
>
> "And when the noble old house could hold no more, the yard was appropriated until the wounded and the dead filled that, and all were not yet provided for.
>
> "Our doctors were deficient in bandages, and she began by giving her old linen, then her towels and napkins, then her sheets and tablecloths, then her husband's shirts and her own undergarments.
>
> "During all this time the surgeons plied their dreadful work amid the sighs and moans and death rattle. Yet, amid it all, this noble woman . . . was very active and constantly at work. During all the night neither she nor any of the household slept, but dispensed tea and coffee and such stimulants as she had, and that, too, with her own hands. . . . She walked from room to room, from man to man, her skirts stained in blood, the incarnation of pity and mercy. Is it strange that all who were there praise and call her blessed?"

Mrs. McGavock personally nursed some of the wounded at Carnton for long periods, such as General William Andrew Quarles, who remained at the plantation for two months. Thus she was viewed by Confederate soldiers as an "Angel of Mercy."

But her strong sense of compassion and concern for the less fortunate had not begun with Lincoln's War.

Carnton Plantation, rear view. (Photographer: Lochlainn Seabrook)

Far earlier she was known to periodically take in two or three orphans from the orphanage in New Orleans to act as household servants at Carnton. She would raise them at the Mansion, educate them, and give them religious training, then later pay to find them suitable homes and employment.

For her unselfish service to the Confederacy, kind heart, Christ-like ways, loving generous nature, and lifelong faithfulness to her husband, children, and relatives, she would later be called "the Good Samaritan of Williamson County."

What follows is a 19th-Century article that discusses Mrs. McGavock and her many wonderful attributes:

>CHRISTMAS OF THE LONG AGO IN THE GOOD
>COUNTY OF WILLIAMSON, by Anna Bland [name of
>newspaper and date of publication unknown]

"Mrs. McGavock, member of one of the most prominent and, at one time, wealthiest families of this section, was mistress of the beautiful and historic Carnton estate, situated near Franklin. She was particularly noted for her charity, and reared in her own home a number of orphan children. It is said that she once gave shelter at one time to seven little waifs. Mrs. McGavock was devoted to the Confederate cause, and did a great deal for its soldiers. The two acres occupied by the Confederate cemetery are on the original McGavock place, and were given by Carnton's mistress and Colonel [John W.] McGavock [a member of the U.C.V.] for the purpose."

. . . Of Mrs. McGavock's love for the Confederacy it is written:

"From the beginning of the civil war until its close her devotion to the Southern Confederacy was unfaltering, and at the end of that struggle until her death she maintained a deep and active interest in the Confederate veterans."

Another writer said of Mrs. McGavock:

"For her unwavering loyalty to the Confederate cause, both in war and in peace, her benefactions to the soldier boys living and honor paid to them in death, a spirit which she shared with her noble husband, she will be ever remembered in this County and section. The Confederate cemetery which bears her husband's name, where sleep hundreds of fallen heroes, was the object of her unwavering and tender devotion."

Her children were also profoundly involved in the Confederate Movement. Her daughter Harriet "Hattie" Young Cowan was not only an active and influential member of the Franklin Chapter of the United Daughters of the Confederacy, No. 14, she also served as its president on several occasions. After her death one writer revealed the depth of Miss Hattie's involvement in the Southern Cause:

> "Born of parents whose lives were so closely identified with the history and welfare of Williamson County, and who donated so much of their time and means to the Confederacy, Mrs. Cowan was reared in an atmosphere of loyalty to "The Lost Cause," and her deep devotion to patriotic work was one of the main factors in her long and useful life."

We will note here that Hattie's husband, Lieutenant Colonel George Limerick Cowan, was a courageous Confederate soldier and a member of both General Nathan Bedford Forrest's staff and his famed Escort. During the postbellum period Lieutenant Cowan served as the treasurer of the "Association of Lt. Gen. Nathan Bedford Forrest Escort and Staff," and was later elected president of the beloved (Confederate) Veterans Association, a group devoted to aiding former Confederate soldiers and their families.[46]

The McGavock Confederate Cemetery, behind Carnton Plantation, Franklin, Tennessee, where nearly 1,500 of the dead from the Battle of Franklin II rest. (Photographer: Lochlainn Seabrook)

Mrs. Mary Bradford Johns of Tennessee.

From Ridley's *Battles and Sketches of the Army of Tennessee*, 1906

HEROINES OF THE SOUTH
By Bromfield L. Ridley, Murfreesboro, Tenn.

Confederate General A. P. Stewart speaks of Southern women "as a race unsurpassed for heroism, for deeds of charity and loving kindness, for self-sacrificing and patriotic devotion to the cause of their country, for unswerving constancy and perseverance in what they knew to be right, and the uncomplaining fortitude with which they accepted defeat and all its adverse consequences." To show the blood that was in them, from wealth they met the conditions that confronted them and submitted to sacrifices cheerfully, going to the washtub, the spindle and the loom to support the widowed mothers and crippled fathers and kindred, until our Southland blossoms with a heroine in nearly every home.

I have read of the heroines in Napoleon's Court, "Families of Cleopatra's enchantresses who charm posterity, who had but to smile at history to obtain history's smile in return;" Mesdames Tallien, [Madame] De Staël, [Juliette] Recamier, Charlotte Corday, of the deeds of Joan d'Arc, of Mollie Pitcher and Deborah Sampson of our Revolution, and Florence Nightingale of England, but when I draw the line of comparison

I can point to women whose names and fame "in the War between the States" will surpass them in acts and deeds that will only die with the echo of time.

The battle of Nashville gave us a heroine whose name General Hood placed on the roll of honor, "Miss Mary Bradford," now Mrs. John Johns. When [George H.] Thomas' Army was pouring the musketry into us and Hood's Army was in full retreat, she rushed out in the thickest of the storm-cloud and begged the soldiers to stop and fight.

The famous raid of [Union] General [Col. Abel D.] Streight with two thousand men, near Rome, Ga., resulting in his capture through the intrepidity of a Miss Emma Sanson [Sansom], was an instance of female prowess long to be remembered. Amidst the flying bullets, thrilled with patriotism, she jumped on behind Gen. Forrest and piloted him across the Black Warrior [River]. The Legislature of Alabama granted her land, and the people lauded her to the skies. When Hood's Army, on the Nashville campaign, passed Gadsden, this young lady stood on her porch and the army went wild with cheers in her honor.

Emma Sansom.

Another heroine in [Confederate] General [John Hunt] Morgan's cavalry tramp, on the line of Kentucky and Tennessee, grew to be a terror in her section. She was as expert in horsemanship as a Cossack dressed in men's clothes and handled a gun with the skill of a cracksman. She bore the name of "Sue Munday," had many encounters and her career was exceedingly romantic.

The old scouts in the West will remember two other heroines through whose aid we were often saved from attack and told when and where to strike. Miss Kate Patterson, now Mrs. Kyle of Lavergne, Tenn., and Miss Robbie Woodruff, who lived ten miles from Nashville. They would go into Nashville, get what information was needed and place it in a designated tree, stump or log to be conveyed to us by our secret scouts. I have often wondered if the diagram of works around Nashville found on the person of Sam Davis was not gotten through them, notwithstanding the impression received that it was stolen from Gen. Dodge's table by a negro boy. Miss Woodruff thrilled the scouts by her many perilous achievements.

But I have a heroine of the mountains who developed in wartimes, yet on account of her obscure habitation and the bitter heartburnings existing between the two factions, so nearly divided in her section, that history has not yet given her name merited fame. I got her record from the Rev. J. H. Nichols, who lived in her section of Putnam County, three miles from Cookeville, Tenn. Her name was Miss Marina Gunter, now Mrs. Joe Harris. Her father, Larkin Gunter, was a Southern man, and some bushwhackers claiming to belong to the Federal Army, resolved to kill him. One night three of them, Maxwell, Miller and Patton, visited his home and told him, in the presence of his family, that his time had come to die. They took him out from the house and in a short time this maiden of seventeen heard the licks and her old father's groans, when she rushed to the wood-pile, got an axe and hurriedly approached the scene. The night was dark and drizzly, and the men were standing by a log on which they had placed her father and he was pleading for his life. She killed two with the axe and broke the third one's arm. He got away at lightning speed, but afterwards died from the wound. She lifted up her father and helped him home. Soon she sought and obtained protection from the Federal General at Nashville. She said afterwards, that upon hearing her father's groans she grew frantic and does not know, to this good day, how she managed it, nor did she know anything until she had cleaned out the platter. This is the greatest achievement of female heroism of its kind that has ever been recorded, and places Miss Gunter on the pinnacle of glory that belongs not alone to patriotism, but to the grandeur of filial affection "the tie that stretches from the cradle to the grave, spans the Heavens and is riveted through eternity to the throne of God on high."

Miss Sue Munday.

They talk about [Union Gen. Philip H.] Sheridan's ride but let me tell of one that strips it of its grandeur—the famous run of Miss

Antoinette Polk, displaying a heroism worthy of imperishable record. She was on the Hampshire Turnpike, a few miles from Columbia, Tenn., when someone informed her of the Federals' contemplated visit to her father's home on the Mt. Pleasant Pike five miles across—said pikes forming an obtuse angle from Columbia. She knew that some soldier friends at her father's would be captured unless they had notice, and in order to inform them, she had to go across the angle that was barricaded many times with high rail and rock fences. There was no more superb equestrienne in the valley of the Tennessee—and she was of magnificent physique. She had a thoroughbred horse trained to her bidding. The young lady started, leaping the fences like a reindeer, and came out on the pike just in front of the troopers, four miles from home. They took after her, but her foaming steed was so fleet of foot, that she got away from them in the twinkling of an eye, and saved her friends from capture.

Antoinette Wayne Van Leer Polk is the full name of this brave girl, given in honor of her maternal grandfather, who was a nephew of Major General Anthony Wayne, of Revolutionary fame, and who was Commander-in-Chief of the army at the time of his death, and whose father was a son of a brave officer in the French and Indian war, while his direct ancestor was a distinguished soldier in the Battle of the Boyne, so that on both sides she was of heroic blood.

Miss Antoinette Polk.

She was not fully grown when she took this famous ride. After the war she went abroad with her father and mother and finished her education in Europe. The health of her father, Andrew Jackson Polk, having failed when in the Confederate Army, he grew worse and died in Switzerland.

Miss Polk had a most brilliant young ladyhood abroad, principally in Rome, where she was beloved by the Princess Margarite, and universally admired. She married a distinguished French soldier of the old regime, the Marquis de Charette de la Contrie, like herself, of heroic stock, and has her home in France. She has one son, a youth of great promise.

I recollect another heroine, a Lieut. Buford of an Arkansas regiment. She stepped and walked the personification of a soldier boy; had won her spurs on the battlefield at Bull Run, Fort Donelson, and Shiloh, and was promoted for gallantry. One evening she came to General Stewart's headquarters, at Tyner's Station, with an order from Maj. Kinloch Falconer to report for duty as scout, but upon his finding that "he" was a woman, she was sent back and the order revoked. She has written a book.

[Here is a sketch of another remarkable woman, Miss Jane Thomas.] Miss Thomas' father arrived where Nashville now is, Dec. 24, 1804. She, the fifth child, was a little tot four years old—born Sept. 2, 1800.

Miss Robbie Woodruff.

During nearly all of her eventful life she has lived in this County, when not in Nashville proper.

She has known many of the National Presidents, and nearly all of the Governors of Tennessee. She kissed [Marquis de] Lafayette, and Sam Houston was as her own brother.

Away back in the other century, her father boarded in the house of Wm. Henry Harrison as a school boy, and his brother, Carter Harrison, visited the Thomas family, coming across the country from Russellville, Ky. "Miss Jane," as she is familiarly called, has given reminiscences of war times from which extracts are made:

"After the battle of Manassas I visited the hospitals in Virginia, stopping first at Lynchburg and then at Charlottesville. I then went to Staunton, to Bath Alum and thence to Warm Springs. Dr. William Bass went to Virginia with me.

"I remained at Warm Springs two months. General Lee was camped on Gauley River near Cheat Mountain and [Union Gen. William Starke] Rosecrans was fortifying on the other side. Cheat Mountain was forty miles from Warm Springs and the sick soldiers were sent there in wagons. One day there were three wagons full of soldiers, all with typhoid fever. Dr. Crump was the physician in charge of the hospital and he asked me to go and see them. In one cottage there were only three beds and six patients. The men were surprised at seeing a lady. One of them was an elegant young physician, Dr. Robert Taylor, from Richmond, Va., and he belonged to Fitzhugh Lee's company of cavalry, made up of the aristocratic young men around Richmond. They were the "Virginia Rangers." I told to the young gentleman that I was an old lady, sixty-three years old, and had gone all the way from Nashville to care for sick and wounded soldiers.

Mrs. Marina Gunter-Harris.

"Dr. Taylor was so very ill that I got a room in the hotel and had him moved to it and nursed him carefully for seven weeks. Afterward his sister, Mrs. Gen. Wickham, wrote me a beautiful letter, begging me to go and see them. Her brother had told them that I had "saved his life."

"I met many distinguished, elegant people while at Warm Springs—among them Gen. Lee's wife and daughter, Maj. Baskerville, Dr. Paul Carrington, Dr. Hunter, Lieut. Bassett, Col. Morris Langhorn.

"I went from there to Hot Springs, where Dr. J. R. Buist of Nashville had charge. Dr. Goode owned the place and his mother, in her beautiful homemade chicken soup and bread which I distributed among the soldiers every day. Before I left home the ladies of Nashville had given me a large supply of clothing, food and medicines.

"[Confederate] Gen. [Robert Hopkins] Hatton was at Healing Springs, where I visited also, but did not stay long. Our own boys who were sick, and whom I nursed were Cad Polk, Sam Van Leer, Jim Cockrill, Robert Moore, Robert Phillips and others. Bishop [Charles Todd] Quintard was there helping to nurse the soldiers, also. Capt. Beaumont died at Warm Springs. His wife and niece, Miss Mary Boyd, were with him."

Comrades would like to see "Miss Jane" at the Richmond reunion. The writer once offended our President by asking his age, and again had bitter response when having asked our first Secretary of War his age, though has he rarely made the mistake to discuss age with a lady. But he asked "Miss Jane" if she seemed old in those days, and she replied spiritedly, "No, sir, and I am not old now!"

In point of devotion and of nursing our soldiers in distress, the sick, the wounded, the women of the South, were all "Florence Nightingales." It would be invidious to discriminate, but I will mention some of the other noteworthy deeds.

I have another heroine—bless her sweet soul. I have forgotten her name [her name was Miss Helen Price, later Mrs. Cato of Rome, Tennessee — Col. L.S.]. One day General Morgan sent a squad of us on a scout and we were pursued by Colonel Funkerhauser's regiment in Denny's Bend of Cumberland river, near Rome, Tennessee. My heroine, a little girl of fourteen, directed us to Bradley Island for safety—a place of some sixty acres in cultivation, but on the river side it was encircled by a sandbar with driftwood lodged on an occasional stubby sycamore. This

Miss Jane Thomas.

sweet, animated little girl brought us a "square" meal, and watched for our safety like a hawk during the day. Thinking it was a foraging expedition, and that they were gone, we ventured to leave late in the afternoon, but ran into them and a running fire ensued. After eluding pursuit, we concluded to go back. In a short time a company of Federals appeared on the island, evidently having tracked our horses. We left the horses behind the driftwood, without hitching, and took shelter under a big fallen tree. The troopers were in ten steps of us at the time. We could hear them distinctly, and one fellow said: "If we catch 'em, boys, this is a good place to hang 'em." Another said, "Let's go down in the driftwood on the sandbar, and bag 'em." Hearts throbbed and legs trembled! We thought we were gone. One of our squad said, "Let's give up," but the rest of us were too badly scared to reply. A frightened rabbit stopped near us, panting, watching and trembling with fear, producing a mimetic effect on our feelings. Ah, if a painter could have pictured that scene, and if a pen could describe that occasion.

Miss Helen Price Cato.

We lay there until nightfall. They did not happen to see our horses and, through a kind Providence, we escaped. Our heroine came to us after nightfall, signaled and we answered. She was so happy over our escape; told us that she saw them leaving, and that they had no prisoners. She mounted her horse, followed on behind them to the toll-gate, two miles away, and learned that they had returned to Lebanon, after which she came to us, brought our supper and put us on a safe road.

Such heroines the Southern soldiers met with often in the disputed territory of contending armies. They evidenced a devotion to country that only might, and not right could subdue.

There was another class more nearly comporting with female character; sock knitters, clothes makers, needle pliers, God servers, revelling in sentiment in touch with the times. From wealth they drank the dregs of poverty's cup, until now, for over forty years, by frugality and dint of perseverance, they have been instrumental in our Southland's blessed resurrection. Female clerks, teachers, "Graphs," phone and type machine operators, and other callings. From authoresses to cooks, they attest a courage and praiseworthiness that exceeds bellicose valor. To the old stranded Southern craft they have been mariners that make the world pause to see us moving again amid the councils of our common country, resuscitated and disenthralled. Posterity will do them justice, historians, poets, and dramatists will chronicle their praises. Charlotte Corday's epitaph was "Greater than Brutus," but that of the Southern woman will be "Greater than Jackson, the Johnstons or Lee, greater than Jefferson Davis, greater than any other heroines of time."

Miss Buford, a Confederate female lieutenant.

SAVED HER FATHER'S LIFE BY KILLING A YANKEE WITH A CORN KNIFE

The following account of the heroic act of Mary Bedichek in saving the life of her father is contributed by Mr. J. M. Bedichek, brother of the heroine, and now principal of the Eddy Literary and Scientific Institute of Eddy, Texas. Mr. Bedichek was under General Frances M. Cockrell in the First Missouri Brigade; his brother, F. A. Bedichek belonging to Parson's Brigade, thus his father and sister were left home alone, his mother having died before the war.

"It was on the night of the 6th of June, 1865, while the most cruel phase of a horrible war was seen nightly, in ghastly murders and lurid flames, that a band of soldiers was seen in father's yard seven miles northwest of Warrensburg, Johnson County, Missouri.

Miss Mary Bedichek, later Mrs. Samuel Campbell.

"Soon a knock was heard at the door. Sister, Mary Bedichek, then nineteen years old, asked 'Who is there?' 'Friends,' said a voice outside. 'What do you want?' 'We want to come in to warm.' 'You have guns?' 'Yes.' 'If you leave your guns outside you may.' 'Oh! well, if that will please you we will.' Whereupon the leader came in. No other seemed to care to enter. Sister closed the door and locked it. The soldier asked if there were any Bushwhackers in the house. 'There is no one but father and me.' 'Your two brothers are in the rebel army eh?' 'Yes.'

"A search of the room was made by the dim light in the fire place. The lamp had been blown out just before the approach of the soldiers as it was time to retire.

"When the militiaman was satisfied that none

but father and sister were in the house he said 'Old man, I've come to kill you,' drawing his pistol at the same instant. 'Ah!' As father gave this laconic answer, he grabbed the pistol and a most terrible scuffle ensued. The assailant having the advantage of the hold on the pistol, wrenched it out of father's hand and began beating him over the head with it.

Mrs. Kate Kyle of La Vergne, Tennessee, friend of Confederate hero Sam Davis.

"Sister was not idle. She ran to the kitchen, seized a very large and sharp corn-knife and soon directed an effectual blow at the uplifted arm. The arm fell. She then with strong and rapid blows chopped his head until he hallooed, 'help, help, for God's sake let me out.' Whereupon one of the party on the outside ran to the North side of the house opened the door, gun in hand, and tried to see which one to shoot. Sister, hearing the door slam against the wall, turned in time and leaping toward him, caught the gun with her left hand and dealt him a severe stroke on his head with the corn knife. He jerked the gun from her, but on giving him another cut on the arm she rushed him out of the door. Then she shut the door on him and locked it, turning the window shade so he could not see whom to shoot.

"Those on the south of the house opened fire into the window and door and with a beam burst the door down. Sister rushed to the door to defend it. No one attempted to come in, but the wounded man staggered to the door and down the steps. His comrades asked him if he was hurt. He replied, 'I am a dead man.' He fell within ten steps of the door and his comrades carried him off.

"Father sent word to Warrensburg that his house had been attacked. Colonel Thomas T. Crittenden, of the Federal Army, later Democratic Governor of Missouri, sent out a scout under Captain Box who soon approached the house and as the company were about to enter our yard he bade them keep back for a minute.

"Sister saw them coming. She thought they were coming for revenge, hence, she took a long dagger and holding it in the folds of her dress awaited at the door the approach of the captain.

"'Well,' said the Captain, 'you have had a battle here, I understand. I can well believe it from the looks of the room.' There were blood, hair, a cut up hat, gloves, etc., strewn around. 'Well, tell me how it happened and all about it.' As sister was telling her story the company soon became so interested by an occasional word which came to their ears that they drew nearer and formed a semicircle close around the door. One said, 'I wish she had killed the other one too.' Another said, 'I wish she had killed the whole outfit.'

"Sister seeing they meant no harm turned and placed her dagger in the dresser drawer, whereupon one of the soldiers said 'Don't you see, she would have fought the whole company.'

"Colonel Crittenden made sister a present of a fine revolver, not only as a mark of his appreciation of her heroism but to emphasize his disapproval of the murder of helpless old men by brutal 'soldiers.' This account is as father and sister told it to me a few months after the terrible tragedy. J. M. Bedichek."

To impress more forcibly my idea of our women, I have a friend who has risen as a poet—Albert Sidney Morton, St. Paul, Minn., who has written, to go with this tribute, a poem on "The Women of the South." It is beautiful, thrilling and true.

WOMEN OF THE SOUTH
Not Homer dreamt, nor Milton sung
    Through his heroic verse,
Nor Prentiss did with wondrous tongue,
    In silver tones rehearse
The grandest theme that ever yet
    Moved brush or tongue, or pen—
A theme in radiant glory set
    To stir the souls of men—
The Women of the South.

Of nascent charms that thrall the gaze,
    On love's most pleasing pain,
Ten thousand tuneful, lyric lays
    Have sung and sung again;
But I would sing of souls, of hearts
    Within those forms of clay,
Of lives whose luster yet imparts
    Fresh radiance to our day
The Women of the South.

When battle's fierce and lurid glare
    Lit up our shady glens;
When slaughter, agony, despair,
    Or Northern prison pens,

Were portions of the sturdy son
        Of Southern mother true.
Who prayed the battle might be won
        Of the gray against the blue?—
The Women of the South.

Our lads were true, our lads were brave,
        Nor feared the foemen's steel,
And thousands in a bloody grave
        Did true devotion seal;
But brightest star upon our shield,
        Undimmed without a stain,
Is she who still refused to yield
        Refused, alas, in vain—
The Women of the South.

No choice was left us but to fight,
        While she was left to grieve;
We battled for truth and right
        Our freedom to achieve—
Assured that death we could embrace—
        But there is not yet born
The Southern man who dare to face
        The silent withering scorn
of Women of the South.

Who bade us go with smiling tears?
        Who scorned the renegade?
Who, silencing their trembling fears,
        Watched, cheered, then wept and prayed?
Who nursed our wounds with tender care.
        And then when all was lost,
Who lifted us from our despair
        And counted not the cost?
The Women of the South.

Then glory to the Lord of Hosts,—
        Yes, glory to the Lord,
To Father, Son and Holy Ghost
        And glory to His Word;
To us is giv'n creation's prize—
        The masterpiece of Him
Who made the earth, the stars, the skies,
        The war cloud's golden rim:—
The Women of the South.[47]

Miss Mary V. Duval of Pulaski, Tennessee, pro-South playwright.

From *Confederate Veteran*, 1898

"THE QUEEN OF THE SOUTH"
A Stage Performance that Educates Correctly

A happy thought induced the preparation of an evening of pleasure and profit at Pulaski during the reunion of Tennessee Confederates held there last month. It is so clearly a stage presentation of much historic value that a liberal account of it is here given. The play was composed and prepared for the stage by Miss Mary V. Duval, teacher of English in Martin College, Pulaski, Tenn. As presented before the reunion of the Tennessee veterans on the evening of October 12, 1898, it was received with much enthusiasm. Gray haired men laughed and wept by turns, and at the final superb scene, where the choice of queen is made, the pent-up feelings of the veterans found relief, at the suggestion of Capt. J. B. O'Bryan, in the old-time, never to-be-forgotten Rebel yell.

Thirty or forty beautifully costumed girls, carrying Confederate flags and other symbols of the Confederacy, united in a contest as to which of all the brilliant galaxy of Southern States deserved to be crowned as the worthiest. A white-covered throne in the center of the stage served as the seat of honor for Miss Pearl Booth, the beautiful young lady who acted in the capacity of presiding genius of the South, holding her court for the purpose of making the award of a queenly crown. Miss Booth is a stately brunette, a native of Pulaski, and a typical representative of the South. Her clear voice was well modulated, and her words were heard distinctly by the multitude present. She represented this character most happily, and her dramatic rendering of some of the most thrilling passages of the drama added much to the success of the entertainment.

Just before the entrance of Miss Booth, a military band played a brilliant overture, and at its close the *Herald*, represented by Miss Martha Rivers, announced the name of each fair contestant, who advanced for the coveted prize. Miss Rivers is a fair blonde, a native of Giles County, and a descendant of one of the oldest Virginia families. Though young, being still a schoolgirl, she displayed excellent composure and rendered her difficult part remarkably well.

Miss Pearl Booth of Pulaski, Tennessee.

The States contending for the prize were represented by the following young ladies: Virginia, Miss Mary Reynolds; Texas, Miss Louise Rhea; North Carolina, Miss Eva Moore; Kentucky, Miss Florence Wilkes; Georgia, Miss Sadie Abernathy; Maryland, Miss Effie Butler; Louisiana, Miss Mary Trigg; Florida, Miss Bessie Braden; South Carolina, Miss Florence Oakes; Alabama, Miss Virginia Carter; Mississippi, Miss Blanche Crawford; Arkansas, Miss Agnes Ezelle; Cuba, Miss Margaret Dupont; Tennessee, Miss Sadie Ballentine. Each presented the best possible record for her State under the circumstances.

In compliment to the Tennessee veterans, the real ending of the play was altered, so that the Volunteer State might receive the reward, which she claimed so beautifully and, as the veterans of course considered so justly. This part was taken by Miss Sadie Ballentine, another fair daughter of Pulaski, who played the queen right royally. She is a handsome blonde of dignified but animated appearance, and her voice, in speaking, was so well modulated as to be heard distinctly by every one present.

After each one had pleaded her cause, reciting the achievements which made her State glorious, the South, descending from her lofty eminence, placed the laurel crown upon the fair brow of Tennessee. The delight of the audience was manifested in long-continued applause, which was only hushed by the uprising of the curtain on the beautiful tableau "City of the Dead," in which the statue of the martyr hero Sam Davis was the principal figure.

The evening will long be delightfully remembered, and Miss Duval has been heartily congratulated upon the success of her play.[48]

Miss Sadie Ballentine of Pulaski, Tennessee.

Rippavalla Plantation, Spring Hill, Tennessee, where Mrs. Susan P. Cheairs served breakfast to Confederate officers in the Fall of 1864. (Photographer: Lochlainn Seabrook)

From Lochlainn Seabrook's *A Rebel Born*, 2010

SUSAN P. CHEAIRS & A CONFEDERATE BREAKFAST

On the morning of November 30, 1864, Susan Peters Cheairs (née McKissack), wife of Col. Nathaniel Francis Cheairs, IV (a close cousin of the author), hosted a large breakfast for a group of Confederate officers at their palatial Spring Hill, Tennessee, home, Rippavilla. The family was well-known for their Confederate sympathies, allowing troops to camp in their yards whenever necessary.

The previous night, at the Battle of Spring Hill, the Confederates had made several errors, losing their best chance yet to subdue the Yanks, and had encamped at Rippavilla for the evening. As the Sun came up the next day, they were determined to push onto Franklin to finish the job.

The breakfast that brisk November morning did not go well, however. Confederate Gen. John Bell Hood, quarreled with his men, in particular Gen. Nathan Bedford Forrest, about the "lost opportunity" the night before. Blame was cast on all sides, but the real responsibility lay with Hood, and his angry officers told him so.

Forrest stormed out, and soon the others followed, making their way north up Columbia Pike to meet their harsh fate on the brown dry fields of Franklin later that day.[49]

Miss Ellen Louise McAdams of Lewisburg, Tennessee.

From *Confederate Veteran*, 1903

SOUTHERN GIRLS ON CAUSES OF THE WAR

Miss Ellen Louise McAdams, of Lewisburg, Tenn., secured the prize for the best story on the war in her school at the last term. The manuscript covers over twenty-seven pages of legal cap, and it is so systematic a history of the causes leading to the war, the tragic years of its existence, and the malevolence of reconstruction that it would make a worthy school reader.

The loyalty of the author to the South while her father is "a mean old Republican" to use his own term jocosely (he is of an old Whig family), makes the fair young woman deserve all the greater credit for her noble vindication of her native Southland. Writing of the devastation and ruin in the South, she says: "The knowledge of these outrages nerved the Southern arms to strike a deadlier blow and overcome all thought of personal fear in every Southern heart. But they could not withstand starvation and the overwhelming odds against them, and so in the gloom of a defeat, glorified by valiant deeds, their tattered flag was furled at

Appomattox and the remnant of the Southern army, worn, grim, battle-scarred, laid down their arms in sorrow and in tears. Thank God, Southern men were no less great in defeat than in victory. They faced toil and poverty unflinchingly, cheered and inspired in the work of building by Southern women who had shown themselves fit mates for heroic souls. We still have a tear for the banner so sadly furled and for all it represents."[50]

Miss Eleanore Felicia Hussey of Columbia, Tennessee, won a prize offered by the UDC for the best paper on "The True Causes of the Civil War," 1903.

Mary and Milly of Tennessee.

From *Confederate Veteran*, 1898

IN HOT PURSUIT: AN INCIDENT OF THE WAR
Mrs. Kate Lee Shaw Nichols, a daughter of one of Forrest's soldiers, gives the following as literally true:

A sultry August noon, with the sun's piercing rays beaming down upon two little figures trudging up a long, dusty lane.
"Somehow it seems awful far to-day, Milly. Maybe, though, it's because I have such a headache."
"Hurry on, Mary; we'll soon be there. Just think how hungry sister must get waiting for her dinner!"
They quickened their footsteps, and soon reached a stone stile leading into a cool, shady yard, in the center of which stood a low, rambling log house, with here and there a room added to suit the fancy of its owner.
When they entered the front room a scene of disorder and confusion confronted them. It was plain that something had happened, for there on the lounge lay Aunt Amelia, sobbing and muttering incoherently. Between her disjointed sentences and outbursts a vague fear seized the children, until they asked in one breath: "Where is George, Aunt Amelia?"
"Those vagabond Yankees took him off to Carthage [Tennessee] a little while ago. Oh, dear me! I know that Miss Sallie will be heart-broken when she hears of it."
Mary and Milly exchanged glances. A fixed determination suddenly filled the hearts of both little girls. Seizing their pink

sunbonnets and darting out of the door, they called back to the dazed old woman: "Tell sister we've gone for George."

In vain she called after them as they sped out the back gate and through the orchard. On through the meadow into the stubble-field ran the panting children, oblivious of briers or stubble. They knew that the road wound around many a broad acre, and, if their strength did not fail them, they could, by going through, overtake the Federal cavalry before they reached the main Carthage pike. Once they paused when a vicious dog pursued them into a yard, where they sought refuge upon an ash-hopper. The noise of the clattering boards and the shrieking children brought the owner to the door in time to witness a ludicrous scene. Perched upon one corner of the dilapidated hopper was a brave little creature, with one arm clasped tightly around the smaller and younger sister, while with the disengaged hand she hurled clods of hardened ashes at their pursuer, and at intervals wailed: "Oh, do come and take your dog away! for we're in a dreadful hurry."

Released from their embarrassing position, they fled without any intelligible explanation. They soon spied blue uniforms mingled with the dust in the distance. Nearer and nearer they drew, until Mary waved her bonnet aloft. The captain drew rein, as did the entire company, and awaited the approach of the flushed little girls. They clambered over the fence, and, walking up to the foremost man, Milly asked timidly: "Are you the captain, sir?"

The surprised officer answered in the affirmative.

"Then, sir, do, oh, please do, give us back George!"

A magnificent bay, bearing a ruddy-faced Dutch man, nickered at the sound of his name and sight of those children.

Not waiting for a reply, the quavering little voice hurried on: "Oh, sir! he was the only horse we had, and we would miss him like he was one of our family."

Mary stole to the horse's side, and, fastening her fingers in his dark mane, she looked up with eyes full of pitiful entreaty. "Oh, Mr. Captain, do let us take him back home, for we do love him ever so good."

In a few polite phrases the young officer tried to explain that all such captures became Gen. Payne's [Union General Eleazer Arthur Paine].

"But, oh, sir, just think how your own little girls at home would feel if some big, strange men were to take away their own dear horse!"

The man's face softened as he turned to the glowering Dutchman and said in a low, imperative tone: "Dismount, and give that horse to these children!"

Then, alighting himself, he took a blanket from underneath his own saddle, and, placing it on George, proffered to assist the happy children in getting up.

What a glad pair they were returning home![51]

As this 1898 ad in a pro-South magazine shows, Nashville's prestigious Vanderbilt University once openly supported the South and proudly associated itself with the Confederacy. Today, however, uninformed anti-South partisans are working hard to turn the school against its own heritage.

From *Confederate Veteran*, 1898

ONE DAY DURING THE WAR
From Miss Mollie Y. Gill (now Mrs. Ogilvie), of Petersburg, Tenn.;

In the summer of 1863 I was going to school in Petersburg, Tenn. One day at recess it was announced that the town was full of Yankees. The next startling thing I heard was that they had my horse, a beautiful roan which my father had given me on condition that I keep her through the war. I stated the case to the teacher, who gave me permission to see if I could recover the animal. Accompanied by a classmate (Sallie Leonard), I went to all the racks in town, but saw nothing of my Kate. Upon turning a corner I saw my mother, and she beckoned us to her. I advanced toward her and saw Kate, among many other horses eating straw. I ran to her, and said, "Here she is! here she is!" and patted her with one hand, reaching up for the halter with the other.

Just then a gruff voice said: "Hold on there! You don't get that horse." I jumped from surprise at being so roughly spoken to, but held the rein and claimed my right.

"Why did you have her hid?" asked the man.

"To keep the Yankees from taking her," I replied.

About this time my mother called me, and I reluctantly went to her. She introduced me to Capt. ____ and told him that I was the owner of the horse. He arose and extended his hand, but I put mine behind me.

He then seated himself, saying: "If you were like a cousin of yours that I know, you could get your horse without any trouble."

I replied that I didn't care about my cousin; that what I wanted was my horse. I then asked a soldier if there was a higher officer about there, and he replied: "O yes! but he is asleep out yonder in that yard."

I asked the soldier to go and wake him and tell him a schoolgirl wanted to speak to him. A young and handsome officer from Maine responded. When I made my business known to him, he laughed, and asked how his men happened to get my horse. I replied that we had her hid and they found her. Then he asked me if I wouldn't give her to the Rebels if I could.

"Yes, sir," said I; "I wish they had her now."

I appealed to him, and asked how he would like for his sister to be in my place. He asked me to quit crying and tell him what other horse I would take for her. I said: "None." He then ordered a man to bring up my horse.

Being supplied with bridle and saddle, I proudly mounted Kate, amid the shouts of many Yankees. A soldier's last words to me were: "I'll follow you and get her back." Kate was scarcely bridlewise, but took me swiftly homeward.

On reaching the home of Uncle Tom Moore, he detained me to learn how I had succeeded, and as we were talking we saw two blue coats coming, and I moved rapidly away. On reaching home I rode into a cornfield and, dismounting, sat on the ground. As I meditated upon my utter helplessness and of our defenders so far away, I feared my pursuers would come suddenly upon me, so I climbed to my saddle and rode to the top of a hill, where I could see two roads, and there I sat and watched the main body leave.

Then I thought of the dreadful stragglers. The crackling of a dry limb startled me, and I turned to find within fifty yards of me the two bluecoats I had seen at my uncle's. I changed my position, hoping they had not seen me, and got behind a broad, spreading sycamore tree. As I sat there so anxiously watching I distinctly heard my name called.

It was by one of our servants, who was picking cotton near by. She called and said: "The Yankees are after you."

I gave Kate the rein, and sped homeward in full view of the enemy as I rode through the cotton and corn fields. My mother opened the smokehouse door, and I hid there. Fearing Kate would make a noise when the other horses came, for those men were on my track, I held the rein with one hand, so that I might cover her nostrils with the other, but she was quiet as they passed. Putting some of the little darkies in the basement, mother followed the Yankees in their search for me. Expecting them at the smoke-house, I had selected a small, hard stick of wood for use if they came. I heard the voice of one of them as he said to the other: "You go and search the barn."

After his companion had left he turned to my mother and said: "I know where your daughter is, and have come for her protection." My mother pronounced a blessing upon him, but he never heard my words of thanks; his consciousness of having done right was better pay than I could give.[52]

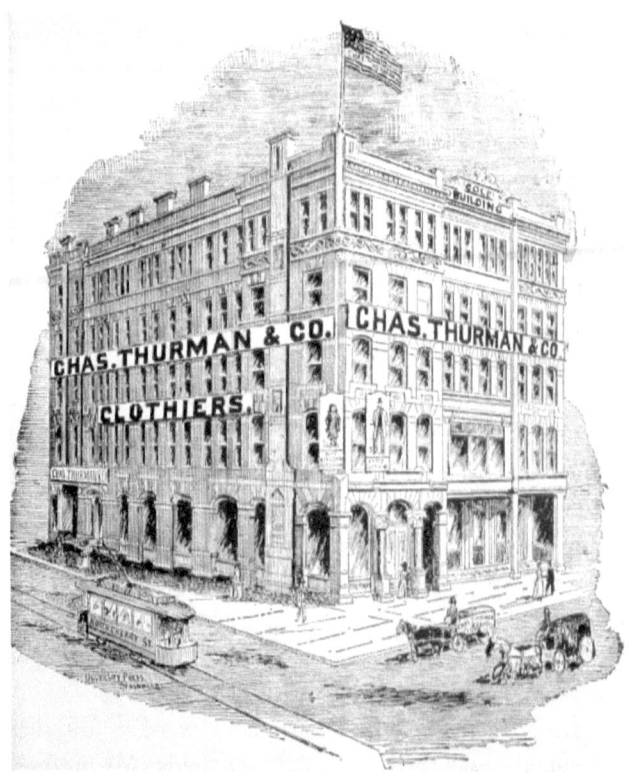

The largest clothing store in the South in 1893, Nashville, Tennessee.

SELENE HARDING OF NASHVILLE, TENNESSEE

From Lochlainn Seabrook's *Encyclopedia of the Battle of Franklin*, 2012

Selene Harding was the daughter of Tennessee General William Giles Harding (son of John Harding, founder of Belle Meade Plantation in Nashville) and Elizabeth Irwin McGavock (daughter of Randal McGavock, founder of Carnton Plantation in Franklin), she was born April 5, 1846, and married Confederate General William Hicks "Red" Jackson on December 15, 1868.

Four years earlier, on December 15, 1864, during the Battle of Nashville (December 14-15, 1864), Selene stood on the stone arm of the front steps of Belle Meade Mansion during a skirmish between the Confederates and the Yanks. To encourage the Rebels, she waved her handkerchief in the air as their cavalry came roaring through her yard. Despite the entreaties of the Confederate troops to get back in the house (as bullets were flying in every direction), she refused to move, standing firm until every last cavalryman had ridden past. Later, eyewitnesses called her "the bravest person on the scene."

Miss Selene died on December 13, 1892, and was first buried at Belle Meade Plantation. In 1906 her remains were reinterred in Mount Olivet Cemetery, Nashville, Tennessee.[53]

Belle Meade Plantation House, Nashville, Tennessee. The author descends from the Hardings. (Photographer: Lochlainn Seabrook)

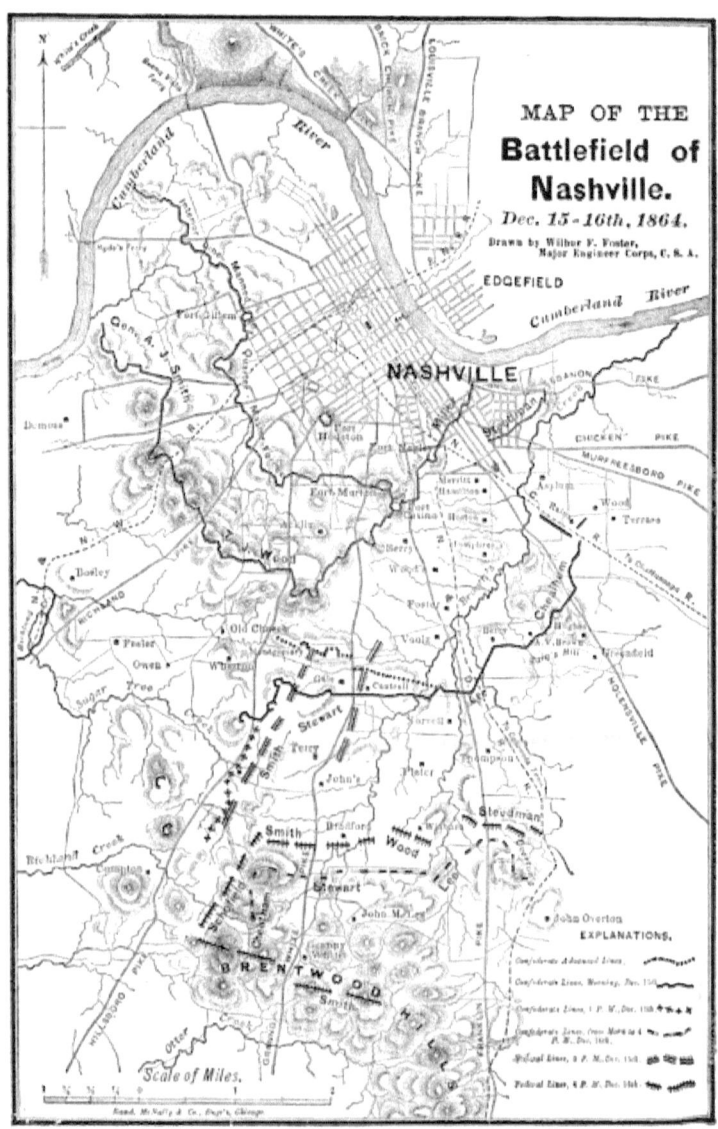

Map of the Battle of Nashville, December 15-16, 1864.

Mrs. Sallie Chapman Gordon-Law of Memphis, Tennessee, known as "the Mother of the Confederacy."

From *Confederate Veteran*, 1904

The venerable Mrs. Sallie Chapman Gordon-Law, of Memphis, Tenn., dedicates some "Reminiscences of the War of the Sixties" to her children, grandchildren and friends, in a neat pamphlet of sixteen pages. Although "Mother of the Confederacy," she still lives to testify in behalf of a people who dared perform their duty as they saw it, regardless of cost, comfort or life.

The story she tells concisely begins with woman's work for our armies in Memphis. Every day but Sunday the women met and sewed for the private soldiers. When her own son went home from school, threw down his books and said, "Mother, I have enlisted for the war," she replied, "You did right, my son."

In the narrative she says: "My home has ever been in the Sunny South; my paternal ancestors, the Gordons of Virginia, my mother's, the Kings of South Carolina, were all rebels of the first revolution; my father, Chapman Gordon (in his teens), with two elder brothers, Nat and Charles, fought in the battle at King's Mountain, and through the entire war.

"My mother's father, too old for the [American Revolutionary] war, sent all his sons and sons-in-law. They fought in and belonged to the command of Generals [Francis] Marion and [Thomas] Sumpter. My second brother, Wyley J. Gordon, was an officer in the U. S. Army, in the War of 1812. My brother, Gen. George W. Gordon, of Columbia, Tennessee, with three sons, fought in the Confederate Army of 1861. My nephew, Gen. John B. Gordon, whose record for valor and heroic deeds is too well known to call for comment, with his three brothers, all fought in the Confederate Army. My nephew, Maj. Augustus Gordon, was killed at the age of twenty-one, while leading a charge at Chancellorsville, Virginia. My brothers, Charles' grandsons and Harvey's sons, were in the Confederate Army. My cousin, Gen. James B. Gordon, of North Carolina, was killed at Brandy Station, near Richmond, in Confederate service. And I know of over thirty brave, heroic privates of my kindred who belonged to the war of the 'Sixties.'

". . . After the battle of Shiloh, many of the wounded were brought to our hospital. I carried many articles of clothing, etc., beyond the lines to our soldiers.

"In our hospital at Memphis, we had domestic wines, lemons, pickles, clothing, and I proposed taking them to our sick soldiers at Columbus, Kentucky. I had large boxes packed and carried them to the hospital there. I made the second trip a few weeks later with more supplies for the sick. The morning after my arrival the battle of Belmont came off. We were on the steamer *Prince*, at breakfast, when Capt. Butler came in, saying: 'Ladies, finish your breakfast, but the yankees are landing their gunboats above.' We jumped up and ran out on the guards and saw the wildest confusion—soldiers running to and fro to get ready for the battle; then the cannonading commenced from the Federal gunboats, with Confederate artillery from the high bluffs. The cannonading was sublimely grand. My own dear boy was there in Gen. Cheatham's command, marching out to battle. It was a grand, victorious battle for us.

". . . The steamer *Prince*, on which we were staying, carried over many wounded Confederates, and among them the brave, heroic Gen. William H. Jackson, whom it was our privilege to nurse and attend. He was dreadfully wounded, and that night many officers came in to see him, Dr. Bell, Surgeon, from Memphis, among the number. Young Dr.

Yandel came in, and Dr. Bell said to him, 'Yandel, I want you to go and detail so many men (I forgot the number), with buckets of water, and go to the battlefield and give those wounded and dying men water.' I went to Gen. [Leonidas] Polk and got an order to have four yankee surgeons taken out of prison to go to the battlefield to attend their wounded, and every one of them refused to go, but ours went.

". . . Standing in the pilot-house with us was a young girl who had gone up to see her brother. She had always lived in Cincinnati with an aunt, her mother being dead and father and brother living in Memphis; when the war commenced her father had gone and brought her home. Young Star had enlisted in the same company with my son. All the way going up on the boat she had been defending the Union; and while the battle was raging, and the musketry mowing down thousands, with tears streaming down her face, she said, 'Oh I wish I had a gun. Oh! for a gun!' 'What do you want with a gun, Alice?' 'To kill the yankees.'

"After the battle was over I went to the hospital to see if I could do anything for the wounded. I was invited in to see the apparently mortally wounded Federal officer, Col. Dorrity. At sight of the wounded man I lost sight of the enemy of my country. I made a glass of lemonade and fed him with a spoon, as one arm was cut off and the other paralyzed. I said to him, 'Col. Dorrity, have you a wife?' He replied, 'Yes, at Cape Girardeau.' At that moment Col. Bethel, Gen. Polk's Adjutant, came in, and I said to him, 'Col. Bethel, will you please take my compliments to Gen. Polk and ask him, as a special favor, to let Col. Dorrity's wife be sent for.' He left immediately, and a courier and a flag of truce were sent for her, by order of the magnanimous, heroic Gen. Polk. At two o'clock P.M. the next day, the wife of the prostrate, paralyzed, wounded husband, was with him.

"The morning after the battle of Belmont, I called at [Confederate] Gen. [Gideon Johnson] Pillow's office, on business, when a little boy came in with a message. He was dressed up in Confederate uniform, with a military cap. I asked, 'Why, my little boy, what are you doing here?' He said, very modestly, 'I belong to the army.' 'What can you do here?' 'Well, yesterday I was on the battle-field, and got down in a sink hole, when I saw a yankee with his gun pointed right at my Colonel, and I fired away and killed him—now, that is what I am doing here.' 'How old are you?' 'Twelve years old.' 'Where were your father and mother to let you come here?' 'Oh! I ran away, and am staying at my uncle's tent, and if you don't believe I killed the yank, come with me and see his watch.' He said to Gen. Pillow, 'Now, I want a furlough to go home and see my father and mother'. . . . He got it.

"After the Federals occupied Memphis, I heard that my dear brother, George W. Gordon, a prisoner from Johnson's Island, was on a boat anchored out in the Mississippi River, very ill. I walked up and down the river bank from nine till five, trying to get permission to go to see him. At last I met Col. Oaks, a Federal officer, who politely said he would send me in a skiff, and I was taken by two Federal soldiers. On reaching the boat, it was filled by Confederate officers, prisoners from Johnson's Island, bound for Vicksburg to be exchanged. I found my brother very ill, so ill I remained with him that night, and Col. Johnson, an elegant gentleman from Kentucky, proffered his berth to me, he sleeping on a blanket in the cabin. . . . I left for Vicksburg next day to nurse and attend to him, driven by a ten year old grandson; but when I arrived at Mrs. Vernon's, sixty miles from Memphis, I heard the sad news that he had died in ten minutes after landing at Vicksburg.

". . . My noble, patriotic brother, the Christian soldier, tried to lead souls to Christ. Regularly, night and morning, he had prayers, and invited all who were disposed to attend.

"Our hospitals all broken up, I felt I must seek a new field in which to work. In our Southern Mothers' treasury was $2,500 in Confederate money, and, with the aid of Mrs. W. S. Pickett, we laid it all out for quinine, morphine and opium, and I carried it into the Confederacy, on my person, distributing it in the hospitals at LaGrange, Ga., and there I had the compliment of having a hospital called for me (The Law Hospital), which many Surgeons and old soldiers still recollect.

"Miss Anna Hardee, [Confederate] General [William Joseph] Hardee's daughter, went the rounds daily with me. We made egg-nogg every day for the pneumonia and typhoid patients, and carried coffee to sick patients.

". . . While at Columbus, Ga., I heard of the terrible destitution of the soldiers at Dalton, Ga., in Gen. J. E. Johnston's division. Thousands of soldiers were having to sit up all night round a log fire, for want of blankets. I was so greatly troubled to hear of the great suffering of the brave heroes who were standing like a "stone wall" between the women and children of the South and the enemy, that after a sleepless night, I went directly to a Ladies' Aid Society, where a number of patriotic women of Columbus, Ga. were at work for the soldiers. I told what I had heard of the suffering, for want of blankets, by the soldiers, and made an appeal to them for aid, telling them if they would furnish the blankets, I would go in person to Dalton and distribute them to the soldiers. With generous liberality, boxes of good things—chicken, ham, sausage, butter, pickles, bread and cake were packed, and I carried them to our Memphis soldier boys at the time I did the blankets.

"On Christmas night I left for Dalton, accompanied by the noble, patriotic President of that Aid Society, Mrs. Robt. Carter. At Atlanta my boxes had to be rechecked to Dalton. I met Dr. LaGree, of New Orleans, who proposed to telegraph Dr. John Erskine to meet us on our arrival at Dalton, at three o'clock in the morning, and he did so.

". . . At Dalton I sent a note to Gen. Hardee, Gen. Johnston being absent, telling him my mission. He came immediately. A courier and carriage were sent to us, and our first visit was to the old 154th Regiment, Gen. Preston Smith's. That night we had quite a levee of Officers. Gen. Hardee said that he had in his division fifteen hundred men without a blanket; Gen. [Thomas Carmichael] Hindman, one thousand; Gen. Cheatham, hundreds; and many other divisions in a similar condition. Gen. Pat Cleburne said socks were a luxury his men did not know; he had not had a pair on for five months.

"That evening a wagon was sent, with twenty soldiers, to receive the blankets I had brought. The boxes had been opened by order of Dr. Erskine; and I distributed the blankets and clothing to those who needed them.

". . . I then returned to Columbus, wrote and published in the papers what I had seen and heard at Dalton, of the great need of blankets for the Confederate soldiers, and made another appeal to that Ladies' Aid Society for more blankets. And they again nobly responded to my request, and went to work with zeal unprecedented, working night and day, taking the last blanket from their beds, cutting up carpets and lining them. I went out and in one hour I collected twenty-five hundred dollars from the business houses, and laid it out in the Columbus factories for jeans and coarse cloth. The women and children worked night and day, and in ten days I returned to the army in Dalton with seven large dry goods boxes, one each for Tennessee, Kentucky, Mississippi, Louisiana, Arkansas, Missouri, and Texas, all packed with five hundred and thirty blankets and coverings, and sixteen hundred pairs of socks, for the soldiers. I then went up to Tunnel Hill where Gen. Cleburne had his division; we rode on sacks of corn, for a freight train carried the Arkansas box to his soldiers. Had the boxes opened at the General's quarters, and as he was very soon to make a speech to his men on re-enlisting, said the box of blankets would do more than anything he could say, showing them the interest the women at home felt in them. But for the generous aid of the noble, patriotic women of Columbus, Ga., I would have been powerless to take those needed stores of blankets and socks to our suffering soldiers.

"After the second effort by the ladies of Columbus, and expecting to make the second trip with blankets, I wrote to Gen. Johnston of my intention, and asked him to send me an escort to Dalton. The difficulty in having to travel with so many boxes, and they to be transferred at Atlanta, was hazardous and annoying. Gen. Johnston sent the escort immediately and we left again for the seat of war, this time accompanied by three ladies, Mrs. Sallie Wilkins, my niece, and a daughter and granddaughter of Gov. [John] Forsythe. We were invited to dine with Generals Johnston, Hindman, [Alfred] Cumming and others, and my escort to dinner at Gen. Cumming's was the Rev. Dr. Stiles. We had four o'clock Confederate dinners, and were always sent for by the Adjutant of the General with whom we were to dine, with a carriage, and always escorted by Dr. John. Gen. J. C. Brown gave a party in honor of my lady friends. His headquarters were out about two miles in a large eight room brick house. The rooms were handsomely draped with Confederate flags, with a splendid band of music in the wide hall. There the Episcopal Bishop and the Presbyterian Rebel woman stood on the same platform under the Confederate flag. Gen. Johnston ordered a grand parade—thirty thousand brave, tattered troops—in honor of my mission to his soldiers. Mrs. Johnston invited me to take a seat in her carriage.

". . . My poor services to my struggling, bleeding country I know was only a drop in the ocean of that gigantic, cruel civil war. Still, for all those years of the 'Sixties,' they were most cheerfully, lovingly, and gratuitously given. In all my trips with supplies for the soldiers, I paid all my own expenses, never asking or receiving so much as a railroad pass or ticket. No, no; my whole heart and thoughts and deepest sympathies were all absorbed in the destiny of my people. For that just cause I would have died, could that sacrifice have brought peace, instead of a surrender, in which all was lost, save honor.

"Could I write all the incidents of my war record of the 'Sixties' a book could not contain them—the many reminiscences of those sad, gloomy, sorrowful years of terror and gloom. Perhaps at fifty years I might have accomplished it, but now, at eighty-seven years, I feel inadequate to the task; still, memories of suffering, blood, and tears at the bedside of the wounded, dying soldier, is indelibly stamped on my memory, and will probably last until the dreams of this fitful, checkered life are over, and I am transported to that 'House of many mansions,' prepared for all who love and serve God. I have had the honor of being called the 'Mother of the Confederacy,' a compliment I esteem higher than any that could be conferred upon me."[54]

The General Confederate Reunion of the UCV and the UDC were held at the Grand Auditorium, now the Ryman Auditorium, Nashville, Tennessee, in the fall of 1896. The Ryman was the home of the Grand Ole Opry from 1943 to 1974.

Mrs. Sarah Ewing Gaut, of Franklin, Tennessee, best known as "Sallie Carter."

From *Confederate Veteran*, 1912

OBITUARY: MRS. SARAH EWING GAUT

Mrs. Sarah ["Sallie"] Ewing Gaut passed away Wednesday afternoon, August 21, 1912, at the home of her daughter, Mrs. R. N. Richardson, in Franklin, Tenn., in her eighty-seventh year. For a year or more her health had been failing, the loss of strength being a gradual surrender to the infirmities of age; but she preserved her mental faculties to the last, evincing in her last days that interest in current events and in her friends which had been so marked a characteristic. With her only two surviving children, Mrs. Richardson and Mr. William E. Carter, of South Pittsburg, at her bedside and the recipient of many attentions from friends, she approached the end without a tremor and serenely passed from that to eternity.

The funeral was held at the Presbyterian church, of which she had long been a member, and the obsequies strikingly attested the wide regard in which she was held.

Mrs. Gaut was a daughter of Alexander C. Ewing, and was born July 12, 1826, on the homestead near Franklin which had been given to her grandfather, Alexander C. Ewing, in 1787 by the Federal government in recognition of his services as a Revolutionary soldier. This farm has been owned by five generations of Ewings, its senior immediate representative being Mr. Alexander H. Ewing. Her parents dying in her childhood, she was reared by Mrs. Sallie McGavock, a neighbor and relative, and when fifteen years old married Boyd McNairy Sims, who had not attained his majority. He was a lawyer and rich planter. They lived near Brentwood, and three children were born to them.

Carnton Plantation, front view, Franklin, Tennessee. (Photographer: Lochlainn Seabrook)

  She was left a widow at the age of twenty-three. After four years she married Joseph W. Carter, then of the State Senate from Winchester and one of the foremost lawyers and public men of the section. Two children were born to them. Mr. Carter died in about three years, and in 1860 his widow moved to Franklin, where she lived nearly a quarter of a century.

  After a widowhood of nineteen years following the death of Mr. Carter, Mrs. Carter in 1875 married Judge John M. Gaut, a prominent Nashville lawyer, and resided there until his death, in 1895. Her last years were spent in the house to which she came a widow over fifty years ago; and never losing interest in the affairs of her time, the fortunes of her friends, and often visited by those whom she had long known and loved, the evening of her days gently passed away and she fell asleep, unmurmuring and at peace.

Her sympathies were strongly enlisted for the Confederate cause, and this she showed in various ways both during the war and subsequent to it. It is said that the first Confederate flag raised in Franklin was the one which she and a number of friends hastily made and placed on the front of her house the day that one was unfurled from the Capitol in Nashville. She was actively connected with the organization of the Daughters of the Confederacy. She was one of the most active spirits also in the Ladies' Hermitage Association. — The *Franklin Review-Appeal*.

Adelicia Acklen of Nashville, Tennessee, daughter of Oliver Bliss Hayes. One of the wealthiest women in America, she was the founder and owner of the beautiful 20,000 square-foot home "*Bellemonte*," today known as Belmont Mansion. Constructed in 1853, today it is part of Nashville's Belmont University. Her nephew, Joel Addison Hayes, Jr., married a daughter of Jefferson Davis.

In an interesting sketch of Mrs. Gaut, "Anna Bland," the Franklin correspondent of the *Nashville Banner*, wrote: "Many interesting incidents in the life of Mrs. Carter [that is, Mrs. Gaut] occurred during the war. It is said that she gave the first positive information to General [Braxton] Bragg that the Federals contemplated an immediate advance on Murfreesboro. She had gone to Nashville upon personal matters, accompanied by two Franklin ladies, and was arrested and taken to headquarters. Hardly knowing what to do to secure a release, she sent for Ex-Gov. William Campbell, her kinsman, to secure her release, which he did. She then asked him to get a pass for her that she might go through the Union lines and return home. This, Governor Campbell said, would be impossible, as no one was allowed to leave the city at that time because of the plan of [Union] General [William Starke] Rosecrans to attack Bragg at Murfreesboro. Realizing the importance of getting this news to General Bragg at the earliest moment, Mrs. Carter determined to hurry to Franklin so as to notify Col. Baxter

Smith, who was in command of cavalry stationed at that place, that the news might be sent on to Murfreesboro. She got a horse and buggy, and with a young boy (Joe Dollis) to drive she started to Franklin. Taking a road leading north from Nashville, she cut across fields and pastures, heading for the Hillsboro Turnpike. As all fences were down, this was done without trouble. Finally the Federal picket lines were safely passed. Once on the Hillsboro Turnpike, the rest of the journey was quickly accomplished. Reaching Franklin, Mrs. Carter sent at once for Colonel Smith, gave him her news, and he dispatched a courier to Murfreesboro to give General Bragg warning of the contemplated attack.

"During the fall of 1863 Mrs. Adelicia Acklen, of Nashville, a cousin and close friend of Mrs. Carter, received the news that her large cotton crop in Louisiana was in danger of being burned by the Federals. [Mrs. Gaut and and Mrs. Acklen, owner of the cotton, went to Louisiana, got the cotton through the blockade, and saved the crop, which they sold for $960,000 gold. Col. L. Seabrook]

Belmont Mansion, Nashville, Tennessee. (Photographer: Lochlainn Seabrook)

"In the winter of 1864, after the battle of Franklin, the bloodiest of the War of the States, where five generals were killed, many of the wounded were carried to the home of Mrs. Carter and tenderly cared for until they were able to be sent to prison. One soldier, Capt. John M. Hickey, who had lost a leg, was never able to be moved, and remained at her home until the close of the war. Dr. J. D. Wallis, who was a surgeon in the Confederate army, stayed with Captain Hickey, and afterwards married one of Franklin's most charming girls, Miss Fanny Park. Captain Hickey moved to Columbia, where after a few years he was married to Miss Fannie Baird. Another of the wounded boys who was cared for in the home of Mrs. Carter was Capt. Matt Pilcher, who married Miss Judith Winston, of Nashville.

"The Federals, knowing of the shelter which had been given by Mrs. Carter to the Confederate soldiers, ordered her to prepare to receive a number of wounded Union men; but a change of orders was made, and the greater number were taken to Nashville, only four being left in the care of Mrs. Carter. She assisted in nursing these as tenderly as she had nursed the Confederates, although they had their own physicians and nurses. In after years Mrs. Carter received letters from many of the Union soldiers who were cared for under her roof thanking her for her goodness and kind treatment.

Historical marker at Belmont Mansion, Nashville, Tennessee. (Photographer: Lochlainn Seabrook)

"A few days after the battle of Franklin, when [Confederate] General [William Andrew] Quarles lay wounded at the home [Carnton Plantation] of Col. John McGavock, which had been turned into a hospital for Confederate wounded, Mrs. Carter visited him. General Quarles told her that if he recovered he was to be married to Miss Alice Vivian, a beautiful Mississippi girl, but that he did not possess a suit of clothes he was willing for his bride to see. Mrs. Carter went to Nashville and bought a suit for him and also an engagement ring for his sweetheart. Mrs. Carter visited them at Clarksville, Tenn., and was royally entertained.

"Soon after the war Mrs. Felicia Grundy Porter, of Nashville, a noble daughter of the eminent Felix Grundy, conceived the idea of raising funds for the disabled Confederate soldiers who had lost limbs. A society was organized for this purpose, and Mrs. Carter was appointed President for the Williamson County branch. Soon after her appointment Mrs. Carter arranged an entertainment to be given for the benefit of this organization, and from it over $7,000 was realized."[55]

MORE ON MRS. SARAH CARTER GAUT
From Lochlainn Seabrook's book *Encyclopedia of the Battle of Franklin*, 2012

Mrs. Carter became famous for sewing and then flying the first Confederate Flag in Williamson County, Tennessee. The beautiful symbol was displayed at her home on Third Avenue North, at Franklin, and was raised by a group of young men. One of these was Southern hero-martyr Confederate Captain Theodrick "Tod" Carter, of the city's celebrated Carter House, where several frightened families sheltered during the Battle of Franklin, November 30, 1864.

Mrs. Carter became well-known for another event: it was at her Franklin home in 1895 that the United Daughters of the Confederacy's Chapter Number 14 was formed. She was a true Southern heroine.[56]

The Carter House, Franklin, Tennessee, epicenter of the Battle of Franklin II, November 30, 1864. Bullet holes can still be seen on the property. One of the Carter sons, Confederate Capt. Theodrick "Tod" Carter, was mortally wounded just feet from his home that day. Earlier he had helped raise Williamson County's first Confederate flag, sewn by Southern patriot and UDC member Sarah Ann Carter. (Photographer: Lochlainn Seabrook)

Southern icon Confederate General Nathan Bedford Forrest of Tennessee fighting at close quarters, cutting down Yanks with his sword—which, against army regulations, he sharpened on both sides of the blade.

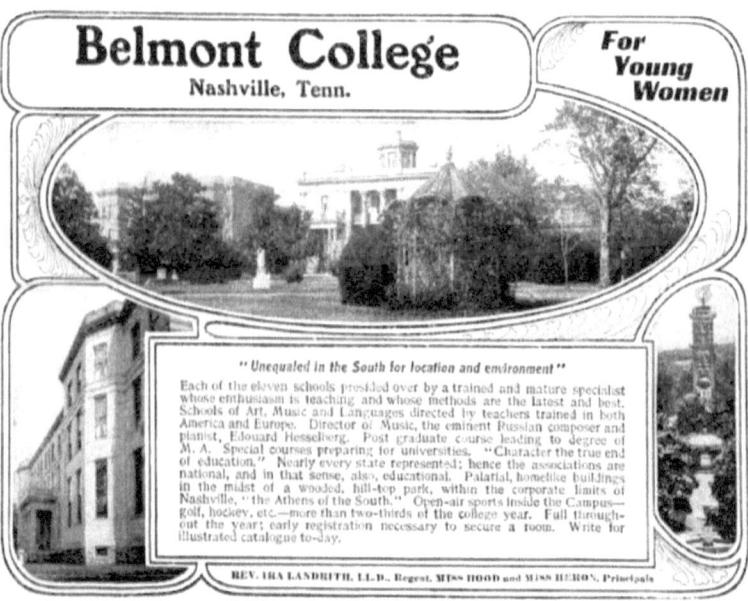

Before liberal anti-South partisans took over America's educational system, Southern institutions were proud to be Southern and were honored to be associated with the Confederacy. This ad in a 1907 *Confederate Veteran*, for example, was placed in the conservative magazine by Nashville's celebrated Belmont College For Young Women (now Belmont University), at a time when "character" rather than left-wing political activism and propagandism was "the true end of education." Belmont Mansion can be seen in the center of the upper image.

TEXAS

Miss Hattie Harn of Texas.

Misses Willie and Maud Lewis of Texas.

Texas belles, L-R: Bessie Polk, Omi Polk, and Lomie Beaumont, of Houston.

Miss Mary Muse Banks of Houston, Texas, Confederate Representative for her state in the UCV Reunion at Birmingham, Alabama.

Mrs. Eleanore Damon Pace of Corsicana, Texas, Confederate Sponsor for her state at the Macon Reunion of the Confederate Veterans. Her father, H. C. Damon, fought for the Confederacy in Virginia under Johnston and Lee.

Mrs. Z. T. Fulmore of Austin, Texas, Chairman of the Tom Green Monument Committee.

Marthy Cozby of Azle, Texas, read a poem entitled "Echoes of the Confederacy" at the State Reunion in Bowie in 1907.

Miss Flora Martin of Texas, Confederate Sponsor for her state.

Miss Decca Lamar West, Confederate Sponsor for the Texas Division, UCV.

UDC sponsored unveiling of the Confederate Monument at Jefferson, Texas, July 10, 1907, with 13 girls representing the 13 Southern states.

Miss Tennie Juliet Odem of Texas sang the song the "Conquered Banner" at the Russellville Reunion in 1894, and was asked to sing it again at the next meeting of the Orphan Brigade.

Mrs. Stella P. Dinsmore, President of the Joseph Wheeler Chapter of the UDC, Sulphur Springs, Texas. General Wheeler wrote to the ladies, thanking them for "the high honor paid him in naming the chapter."

Confederate Monument erected by the UDC at Waxahachie, Texas.

Miss Ida Richardson Hood of Texas, Confederate Sponsor for the Texas Division, UCV, at the Atlanta Reunion, 1898.

Miss Agatha Wright of Gainesville, Texas.

Mrs. W. P. Lane of Fort Worth, Texas, Secretary for the Texas Division, UDC.

Mrs. Wharton Bates of Houston, Texas, Treasurer of the Texas Division, UDC.

Mrs. James Gaines Carloss, Confederate Sponsor for the A. P. Hill Camp, Texarkana, Texas, Dallas Reunion.

Mrs. Cone Johnson, President Texas Division, UDC.

Miss Edith K. Ellis of Fort Worth, Texas, Assistant Secretary, Texas Division, UDC.

Mrs. Seabrook W. Sydnor of Houston, Texas, first Vice President of the Texas Division, UDC.

Mrs. Kate Cabell Currie of Texas.

From *Confederate Veteran*, 1895.

THE DAUGHTERS' WORK AT DALLAS, TEXAS

Mrs. Kate Cabell Currie, President Daughters of the Confederacy for the great Texas, writes quite at length, of the good work being done in Texas. Her local organization at Dallas has been diligent during the sixteen months of its existence. The membership is two hundred, and with their enthusiasm they have secured $3,000, which is now in bank, towards a Confederate Monument; and as they are to have a percentage of gate receipts at the Fair October 24th, and have the promised co-operation of many Veterans and Daughters in various counties, they expect to add $1,000 to the fund on that day. Last year, with many disadvantages, they secured $694 on their day at the Fair. The ladies of Sherman, Paris, Melissa, Lancaster, Hutchins, Terrell, Forney, Waxahachie, Weatherford, Mexia and Pilot Point have promised generous donations.

Mr. Couts, of Weatherford, has a beef fattening, and others yet to report, are doubtless doing likewise. So, Veterans who once knew not "marrow in the bone" may expect to enjoy the fat of the land at Dallas, October 24th. Mrs. Currie writes:

> "The noble old Veterans will be with us. Each mail comes loaded with words from privates and chieftains that they will come to honor the true women of the Southland, and to aid us in telling the story of Confederate bravery, suffering and patriotism.
>
> "Miss Lucy Lee Hill comes as our guest. Mrs. Willis, daughter of Gen. Sterling Price, and Mrs. Robertson, daughter of Gen. Dick Dowling, will be of the many with us to dispense hospitality to the Veterans.
>
> "Mrs. L. L. Jester, the 'Song Bird of Texas,' will sing only on the 24th, just to please the Veterans. She is proud of the title Daughter of the Confederacy. Her magnificent voice is known throughout the 'Lone Star State' and the Republic of Mexico. She will be accompanied by Sousa's band.
>
> "The concert and reception for Veterans will take place in Music Hall from 10 A.M. until noon. There will be a meeting at 3:30 to perfect the state organization, which is growing rapidly."

Mrs. Currie has just organized an Association at Terrell. There are Associations in Sherman, Victoria, Alvin, Galveston, Houston, Coleman, while Corsicana, Ennis and Salado have written for instructions. During the months of June, July, August and September, Mrs. Currie wrote with her own hand nearly three hundred letters. The spirit of "Old Tige," in unceasing zeal for the honor and glory of Southern heroes, is undaunted in her.[57]

Mrs. Katie Cabell Muse (née Cabell), of Dallas, Texas, fourth president of the UDC.

From *Confederate Veteran*, 1907

MARRIAGE OF MRS. KATIE CABELL

The fascinating and beautiful daughter of Gen. W. L. Cabell, of Dallas, has become the wife of Judge J. C. Muse. While the United Daughters of the Confederacy preserve a history of their organization, and especially while the older members live, there will be a charming memory of Mrs. Katie Cabell Currie, who served two terms as President, and whose administrations were a credit to the great cause this organization of Southern women was created to perpetuate.

Zealous for principles, Mrs. Currie was conspicuously impartial in her rulings; and when trouble brewed, she was so tactful as to bring smiles to delegations instead of frowns and angry words. Since her active official relations with the U.D.C., she has been diligent in looking after the comfort of her venerable father, and many a veteran will cherish the fond interest she has ever displayed in "Daddy" at Confederate Reunions.

A Dallas paper in giving account of the wedding, which took place at the residence of General Cabell, states: "Before the ceremony

Mrs. Henry Hymes sang 'Call Me Thine Own,' and Mr. Farris played the wedding march. Gen. R. M. Gaino [Richard Montgomery Gano], the venerable Chaplain of Camp Sterling Price, officiated, General Cabell giving the bride away. The house was radiantly embowered in flowers. The Confederate colors, white and red, predominated in the decorations, and formed an attractive floral background for a profusion of bride roses and white carnations. Four hundred names were inscribed in the 'guest book.'

"The Sons of Confederate Veterans, Camp W. L. Cabell (of which Judge Muse is a member), and Camp John H. Reagan were well represented, and with them came a bright bouquet of pretty girls. The universal esteem in which Judge Muse and his bride are held was eloquently attested by a glittering array of costly bridal presents.

"Mrs. Muse is a gracious, attractive woman, whose wit, poise, and intellectual charm bespeak the culture and refinement of Southern ancestry, education, and environment. Judge Muse is a courtly and accomplished gentleman, a brilliant and successful lawyer. The Cabell home has long been the 'Liberty Hall' of the old Confederacy. Rarely does so close and admirable a tie bind father and daughter. Ever tenderly solicitous for his health and interest, proud of his record as a soldier and commander as well as a civilian, Mrs. Muse has been an ideal example of filial devotion. He has enshrined her in his heart, and cherishes with pride all the noble work she has accomplished for the Confederate cause and the veterans."[58]

Miss Katie Daffan of Ennis, Texas, Confederate Sponsor for the Trans-Mississippi Dept., SCV.

Another photo of Miss Katie Daffan, with Confederate flag.

From *Confederate Veteran*, 1907: "Confederate Flag in Michigan Business Advertisement: *Collier's Weekly*, back cover page, for March 9, 1907, contains a conspicuous advertisement by the Olds Motor Works, Lansing, Mich. . . In December previous a party of men left New York City for Florida in an Oldsmobile 'Λ' and they had finished the trip of fourteen hundred miles to Daytona, Fla., on January 12. The purpose of the advertisement is to show the great power of the machine through muddy roads. Any favor to the company by this notice is gratuitous, and it is given as the first illustration known by the *Veteran* of any Northern concern giving prominence to the Confederate flag. Let it not be the last. That flag is clean enough in its record to be the pride of humanity at the North or elsewhere, as in the South, and it should not be regarded as inappropriate for the families of men who faced it to ornament their homes. It should be the pride of every American, and the tendencies are that way. The time will never come when patriots and Christians can taint the 'bonnie blue flag' with dishonor."[59]

VIRGINIA

Mrs. Mary Anna Jackson (née Morrison), wife of Confederate General Thomas "Stonewall" Jackson, of Virginia.

Julia Jackson Christian of Richmond, Virginia, the only child of Confederate General Stonewall Jackson.

Mrs. Thomas S. Bocock, first Honorary President of the Richmond, Virginia, Chapter, UDC.

Mrs. Mary G. Prichard of Virginia, "an original unreconstructed female rebel 91 years of age," and the proud mother of four Confederate soldiers.

The First Confederate Choir of the Stonewall Camp, whose purpose was to revive old patriotic Confederate war songs and sing them at meetings of the Confederate Veterans. The group performed for the first time at Trinity Church, Portsmouth, Virginia, on January 19, 1907, for the 100th birthday celebration of Robert E. Lee. Top row, L-R: Miss Sophia Nash; Mrs. W. H. Dashiell; Miss Janie Neely (First Lieut.); Mrs. Robt. Ridley, Jr.; Miss Maud Walker; Miss Louise Wilson. Middle row, L-R: Miss Emma Williams; Miss Reita Renn; Mrs. J. Griff Edwards (Captain); Miss Sadie Wilkins; Mrs. S. W. Harris (Second Lieutenant). Bottom row, L-R: Miss Delia Beale; Mrs. Frank L. Crocker; Miss Elizabeth Neeley; Miss Bessie Ridley (Adjutant).

Miss Mildred Kay Harrison, Confederate Sponsor for the Pacific Division, Richmond Reunion.

Miss Lizzie Clarke of West Point, Virginia, Confederate Representative for her state in the UCV Reunion at Birmingham, Alabama.

Mrs. C. W. Hunter of West Appomattox, Virginia, the first President and organizer of the Appomattox Chapter, UDC. The daughter of a Confederate soldier (J. C. Jones) she fought to have historically accurate, South-friendly textbooks put into Southern schools.

Miss Varina Anne Davis, of Richmond, Virginia, was the youngest of the children of Confederate President Jefferson Davis and his wife Varina Howell Davis. An author, "Winnie," as she was nicknamed, was fondly known as the "Daughter of the Confederacy" for her love of Confederate principles. Lamentably, the unmarried 34 year old died in 1898 after contracting a serious illness.

Mrs. Nannie Seddon Barney of Fredericksburg, Virginia, President of her state's Grand Division, UDC.

Mrs. Fitzhugh Lee of Virginia, third President of the UDC. Her husband was a Confederate general, a governor of Virginia, and a nephew of Gen. Robert E. Lee.

Ninety foot Confederate Monument erected at Richmond, Virginia's Hollywood Cemetery by the Ladies Memorial Association.

Norfolk, Virginia, c. 1863. Confederate soldiers being welcomed by their ladies as they are transferred back onto Confederate boats by Union officials under a flag of truce. (Artist: Alfred R. Waud)

Mrs. Minnie Louise Hill Briggs of Norfolk, Virginia.

From *Confederate Veteran*, 1912

MARRIED, DIED, AND BURIED UNDER THE FLAG
Obituary: A True Daughter of Virginia—Her Connections

Mrs. Minnie Louise Hill Briggs, wife of George L. Briggs, of Norfolk, Va., died in Washington, D. C., April 25, after a short illness, and was buried at Culpeper, Va., April 27, the home of her ancestors. She was a daughter of the late Henry Hill, Jr., and granddaughter of Henry Hill, major and paymaster in the U. S. army, who resigned in 1861 and became colonel and paymaster-general of the Virginia Confederate forces. She was a grandniece of the renowned Lieut. Gen. A. P. Hill, whose name was last on the dying lips of Gens. Lee and Jackson.

Mrs. Briggs was married three years ago under a Confederate flag, and, by a strange coincidence, her death occurred under the same Confederate flag, on the anniversary of her marriage.

Some years ago Mrs. Briggs (then Miss Hill) and her twin sister, Miss Frances Ambrose Hill, were officially decorated by A. P. Hill Camp, U.C.V., Petersburg, Va., in recognition of the distinguished services of their relatives and the worthiness of the recipients of the decorations. She was buried with this badge upon her bosom and with the Confederate flag across her form, beneath which she was married and died. The Culpeper and Norfolk Daughters sent beautiful floral designs, and the grave was hung with white cloth, white flowers being tastefully arranged thereon.

Mrs. Briggs was a zealous friend of the *Veteran*, contributed to its pages, and did much to increase its circulation and advance its usefulness. Mrs. Briggs was a zealous and beloved member of the Culpeper Chapter of Daughters of the Confederacy, and subsequently of the Norfolk Chapter. She was untiring in her devotion to Confederate memories and the relief of needy Confederates. Her nature was charitable, loving, and winsome, and she possessed sublime Christian faith. A large circle of devoted relatives and friends mourn her untimely death.

The father of Mrs. Briggs and Miss Hill, the late Henry Hill, Jr., died during their childhood. He entered the Confederate army at the age of seventeen, and served through the war in the Fourth Virginia Cavalry, under Gens. J. E. B. Stuart, Fitzhugh Lee, and W. C. Wickham. He it was who took the body of Gen. A. P. Hill (his uncle) from Petersburg to Richmond the day Gen. Hill was killed, April 2, 1865, and the lines of Lee's army were broken. Gen. Lee directed that an ambulance be furnished for the purpose. The body was coffined in Richmond during the night of the evacuation of the city, after which Mr. Hill and Col. Hill, his father, recrossed the bridge over the James River while it was in flames, and buried the body of Gen. Hill in a family burial-plot near Richmond. The remains were afterward removed to Hollywood Cemetery, and finally were reinterred beneath the statue and pedestal erected to Gen. Hill's memory at Richmond and dedicated in 1892.[60]

A drawing showing Southern women making clothes for Confederate soldiers, 1864. (Artist: Adalbert John Volck)

From *Confederate Veteran*, 1908

"CAPTAIN" SALLY LOUISA TOMPKINS

Miss Sally Louisa Tompkins, of Mathews County, Va., a daughter of Col. Christopher Tompkins (deceased) and Maria Booth Patterson, enjoys the distinction of being the only woman who was an "officer in the Confederate States army." During the four fiery years of Southern trial this pure, saintly, and heroic young patriot displayed throughout as undaunted heroism, as devoted zeal, as steadfast loyalty in behalf of the storm-cradled nation that sleeps as the world's civilization can boast. In recognition of her inestimable service rendered the sick and wounded of the South, for whose benefit she exhausted her once munificent patrimony, in the year 1863 she was regularly commissioned a captain of cavalry in the Confederate army. Verily there were many who called her blessed.

Drawing of a stained glass memorial to Sally Louisa Tompkins, with Robertson Hospital at the top and a rendition of John 10:10: "I am come that you may have everlasting life."

Immediately after the first battle of Manassas the Confederate government called upon the citizens of Richmond, Va., to care for the sick and wounded returning from that memorable engagement. And on July 31, 1861, just ten days succeeding that battle, Miss Tompkins, entirely at her own expense, opened for their benefit (corner of Main and Third Streets) the "Robertson Hospital," which continued uninterruptedly its mission of mercy until July 13, 1865. It was the only private hospital that survived the conflict there. During that time 1,390 of the sons of Dixie's land were tenderly nursed and cared for. At one time an order was issued for the closing of all private hospitals and the removal of all the soldiers to public hospitals, the intent of the Confederate government being to reduce the number of hospitals and correspondingly increase their efficiency. Indeed, it was feared that some hospitals were harboring men more battle-scared than battle-scarred.

Before the order could be executed, however, even while ambulances were in waiting at the door, "Captain Sally" strenuously insisted that the register of her hospital should first be exhibited before President Davis, wherein were accurately shown the number of patients received, the death rate (miraculously low), and the phenomenally large percentage of those returned to duty. These facts induced President Davis to revoke the order, in so far as it applied to the "Robertson Hospital."

For their long-continued, self-sacrificing assistance in her hospital work "Captain Sally" was especially indebted to Mesdames Elizabeth Semmes, James Alfred Jones, Mary Randolph Page, Ellen Tompkins Bowen, William Grant, John Peyton McGuire, and Misses Randolph Tabb, Elizabeth Davenport, Rebecca Churchill Jones, and Augusta Tabb. Mrs. Dr. John Spotswood Welford loaned her an efficient servant, "Sally," who acted as hospital cook, and Benjamin Ficklen, Esq., and Captain Snaden, who acted as blockade runners, furnished innumerable supplies of value, including chests of tea, sacks of coffee, and money.

Attached to the hospital were four slaves belonging to "Captain Sally": Betsey Curtis and Betsey Ashberry (known by the soldiers to whom they tenderly ministered as "Sad Betsey" and "Glad Betsey," respectively) and Peter Smith and Churchill Smith Peter Smith [who] finally ran off. Upon his return, after the close of hostilities, he was profuse in his apologies to Miss Sally, assuring her that his sole reason for leaving was that he knew the slaves would be set free and he didn't want her to lose him.

Among the soldiers desperately wounded but who eventually recovered was one from North Carolina, who, with his eight brothers, had enlisted at the beginning of the conflict; seven of those had already nobly yielded up their bodies to their country, their souls to their God. A purse was quickly made up and the aged mother sent for to come and see her suffering boy. On arriving she calmly yet proudly declared that had she nine other sons she would gladly also give them up to battle for the cause. On one occasion two North Carolinians occupied the same ward, each ill with typhoid fever. In his delirium one struck the nurse as she attempted to administer his medicine, whereupon the other sprang from his cot, declaring with true Southern gallantry: "No man shall ever strike a woman in my presence."

    . . . It has well been said that if we secure a lofty ideal and a noble model on which to shape a well-rounded and perfect womanhood, combining the pure patriotism, the rugged virtues, the winning modesty, and the tender graces of Spartan mother, Roman dame, and Carthagenian maid, we have but to take a retrospective glance down the corridors of memory for about four decades to find it in that heroic sisterhood of martyrs and patriots, the women of the Confederacy.

We should love to teach our children
Of our heroes who are dead,
Of the battle scars they carried,
Marching to a soldier's tread.

Of their loyal hearts so tender,
All aglow in Truth's array,
And the many recollections
Of the boys who wore the Gray.

And so long as Time speeds onward
And there is a heaven of love
God shall watch our silent sentinels
Sleeping from the world above.

And he'll guard the sacred memory
Of the old Confederate Gray
Throughout Time's eternal pages
When the last one's passed away.[61]

Mrs. J. Griff Edwards of Virginia.

From *Confederate Veteran*, 1912

AT HEAD OF THE CONFEDERATE CHOIRS

Mrs. J. Griff Edwards [née Nelson] organized the Confederate Choir which became first known as "Portsmouth Choir, No. 1," and this Choir made its first appearance in Trinity Episcopal Church, Portsmouth. Va., on Gen. Robert E. Lee's one hundredth anniversary. There are now thirty-five Choirs throughout the South, from Seattle, Wash., to Gainesville, Tex., and from Fayetteville, Ark, to the Atlantic Coast. These Choirs have sung at all the Reunions from Richmond to Little Rock, and have tried to tell of their love for the dear old heroes of the sixties, through the immortal songs of Dixie Land. They also chant the requiem of the dead at the graveside of a departed veteran. Apart from trying to preserve the dear old songs of the South, the Choirs aid in every way all other Confederate organizations when called upon. An exchange from Virginia states of Mrs. Edwards:

> "These Choirs are to revive old war songs, and the patriotic lady, Mrs. J. Griff Edwards, who organized the Confederate Choir No. 1 as auxiliary to Stonewall Camp, C. V., of Portsmouth, Va., will be blessed by the old veterans throughout the land. The best blood of Virginia flows in the veins of this sweet-voiced daughter

of Dixie, and her unselfish patriotism is a bright heritage from distinguished ancestors, who are famous for great valor and noble self-sacrifice for their country. She is a direct descendant of Secretary William Nelson, of the Colony of Virginia, the father of Gov. Thomas Nelson and Maj. John Nelson, of Yorktown fame.

"Her father, William Nelson Boswell, entered the Confederate service at eleven years of age as a drummer in his father's company, and his soldierly bearing on drill so attracted the attention of President [Jefferson] Davis that he with his own hands presented the little drummer with a sword.

"The grandfather of Mrs. Edwards, Col. Thomas T. Boswell, personally in 1861 uniformed Company A, 56th Virginia Regiment, Pickett's Division, and served as its captain until the last of the war, when he was promoted to major and then to lieutenant colonel of the 1st Virginia Reserves, stationed at Staunton River Bridge, in Charlotte County. He married Martha Nelson, of the family indicated above."

This notice will interest a multitude who have heard Mrs. Edwards sing "I'm Glad I Live in Dixie" as no one else ever has or ever can.[62]

Mrs. Edwards with Confederate Battle Flag.

Confederate soldiers and families evacuating Mechanicsville, Virginia, as Union troops begin shelling the area. (Artist: Alfred R. Waud)

Damaged engraving of the funeral of Confederate cavalry Captain William D. Latané, the only Confederate who lost his life during Jeb Stuart's raid on the Union army near Richmond, Virginia, June 13, 1862. The funeral took place on Summer Hill Plantation. As all the able-bodied men were away on the battlefield, only women, children, and servants were in attendance. The service was performed by Mrs. Willoughby Newton (center).

From *Confederate Veteran*, 1895

ANNE LEE MEMORIAL ASSOCIATION

Appeal to the women of the South: The first monument erected "by women to a woman" was that to Mary [Ball], the mother of Washington. Now the time has come when every Southern woman must feel that the second so erected should be to the memory of the mother of Robert Edward Lee, Virginia's noble chieftain.

Of his mother [Anne Hill Carter] Gen. Lee once said, "All I am I owe to my mother." And her grandson, Gen. Fitzhugh Lee, writes of her, "I have always heard that to her noble influence the perfect formation of Gen. Lee's character was due."

Thus to Anne Carter Lee, the South owes her illustrious leader, whose brave deeds, honorable record and noble patriotism won for him undying fame and honor, and the love and devotion of a grateful Confederacy.

The women of Alexandria, Va., prompted by a desire to commemorate the virtues of the mother of Robt. E. Lee, propose to erect, in that city, a monument to her memory.

It was in Alexandria, in the beautiful yard of old Christ Church, of which he was, at that time, a vestryman, (and in which Gen. Washington had in earlier days occupied a similar position) that Gen. Lee announced his determination to cast in his lot with his native state in the pending conflict, stating his purpose to leave next day to join the Army of the Confederacy, and "offer his sword in defence of his native land."

('Tis said to have been the identical spot General Washington first "openly" expressed his intention to join the Army of the Revolution.)

No better place could be selected for the erection of such a monument. Her home was there, she was a member of the old Church, and but a few miles off her remains lie buried.

Will it not afford pleasure to our sisters of the South to unite with us in securing a fund to enable us to raise a shaft to the memory of Anne Lee? We are so fully assured of your sympathy and equal interest, that in making this appeal for your help and co-operation, we are satisfied we shall not ask in vain.

If there are some who cannot become members of the Association by reason of their inability to pay the sum required for membership they need not be deterred from helping; let such persons give what they can; any contribution, however small, will be acceptable. Many there are able to make liberal offerings; from such we shall be only too happy to accept gifts in such measure as they may elect.

All contributions should be sent to the Secretary, who is required (Art. IV By-Laws) to "receive all monies and pay them over to the Treasurer."

Alice E. Colquhoun, Secretary,
818 King Street, Alexandria, Va.

Mrs. W. J. Boothe, Treasurer, Alexandria.

This appeal comes to you from the Anne Lee Memorial Association, chartered July 23, 1895, in Alexandria, Virginia.

Trustees: Judge J. K. M. Norton, Capt. Wm. A. Smoot, Col. L. W. Reid, Henry Strauss, G. W. Ramsay, M. B. Harlow, Edgar Warfield, Julian T. Burke, C. C. Carlin, Douglas Stuart.

Lady Managers: President, Mrs. L. W. Reid; Vice President, Miss Sallie Stuart; Recording Secretary, Miss Alice E. Colquhoun; Corresponding Secretary, Miss Katherine H. Stuart; Treasurer, Mrs. W. J. Boothe.

Mrs. Mary B. Washington, Vice President for Tennessee, suggests the giving of mites by the multitude. Let all Tennesseans interested write to Mrs. J. E. Washington, Cedar Hill, Tenn.[63]

Confederate Gen. Stonewall Jackson of Clarksburg, Virginia (now West Virginia).

The Confederate White House, Richmond, Virginia.

Mrs. Carrie Selden Kirby Smith of Virginia.

From *Confederate Veteran*, 1907

OBITUARY: MRS. EDMUND KIRBY-SMITH

The Kirby-Smith Chapter, U.D.C., of Sewanee, Tenn., has sustained another very sad loss in the death of Mrs. Edmund Kirby-Smith, their honorary charter member. She had been identified with Sewanee life for thirty-two years, her husband, [Confederate] Gen. E. Kirby-Smith [Edmund Kirby Smith], having come to the University of the South as professor of mathematics in 1875. She was Miss Caroline Selden, of Lynchburg, Va., married when she was very young, and was one of the most devoted wives and mothers ever known.

One never associated death with Mrs. Kirby-Smith. Her life was so kindly, her temperament so cheerful, and her warm heart went out to those around her with such childlike simplicity, touching the most callous and endearing her to all, that it seemed that she might be spared for many years more. She represented the type, now almost passed away, of warm Southern hospitality, and nothing delighted her more than entertaining the veterans at her home when the Chapter distributed crosses of honor each year on the 3rd of June, and those who attended these reunions will recall her smiling, hearty welcome and cheerful words for all.[64]

Women from the United Daughters of the Confederacy, Virginia Division, 1898.

WASHINGTON, D.C.

UDC members in Washington, D.C., 1912.

Mrs. Alice Pickett Akers of Washington, D.C., made the following famous comment: "I had rather have my picture in the *Confederate Veteran* magazine than in the White House." Both her father and her husband (Major Albert Akers) fought proudly for the Confederacy.

A member of the United Daughters of the Confederacy, in Washington, D.C., 1912.

June 4, 1938, celebration of the birthday of Confederate President Jefferson Davis at Washington, D.C., proof that our Southern chief executive was once honored in America's capital city. From L-R: Senator Walter F. George of Georgia; Miss Imogene Smith, President of the Charles M. Stedman Children of the Confederacy; Mrs. Walter D. Lamar, National President of the Daughters of the Confederacy.

Mrs. Letitia Tyler Semple of Washington, D.C.

From *Confederate Veteran*, 1894

FOUNDER OF THE FIRST CONFEDERATE HOSPITAL
By Mrs. Alice Trueheart Buck, Washington, D.C.

Among the Southern veterans residing in the National Capital are some noble women, whose sacrifices and devotions to our cause have never been recorded in history. The frosts of time have whitened their heads like the old soldiers, but the purity and beauty of their hearts is not marred. One of these, Mrs. Letitia Tyler Semple, daughter of Ex-President [John] Tyler, established the first hospital in the South.

When the war commenced she was in New York with her husband, who was Paymaster in the United States Navy, stationed at New York. They immediately came South and cast their fortunes with our people—he taking a position on the *Alabama* and she on another, and sometimes the more trying battle ground. In Philadelphia, on her way south Mrs. Semple met a friend who suggested to her that more soldiers died from sickness than the bullet, and that she inaugurate a movement for the establishment of hospitals, which she did as soon as she reached Richmond, in May 1861. She arrived there the day the blockade set in.

There she met her father who was a member of the Confederate Congress, and he obtained permission of Mr. Pope Walker, Confederate Secretary of War, to establish a hospital at Williamsburg. Mrs. Semple's appeal to the ladies of Williamsburg was heartily responded to. Col. Benj. S. Ewell was in command of the Peninsular, and with other gentlemen encouraged and assisted the move. The Female Seminary which stood upon the site of the Colonial Capitol, was selected for the purpose desired. The ladies went to work diligently, Mrs. Semple making the first bed with her own hands. Very soon seventy-five cots were in place. Dr. Tinsley, now a practicing physician in Baltimore, and Dr. W. C. Shields were the surgeons in charge. Very soon troops from different points were centered there. About that time Mrs. Semple left Williamsburg and returned after the battle of Bethel, June 10.

There were then so many refugees from Hampton and other places, and so many sick soldiers (none wounded as yet) needing attention and comforts, that William and Mary College, the Court House, and several churches were taken for hospitals, Dr. Willis Westmoreland in charge. Dr. Westmoreland sent a message to Mrs. Semple's residence asking her to inspect the situation, which she did, and when she found so many needing more than the kind citizens could immediately supply, she went to Richmond the next day for supplies. General Moore rendered all the assistance he could, and the people of Petersburg, Pittsylvania and other places contributed liberally of food, clothes and bedding. The first death in the hospital was that of young Ball, Company A of Fairfax County, Va. The young hero gave up his life for his country, and that was all that was known of him there, but the lady who received the tender look from the soft blue eyes, and smoothed his golden hair for the last time never forgot him. It is to be hoped his family found his remains.

The New Orleans (French) Zouaves, and Captain Zachary's troops were stationed there at that time, and the ladies made and presented a flag to them, the address being made by Mr. Edwin Talliaferro. [Confederate] General [John Bankhead] Magruder now took command of the troops. Among them was a brigade from Georgia under General McClaus [Lafayette McLaws]. Colonel Ewell also was there with his regiment awaiting orders. All of them gallantly assisted the ladies in their work.

Knowing the part Mrs. Semple had taken in the noble work, Colonel Ewell asked General McClaus [McLaws] if he had called upon her. He answered, "No, but I'll go directly." When he returned from his visit to Mrs. Semple and the Colonel asked him what he thought of her, he said, "Why sir, I hadn't been in that room five minutes when, if she had said to me, 'McClaus, bring me a bucket of water from the spring,' I would have done it."

So the women of that day helped the cause by cheering the living and caring for the sick and wounded, and the beautiful woman who inaugurated such a glorious work still smiles encouragement to every generous and loyal deed for the good of our loved Southland. The women of this generation also have a work to do, and they are banding together for the purpose.

In Washington, besides the soldiers and their families, there are needy ones from every State who have been shipwrecked on the sea of life. Our Southern Relief Association is composed of about three hundred women who labor zealously in caring for this class, those who have no friends to help them. It is refreshing to meet with an organization so generous and loyal in spirit and practice. When preparing for entertainments wealthy women don their aprons and work by the side of those who are poor, oft times without knowing each other's name. Every Southern heart that beats over a well filled pocket should open it now, for soon our veterans will "pass over the river." There they will neither want nor suffer. While honoring the dead let us not forget the living.[65]

Miss Mary Hayne of Washington, D.C.

From *Confederate Veteran*, 1909

THE WORK OF MISS MARY HAYNE
By Elizabeth Jacobs

The *Veteran* for October contains an article regarding some Confederate prisoners confined during a period of the Civil War in Fort Warren, Boston Harbor. There was also a copy of their pictures taken at that time, now the property of Miss C. M. Davis, of Fernandina, Fla.

In Washington, D. C., there resides an old lady who during the Civil War rendered invaluable services to the Confederacy and incidentally to the United States, services so valuable that they are to-day on record in the War Department.

In 1863 Miss Mary Hayne, then a charming, beautiful young lady, was solely instrumental, making her appeal to Mr. Lincoln, in having one hundred and sixty-three Confederate prisoners exchanged, some of whom were condemned to be shot as traitors to the United States government, among them being Charles M. Reid, noted throughout both armies for his gallantry and daring. Captain Reid was a native of Mississippi, a graduate of the naval school at Annapolis, and a nephew of President Davis.

I have a full account, published in a *New York Sunday Herald* during 1863, of the capture of Captain Reid at New Orleans, with his boat, the *Ram*, and the following gentleman, his associate officers: Lieut. W. H. Wall (executive officer), Surgeon Addison, Midshipman J. P. Blank, H. Scott (pilot), and others, together with two of her crew. They were brought to New York on the United States boat *Florida*, Lieutenant Commander Webb, sometime in the spring of 1863, and were sent to Fort Preble, Maine, and from there transferred to Fort Warren, Boston Harbor. After they were exchanged in 1864, Captain Reid went into active service again, taking command of the Confederate boat *Florida No. 2*. As before, his daring and brave spirit led him to many deeds of valor. He was again taken prisoner and returned to Fort Warren, where he remained until near the close of the war, when, through Miss Hayne's personal appeal to President Andrew Johnson, he was again released, this time to return no more to fight for the beloved republic whose star was about to set.

In 1864 Samuel Sterrett, son of Commodore Sterrett, was incarcerated as a political prisoner in Fort Warren. Commodore Sterrett was killed in a naval engagement somewhere between the Florida coast and Cuba. His son, Samuel Sterrett, who was with his father at the time, was captured with the boat and all on board and imprisoned, as mentioned above.

Miss Hayne went to the President, accompanied by [Confederate] Secretary [of the Navy Gideon] Welles, and interceded so successfully in his behalf that the Chief Magistrate telegraphed to the authorities at Fort Warren, and Mr. Sterrett was released the following day. Miss Hayne has now a personal letter from Mr. Sterrett thanking her for what she did for him.

At the solicitation of the Sisters in charge of Kearney Hospital, Boston, Miss Hayne appealed to President Johnson in behalf of a gentleman from Baltimore, Md., a Mr. Mullen. He had been in prison for some time, and his health was deeply impaired and his eyesight almost gone. The Sisters had succeeded in having him transferred to the hospital, and his mother in great grief finally appealed to Miss Hayne and she to the President, who again granted her request.

Miss Hayne is a noble woman, actuated by sympathy for those who suffered for the cause they deemed just. Her deep interest was accentuated by the fact that she was the fiancee of Captain Reid. Her brother was Gen. Barnwell Hayne, of South Carolina.

I have in my possession a photograph of Captain Reid and his men taken just before they left Fort Warren, with the request that it be sent to Miss Hayne.

In those days she had youth, beauty, wealth, and hosts of friends; to-day she is in Washington bereft of home and fortune and the friends of her better days. Any one desiring further information about this noble woman can address Mrs. Elizabeth Jacobs, 1226 Twelfth Street N.W., Washington, D.C.[66]

From the cover, UDC members in Washington, D.C., at the 1912 UDC Convention. Top left: Mildred Lewis Rutherford, Historian General, UDC. Bottom left: Mrs. Anna Mitchell Davenport Raines, co-founder of the UDC.

THE HOMELAND
By Emma Frances Lee Smith, Washington, D.C.

O, the homeland is the land we love!
Gray are the skies that brood above
The drifting snows of the hardy North,
Where from seashore and valley we hurry forth
On the path where honor and duty lead
To a stricken world in its bitter need;
      But the homeland, the clear land,
      The homeland is the land we love—

Where the moonlight falls in golden gleams
Over orange groves and whispering streams,
Where the mocking bird in the jasmine bowers
Chants his love through the drowsy hours.
Sons of the men who wore the gray,
Rank on rank we have marched away
      From the homeland, the dear land—
      O, the homeland is the land we love!

From mountain and desert, from ranch and plain,
From search for pleasure and hope of gain,
From mine and from forest, from river and hill,
The men of the West are coming still;
Firm is our faith in the glorious prize
Which we see in the future with steadfast eyes
      For the homeland, the dear land,
      The homeland, the land we love.

As we look our last on the clear home lights,
When the troop ships glide through the solemn nights,
Should we feel in the dark the stealthy blow,
The thrust of a savage and cunning foe,
Calmly we'll die, if need there be,
And our young lives offer for liberty
      And the homeland, the dear land,
      For the homeland is the land we love.

If, braving all perils by shell and fire,
We see the end of our long desire
And look with joy on a world restored
By the might of our swift-avenging sword.
With a sigh for our dead in their lonely graves
We'll set our course o'er the swelling waves
      To the homeland, the dear land—
      O, the homeland is the land we love![67]

WEST VIRGINIA

Mrs. Wayne P. Ferguson of Kenova, West Virginia, is the wife of General Ferguson, Brigade Commander of the Second Brigade, West Virginia Division. She was matron of honor of the West Virginia Division, UCV, at the Macon, Georgia Reunion in May 1912.

Miss Jean Miller, daughter of Judge James H. Miller, of Bellepoint, West Virginia, was Maid of Honor for the West Virginia Division, Sons of Confederate Veterans, at Macon, Georgia.

Miss Texa Jordan of Wheeling, West Virginia, Confederate Maid of Honor to the New Orleans Reunion.

Miss Annie D. Lewis, Confederate Sponsor for West Virginia.

Victorian celebrity Maria Isabella Boyd, better known as Belle Boyd: Southern heroine, Confederate spy, author, actress, wife, mother, adventurer, and lecturer, from Martinsburg, West Virginia.

Another view of Miss Belle.

The Belle Boyd House, Martinsburg, West Virginia. Miss Belle's real life story reads like a novel: at the start of the War she killed a Union soldier who insulted her mother; she worked as a courier-spy for such Confederate generals as Stonewall Jackson and P. G. T. Beauregard; she was exiled once, arrested six times (once at sea), and imprisoned three times; she later married one of the Yankee officers who arrested her; she wrote a book called *Belle Boyd, In Camp and Prison*; she toured the U.S., lecturing on her wartime exploits; she became a stage actress; she married several more times and bore at least five children; in 1900, while speaking in Wisconsin, the 56 year old "Siren of the Shenandoah" died of a heart attack, and was buried in Spring Grove Cemetery, Wisconsin Dells.

WISCONSIN

Mrs. Alice W. Waterman, of Madison, Wisconsin. Though born in the South, Mrs. Waterman spent her last years living in the Badger State, where this "noble woman" tended the graves of 139 Confederate soldiers at "Confederate Rest Cemetery" in Madison. Of her work at the graveyard it was noted that she "had the grounds inclosed with a board fence and ornamented with beautiful shade trees and hedges, and every grave was properly marked with a headboard."

In this 1909 railroad ad targeting travelers to the UCV Reunion at Memphis, Tennessee, a Confederate veteran on the left and a Union veteran on the right grudgingly shake hands. As is tacitly illustrated here, profound social, cultural, political, religious, and philosophical differences have always existed between the South and North. Progressive Yankees, like Abraham Lincoln, have long hoped to Northernize the South in an attempt to turn Dixie into an exact replica of the North. Traditional Southerners, like Jefferson Davis, however, were not interested in this idea in the 1860s, and they are still not interested in it today. Like oil and water, as of 2016 a sociopolitical map of the U.S. shows that the 300 year old gulf between the conservative, agrarian, religious South and the liberal, industrial, atheistic North remains as wide and deep as ever—with no sign that the two will ever merge as one.

MISCELLANEOUS

Miss Mary Amelia Smith.

Miss Mary Willingham, Confederate Sponsor for Forrest's Cavalry Corps.

Margaret "Maggie" Howell Davis Hayes and Varina Ann "Winnie" Davis, daughters of Jefferson Davis and Varina Howell Davis.

Unidentified Southern woman, wife of a Confederate soldier, 1861-1865.

"Kentucky Honors Her Southern Sisters: Bowling Green Reunion," 1895. Bottom row, L-R: Miss Daisy Price of Kentucky; Miss Margaret F. Wintersmith of Georgia; Miss Mary Parks of Missouri; Miss Sally G. Marshall of North Carolina; Miss Margaret Taylor of Arkansas. Middle row, L-R: Miss Hyde Baker of Tennessee; Miss Mary Dulaney of Louisiana; Miss Enola A. Chandler of Mississippi; Miss Elizabeth D. Hines of Virginia. Top row, L-R: Miss Emma Wintersmith of South Carolina; Miss Willie A. Perry of Alabama; Miss Clair Stark of Florida; Miss Margaret Kennady of Maryland; Miss Lou Mitchell of Texas.

Miss Louise Dudley, Maid of Honor for Forrest's Cavalry Corp.

Mrs. Alexander B. White, 10th President General UDC.

Mrs. Ridgley (or Ridgely) Brown with an eleven-star First National Confederate Flag, 1861-1865.

Confederate graves at Charleston, South Carolina, being tended by loyal Southern women, c. 1903.

Presentation of the UDC flag to the Nashville Chapter in 1912.

Miss Bettina Ruth Bush attended the UCV Reunion in New Orleans, 1903.

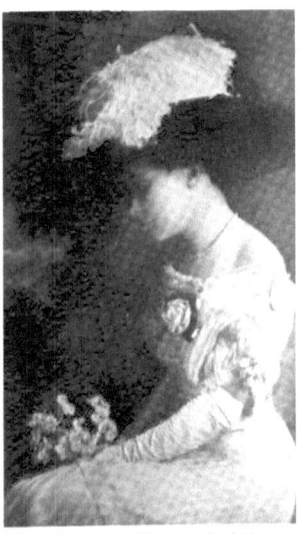

Miss Alleen Smith, Maid of Honor for Forrest's Cavalry Corps.

Miss Marie Brevard, Assistant Adjutant, General Forrest's Cavalry Corps.

Mrs. Lucy Bradford Mitchell, a relation of Confederate President Jefferson Davis.

Unidentified Confederate woman, 1864-1865.

Four Generations of President Jefferson Davis. Center: Varina Howell Davis, wife; with Margaret Davis Hayes, daughter; Mrs. Gerald B. Webb, granddaughter; and Varina Margaret Webb, great-granddaughter.

Unidentified Southern woman in mourning clothes, wearing a brooch containing a photo of a Confederate soldier, probably her late husband. The child is wearing a Confederate kepi, 1861-1865.

L-R: Mrs. Maggie Johns (President UDC at Corinth, Mississippi), Mrs. G. W. Bynum (Matron of Honor), Mrs. M. B. Curlee (Matron of Honor); all were UDC members and wives of Confederate officers.

Southern heroine Miss Emma Sansom, claimed by three states: Georgia, Alabama, and Texas. As a young girl she achieved everlasting fame when, on May 2, 1863, near Gadsden, Alabama, she helped Confederate General Nathan Bedford Forrest locate a "lost" river ford on Black Creek. Her act saved Forrest and his fearsome "critter company" at least three hours, enabling him to score another decisive victory for the Southern Cause.

Miss Virginia Van Zandt, Confederate Sponsor for the Trans-Mississippi Dept., UCV.

Unidentified Confederate woman with framed photo of a Confederate soldier, 1861-1865.

Constance Cary Harrison, one of the three women who sewed the first set of Confederate flags in 1861.

"Southern Beauties at Birmingham, Alabama." The young lady State Representatives at the 1894 Reunion of United Confederate Veterans at Birmingham are as follows. Bottom row, L-R: Adele McMurray (Tennessee) and Bessie B. Henderson (North Carolina). Middle row, L-R: Lula Montague (Maryland); Etta Mitchell (Mississippi); Adele Hayne (South Carolina); Laura Boone (Texas); and Ada Vinson (Louisiana). Top row, L-R: Annie McDougald (Georgia); Carrie T. Cochran (Alabama); Lizzie Clarke (Virginia); Elenora Graves (Kentucky); and Elizabeth Pasco (Florida).

Confederate girls, L-R: Mary A. Jones; Frances B. Hoke; Ellen D. Hindale; Adelaide B. Snow. These four young ladies were selected to ride in the procession when Jefferson Davis' body was received at Raleigh, North Carolina.

Unidentified Confederate woman and child, 1861-1865.

Unidentified Confederate woman, with soldier husband and child, 1861-1865.

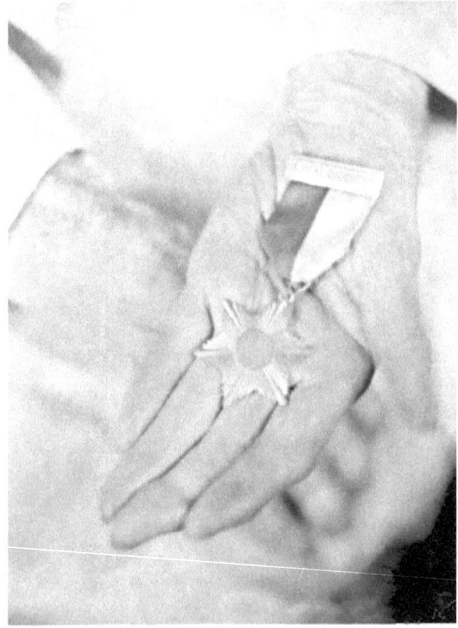

An early "Real Daughter" UDC pin, for first generation descendants of Confederate veterans. (Photo courtesy Lani Burnette Rinkel, UDC)

A group of UDC members with a Confederate veteran and the beautiful Confederate Battle Flag, a conservative Southern symbol of small government, states' rights, and personal freedom, c. 1930s. (Photo courtesy Lani Burnette Rinkel, UDC)

Sponsors and Maids of the United Sons of Confederate Veterans. From top center clockwise: Miss Nannie Pulliam of Ardmore, Indian Territory, State Sponsor; Miss Lucy Powell Randle of Union Springs, Alabama, State Sponsor; Miss Margaret Allison of Lake Charles, Louisiana, State Sponsor; Miss Heloise Sims of Donaldsonville, Louisiana, State Maid of Honor; Miss Anastasia Pickett of Union Springs, Alabama, State Maid of Honor. Center: Miss Margaret Wilkinson of St. Louis, Missouri, State Sponsor.

Jefferson Davis, Jr., born in 1857, Washington, D.C., son of Confederate President Jefferson Davis and Varina Howell Davis. He died in 1878 of yellow fever at Memphis, Tennessee.

Jefferson Davis, III, born 1884, Memphis, Tennessee; the son of Joel Addison Hayes, Jr. and Margaret "Maggie" Howell Davis. Born Jefferson Davis Hayes, at age five his surname was changed to Davis "that the family name might not die out forever." He passed away in 1975 and was buried in Colorado Springs, Colorado. His descendants today spell their surname Hayes-Davis.

Unidentified Confederate family, 1861-1865.

Dr. Alexander Harris of the Fifteenth Virginia Infantry Regiment, with his wife after the War.

Three of our greatest Confederate Generals, L-R: Stonewall Jackson, Joseph E. Johnston, Robert E. Lee.

Miss Jeannette Falconer Rathbone, Confederate Sponsor for the Army of Northern Virginia Dept.

Miss Juliette Opie Tabb, Confederate Maid of Honor for the Army of Northern Virginia Dept.

Victorian cover sheet of the meeting notes of "The Confederate Veteran of New York," 1896.

Kuuleme Stephens, another modern day supporter of the Southern Confederacy. (Photo courtesy Lani Burnette Rinkel, UDC)

Miss McGibbon, Confederate Sponsor for Kentucky.

Miss Daisy H. Harrison, Confederate Maid of Honor for the Pacific Division, UCV,

"Lee and His Generals." (Artist: George B. Matthews)

"Prize Carriage," UDC Exhibit, Chapter No. 567, Texarkana, Texas, street fair, April 25, 1903; prize: $50.00.

Carr-Burdette College, Sherman, Texas, the "Petite Wellesley of the South," as it looked in 1903; founded by Mrs. O. A. Carr, a "true Daughter of the Confederacy," for "the higher education of Southern girls."

Confederate General Nathan Bedford Forrest of Bedford (now Marshall) County, Tennessee, considered by many to be the finest and most able officer on either side of the War. When asked how he managed to survive the conflict's many dangers, including numerous near-fatal wounds, hand-to-hand combat, attempts on his life, and being personally hunted by Sherman, the intrepid warrior credited the prayers and support of his wife Mary Ann (née Montgomery).

Black servant women were nearly as important to maintaining Dixie during Lincoln's War as their white mistresses. Contrary to our Northern oriented "history" books, nearly all remained on their home farms and plantations, supporting the Confederacy in a thousand different ways. The servant couple shown here are Susan and George Page, who worked for the Dabney family of Raymond, Mississippi.

Confederate General James Ewell Brown Stuart, of Patrick County, Virginia, better known by his initials as "Jeb" Stuart.

Miss Mary C. Kimbrough of Greenwood, Mississippi.

From *Confederate Veteran*, 1894

PEACE ON EARTH, GOOD WILL TOWARD MEN

She was a tiny maid of three, but she sat upright on the cushioned seat of the well-filled passenger coach with a certain majesty and grace that pleased the more thoughtful travelers, who stopped now and then to hear her quaint, childish prattle. She was unconscious of any interest she had awakened, and told story after story of her home, dolls, playmates, and games to the lady with whom she was traveling.

Then she grew confidential and climbed into her companion's lap, and this gave a place at their sides to the gentleman who wished to join them a moment later. The tiny bit of precious humanity noticed, in her quick, intelligent, sympathetic way, that an empty sleeve hung at the gentleman's right side, but she looked out of the window, apparently lost in thought.

After a while she spoke, but her eyes seemed still to regard the passing scene: "My farver's farver was in the war, and one day when they had a battle he saw ever and ever and ever so many poor men, who had little chillun at home, killed wite there before his eyes: and they was bewied [buried] wite there, and nobody could tell their names, and their little chillun never could see them any more."

She never seemed to see the empty sleeve, but the gentleman was conscious she had done so, and that the dear little mind had tenderly grasped the truth, that he was one of those who had been "in the war," and that his arm had been left with the unnamed dead on some battlefield—maybe the one where her " farver's farver " had fought. As he rose to leave the train he kissed the child and the little one's companion saw a tear on his furrowed cheek. Are there angels who gather tears such as this for chaplets of pearls in heaven? Then what celestial seas of tears from our great war of sacrifice for principle![68]

During the Great War there were four million African-Americans living in the South. Some 500,000 of them were free, a group of which 25 percent were slave owners—many owning not just black servants, but white ones as well. The vast majority of Southern blacks supported the Confederacy, with at least 1 million serving in the Confederate military in one capacity or another, most voluntarily. Donning Confederate gray they fought to help counter the tyrannical unconstitutional policies of big government Liberal Abraham Lincoln, who they knew as "Marse Linkum." Southern black women, like the young governess pictured here, were especially enthusiastic about a Confederate victory. Few if any wanted to be forced from the "sunny South," where generations of their families had lived in relative peace and comfort alongside their European-American counterparts, whom they considered their second family, their "white family." Whatever their skin color or nationality, Southern women as a whole formed the foundation of Southern society while their menfolk were away, working harmoniously to hold their homes and businesses together, while providing food, clothing, medical care, and general feminine ministrations to the region's beloved "men in gray."

Margaret "Maggie" Howell Davis Hayes.

From *Confederate Veteran*, 1909

OBITUARY: MARGARET HOWELL DAVIS HAYES

In the death of Margaret Howell Davis Hayes [July 12] the last link of the family of Jefferson Davis is broken. One by one, like beads slipping from a chain, they have passed away, and in the cemetery of Richmond is gathered what was once a large family—father and mother, four sons and two daughters, and the tiny grandson who only came to bloom and fade.

Margaret Hayes was the oldest child of Jefferson Davis and his wife, Varina Howell, and, aside from the claim of the first child to an especial love, she was doubly dear to Davis as bearing his mother's name. The tie between the two was an unusually close one, arising from similarity of tastes and the trend of thought. "Polly," as was his pet name for her, was ever his companion, and when together neither seemed to need nor care for other companionship.

Margaret Davis was educated at a convent in Paris, where Margaret of Italy and Princess Margaret of Bavaria were her closest friends. To distinguish her in this trio of namesakes, she was called Pearl, the meaning of her name, and that jewel entered largely into her life pleasures. The friendship for the two Margarets never was lost nor laid aside. During the time of her absence in France Mr. Davis said there was an aching void in his heart that nothing could fill. He was a man who took bright views of circumstances; but sometimes even to him the horizon darkened, and, like Saul with the harp of David, nothing could soothe nor comfort him like his daughter's singing. She had a voice never powerful, but of unusual sweetness and pleading pathos—a deep, velvety contralto, haunting in the tenderness of melody that won its way into all hearts, swaying the listener to nobler deeds and truer aspirations.

After graduation, Miss Davis returned to Memphis, where her father and mother were living at the time. Here she became at once a leading social favorite. She was very young, only eighteen; but even then she possessed the wonderful magnetic charm, the gracious personality that marked her maturer womanhood. In Memphis Miss Davis met Mr. Joel Addison Hayes [Jr., a nephew of Adelicia Acklen], the second son of Joel Addison Hayes [Sr.], of Nashville, and grandson of Oliver Bliss Hayes, one of the pioneers of the capital of Tennessee.

The first view Miss Davis had of Mr. Hayes was at Calvary Church, where as vestryman Mr. Hayes took up the offering. On her return from the service Margaret said to her mother that she had seen the man she felt sure she should marry. Her premonition was amply justified, for an ideal love affair followed the introduction, and the first of the January [1876] following the wedding took place in Calvary Church. The world was clad also in bridal white, and the joy bells that welcomed the newborn year rang in one of the happiest married lives possible to humanity; for with these two, lovers always, duality ceased to exist and unity of love and purpose took its place. Miss Davis went to the altar on the arm of her noble father, and [her sister] Winnie [Varina Ann Davis], then a child of eleven, was maid of honor, while [her brother] young Jeff Davis, then in his early twenties, was groomsman. A grand reception followed, where all of Memphis society came with good wishes for the fair bride and noble groom. At this reception the wedding cake served was brought from England, and had been buried in hermetically sealed tins for fifty years. The remnant of the cake was then sealed, and was opened again for the wedding of Varina, the oldest daughter born to the young couple.

Mr. and Mrs. Hayes lived for many years in Memphis, where Mr. Hayes was very prominent in banking circles. Here were born the tiny boy who bore the name of Jefferson Davis, but who lived only three months; Varina Howell, who is named for the maternal grandmother; Lucy White, who bears the name of her father's mother; and Jefferson Davis Hayes, who by the act of the Legislature of Louisiana became Jefferson Davis, receiving the name in baptism over the coffin containing the body of President Davis.

Mr. Hayes developing throat trouble, the doctors ordered him to Colorado, which climate proved so attractive that the family moved there, making their residence in Colorado Springs, where Mr. Hayes became the leading banker of the State. Their home on Cascade Avenue was one of the show places of the city, and was fitted with every luxury money could buy. Here was born the youngest boy, Billy, named for the passionately loved and never-forgotten brother who was killed by a fall over the balustrade on to the stone floor in the White House of Richmond during President Davis's term of office.

At this home was solemnized the marriage of Varina Howell Hayes, who wedded Dr. Gerald Bertram Webb, a descendant of an English ducal family. To this marriage have been born three children—Margaret Varina, for her grandmother, Mrs. Hayes, and great-grandmother, Mrs. Davis (this little lady, self-styled Marko, was the pet and constant companion of Mrs. Hayes), Gerald Bertram, the only great-grandson of Mr. Davis, and Robina, named for her English grandmother. Dr. Webb is a specialist, and has more than a national reputation.

Mrs. [Margaret Howell Davis] Hayes impressed her vivid personality upon all who were so fortunate as to know her. She was brilliant in conversation, gracious in manners, and of so intense a magnetism that even without her great beauty she would have been observed in any assemblage. In person she was tall and built upon grand lines. Her face was almost pure Greek in outline, with large, dark velvet eyes that could flash and sparkle in conversation, soften to winning tenderness to a child, or brim over with tears at some tale of suffering, for she had the brain of a statesman united to the tender heart of a child. Her complexion was the creamy richness of a magnolia petal, and was framed in masses of dark hair that her fifty-four years never touched with silver.

Mrs. Hayes had never been strong since her mother died—nothing organic, nothing the wisest doctors could grapple; but within the last six months the want of vitality crystallized into a general implication of the functions. Like a flower fading, she gradually wasted away. Her room was a floral bower with love tokens from many friends sent day by day, and everything in the power of humanity to aid or comfort was at her bedside. Her sufferings were past words to express, but even her nurses never heard a groan nor murmur. Her husband and all her children were around her, and her little grandchildren made her room their play place. To them "Mamie," as they called her, was only another and more delightful child, one to be amused with blocks and to be interested in their pet puppy and kitties. They brought to her bed the wild flowers they gathered, the flowers that faded from their little hot hands as the human flower was fading from the fever heat of disease.

On Sunday, July 18, 1909, as the sinking sun was touching Pike's Peak into golden splendor, death came with healing touch and tender claspings, and she fell quietly into that sleep whose wakening was to be with her loved ones in Paradise.

TRIBUTE FROM THE C.S.M.A.
In a tribute to the memory of Mrs. J. A. Hayes, Mrs. W. J. Behan, President of the Confederated Southern Memorial Association, wrote from New Orleans, La.: "In the passing of this noble daughter of President Davis the last tie that united the women of the Confederacy with the parent branch of the Davis family has been severed. Mrs. Hayes was in every sense a true daughter of the South and a worthy descendant of a grand sire. Her life was replete with the splendid traditions of a brave people, and as sister, daughter, wife, and mother she fulfilled all the obligations of a true woman. She will be deeply mourned by her associates in the Confederated Southern Memorial Association, and her name will be held in loving and sacred remembrance for all time to come."

EXPRESSION FROM THE U.D.C.
In an official notice of Mrs. Hayes's death Mrs. Cornelia Branch Stone,

President General U.D.C., states: "It is requested that Chapters of our Association recognize the great loss by holding memorial services in honor of our distinguished dead. With deep pain we realize that in her life the last link is broken that bound us to that dear household in the White House of the Confederacy. We can no more stand in her gracious presence; but we can recall with pride that in her personality she nobly represented the exalted character and splendid qualities of heart and mind, the heritage of her illustrious lineage, for she lived and died a worthy daughter of our great chieftain, Jefferson Davis, and Varina Howell Davis. She has left to us a precious legacy in her children—two sons and two daughters. These we will cherish in our hearts and memories as representing all that is left to us of the descendants of that great man, scholar, statesman, and soldier, Jefferson Davis. Our loving, tender sympathy goes into the home now so desolate."[69]

Mrs. Margaret "Maggie" Howell Davis Hayes, wife of Joel Addison Hayes, Jr., with her grandchildren, from L-R: Margaret Varina Webb, Gerald Bertram Webb, and Robina Webb. Maggie was the only surviving daughter of President Jefferson Davis.

Miss Josie Frazee Cappleman of Okolona, Mississippi.

"OUR SOUTHERN GIRLS" - A POEM, 1898
By Josie F. Cappleman

Greeting, daughters of the Southland,
'Tis a plea to-night I bring;
From the fullness of my feelings
Of our Southern girl I'd sing;
From the realms of truth and glory,
With their rich and radiant flowers,
A wreath I'd cull and crown her,
This Southern girl of ours.

Waken, soul, and let me paint her—
Paint her picture with my pen,
Even as I sometimes see her;
In the mazy walks of men;
'Tis a face all pink and dimpled—
A cameo set in curls,
With eyes the brightest, shyest—
One of our Southern girls.

She's a well-poised, queenly creature
As she moves to tune and time,
And graceful as the lily
Of her own soft, sun-kissed clime;
With an air half pride, half pathos,

A voice like brooklet's purl;
With ways that haunt and hold one—
Our gracious Southern girl.

Hers a heart as pure as star gleams,
And fresh as heavenly flowers,
Whose fragrant pearly petals
Mark the ages—not the hours;
'Tis a heart sweet-tuned, responsive,
A heart that throbs and thrills
With the tenderest emotions
A Southern bosom fills.

Hers the mind for plan and action,
Hers the will to dare and do,
Hers the courage of conviction,
Hers the soul of all that's true.
On the page of art and science
Her bright-winged thoughts unfurl,
Keeping mental pace with masters—
Our brainy Southern girl.

Duty calls, and soft she cometh,
Not, O men, to take your place,
Not unmaidenly and mannish
Would our girl with you keep pace;
Not her wish to rule or rob you,
Nor one right to take away,
But she needs to work as men do,
And as *men* to win her pay.

Then O aid her in her efforts;
Ward off the rude and rough,
And kindly smooth and soften;
The road is hard enough;
In the shop, the store, the office,
The printing room's mad whirl,
Stand by and guard and guide her—
Our brave-souled Southern girl.[70]

Real Daughters of the Confederacy, from the Katie Daffan Chapter, Texas. (Photo courtesy Lani Burnette Rinkel, UDC)

A Confederate drummer boy from Kentucky who died in battle, fighting the tyranny of the Liberal North.

Ellen Barnes McGinnis, a beloved free biracial servant of Jefferson Davis and his family. She was born in Richmond, Virginia, about 1839, and was with the Davises during their capture in Georgia; she continued to care for the family while President Davis was imprisoned at Fort Monroe. (Photo courtesy Teresa Roane)

Confederate Private Edward A. Cary of Company 1, Forty-Fourth Virginia Infantry Regiment, with his sister Mrs. Emma J. Garland, 1861-1862.

21st-Century Confederate supporters Candy White (left) and Manny Vega (right) of the Virginia Flaggers. (Photo courtesy Lani Burnette Rinkel, UDC)

Contrary to Yankee mythology, in 1860 there were 500,000 free African-Americans living in the South (1/8 or 12.5 percent of the total Southern black population). Of these, at least 250,000 were free black women, like the one pictured here, nearly every one who sided with the Confederacy. Into the present day their enlightened descendants continue to advance the Southern Cause and its call for small government, personal liberty, and states' rights.

Unidentified Confederate couple, 1862.

A UNITED DAUGHTERS OF THE CONFEDERACY RITUAL "RESPONSIVE SERVICE" - 1916

LEADER

We have met together, our Heavenly Father, to study and to discover the truth of history. Keep out of our hearts all bitterness—knowing that bitterness engenders strife; keep out of our minds all narrowness, knowing that narrowness weakens character; keep out of our hearts all injustice, knowing that injustice is sinful.

May we measure ourselves by Thy measuring rod, and give to all their due, fully, freely and fairly.

ALL

Lord, who shall abide in thy tabernacle?
Who shall dwell in thy holy hill?

He that walketh uprightly and worketh righteousness, and speaking the truth in his heart.

He that slandereth not with his tongue, nor doeth evil to his friend, nor taketh up a reproach against his neighbor.

In whose eyes a vile person is contemned: but he honoreth them who that fear the Lord. He that sweareth to his own hurt and changeth not.

He that putteth not out his money to usury, nor taketh reward against the innocent.

He that doeth these things shall never be moved.

LEADER

Let the words of our mouths, and the meditations of our hearts be acceptable in thy sight, O Lord, our Rock and our Redeemer. Amen.[71]

Sarah A. Dasher with her husband, a Confederate soldier, 1861-1865.

Yankee sheet music for the song "Chicora," "Respectfully dedicated to the Patriotic Ladies of the Southern Confederated States of North America," 1861.

Teresa Roane of Richmond, Virginia, a strong modern day Confederate supporter and a Southern historian working for the preservation of Confederate history. (Photo courtesy Teresa Roane)

Right, Lani Burnette Rinkel, one of our most ardent Confederate supporters, with her grandson Seth Bonetti, flagging in Lexington, Virginia. (Photo courtesy Lani Burnette Rinkel, UDC)

Decoration of Confederate graves in Oakwood Cemetery, Chicago, Illinois, 1894.

A UDC group at their Annual Convention, this one at Charleston, South Carolina, November 1903. Among the male guests is the state Governor Duncan Clinch Heyward and the city's Mayor James Adger Smythe.

If I were asked . . . to what the singular prosperity and growing strength the American people ought mainly to be attributed, I should reply: To the superiority of their women.

Alexis de Tocqueville
1840

APPENDIX A: THE CONSTITUTION OF THE UDC, 1895

From *Confederate Veteran*, 1895

UNITED DAUGHTERS OF THE SOUTH — DAUGHTERS OF THE CONFEDERACY PERFECT A GENERAL ORGANIZATION

The National Order of the Daughters of the Confederacy [today known as the United Daughters of the Confederacy] held its annual session in Atlanta on Nov. 8th, Mrs. Caroline Meriwether Goodlett, of Tennessee, presiding. After considerable argument as to credentials, delegates from the various Divisions and Chapters were admitted to the floor.

The minutes of the last annual meeting were read as well as those of a called meeting in Nashville last spring. They were adopted. The convention then went into consideration on changes and amendments of the Constitution. The Committee comprised of Mrs. John P. Hickman, of Tennessee, Chairman; Mrs. Smythe, of South Carolina; and Mrs. Parsley, of North Carolina, submitted two reports. One of the reports was submitted by Mrs. Smythe and Mrs. Parsley, and the other by the Chairman. Both were read in full. Being put to the vote, the majority report was accepted as a basis upon which the amendments were to be made. It was read section by section, and the consideration occupied the entire afternoon. A number of changes were made, the most notable of which was that of the name from National Daughters of the Confederacy to United Daughters of the Confederacy.

The Constitution as it now stands is published herewith in full, and other changes may be observed by comparing the new Constitution with the old. Officers elected for the ensuing year are as follows: Mrs. John C. Brown, Nashville, Tenn., President; Mrs. L. H. Raines, Savannah, Ga., Vice President; Mrs. Isabelle M. Clark, Nashville, Tenn., and Mrs. J. Jefferson Thomas, Atlanta, Ga., Recording and Corresponding Secretaries; Mrs. Lottie Preston Clarke, Lynchburg, Va., Treasurer.

The Convention then heard a letter from the Jefferson Davis Monument Committee, in Richmond, through President J. Taylor Ellyson, urging upon the Daughters the necessity of devoting time and labor to the aid of the Jefferson Davis Monument Fund. This request was formally recommended to the Divisions.

The work of the *Confederate Veteran* in our general cause was reported, and the *Veteran* was made official organ of the United Daughters of the Confederacy.

The constitution is as follows:

ARTICLE I.—NAME

Section I. The name or title of the Association shall be The United Daughters of the Confederacy.

Sec. II. Each State Organization shall be known as a Division, and designated by the name of the State in which it is located, and each local organization in that State, as a Chapter of the said Division, to be numbered consecutively, and any name selected by such Chapter.

ARTICLE II.—OBJECTS

The objects of this Association are educational, memorial, literary, social and benevolent; to collect and preserve the material for a truthful history of the war between the Confederate States and the United States of America: to honor the memory of those who served and those who fell in the service of the Confederate States, and to record the part taken by Southern women, as well, in the untiring effort after the war in the reconstruction of the South, as in patient endurance of hardship and patriotic devotion during the struggle; to cherish the ties of friendship among the members of the Society, and to fulfill the duties of sacred charity to the survivors of the war and those dependent upon them.

ARTICLE III.—ORGANIZATIONS OF CHAPTERS

Section I. Those women entitled to membership are the widows, wives, mothers, sisters, nieces and lineal descendants of such men as served honorably in the Confederate Army, Navy and Civil Service, or of those persons who loyally gave material aid to the cause. Also, women and their lineal descendants, wherever living, who can give proof of personal service and loyal aid to the Southern cause during the war.

Sec. II. Each State Division shall furnish blank applications for membership to be used throughout that Division. These blanks may differ in form, but must not conflict with the qualifications of membership as set forth in this Constitution. The mode of electing and admitting members may also vary with each Division, provided, again, the qualifications for membership be not inconsistent with this Constitution.

Sec. III. Seven or more women in any State in which no Division exists, may organize a Chapter and be chartered on application to the United Daughters of the Confederacy and all Chapters subsequently formed in that State shall apply through the first Chapter to the United Daughters of Confederacy for their Charters. A fee of three dollars shall be paid to the United Daughters of the Confederacy for each Charter. Each Chapter shall report annually to the United Daughters of the Confederacy, and shall on the first day of each succeeding February pay into the Treasury of the United Daughters of the Confederacy the sum of ten cents for each and every member who may at such date be in good standing on the roll of such Chapter. Provided, however, that nothing in this Constitution contained shall be construed as preventing any Division or Chapter from becoming legally incorporated under the laws of the State in which it is located, should it desire to do so.

Sec. IV. The United Daughters of the Confederacy suggest that the annual meeting of all Chapters be held on Gen. Lee's birthday, January 19th, or if that day falls on Sunday, then on the day following.

ARTICLE IV.—ORGANIZATION OP STATE DIVISIONS

Section I. When three or more Chapters shall be organized in any state, it shall be the duty of the first or Charter Chapter to call a Convention for the purpose of organizing a State Division. Such Convention shall be held at a time and place to be designated by the Charter Chapter, at which Convention each Chapter shall be entitled to one vote for every twenty-five members or fraction thereof if such fraction be not less than seven.

Sec. II. Such State Division shall be organized by the adoption of a Constitution and By-laws, none of which shall be inconsistent with any of the provisions of this Constitution, and by the election of a president and other proper officers. Any one or more representatives from any Chapter shall be authorized to cast the full vote to which such Chapter may be entitled. In case a Chapter is unable to send a delegate its vote may be cast by proxy.

Sec. III. From and after the organization of such State Division, all Chapters in such State shall be organized upon proper application for their Charters to the United Daughters of the Confederacy, through the Division.

ARTICLE V.—CONVENTIONS OF U.D.C.

Section I. Conventions of United Daughters of the Confederacy shall be held annually on the second Wednesday of November, at such place as designated by the preceding Convention.

Sec II. Each Chapter shall be entitled in all Conventions of the United Daughters of the Confederacy to one vote for every twenty-five members or fraction thereof not less than seven, provided that when a Chapter has less than twenty-five members it shall be entitled to one vote. Any one or more representatives from any such Chapter shall be authorized to cast the full vote to which such Chapter may be entitled. Any Chapter not able to send a delegate may send the vote by proxy.

ARTICLE VI.— OFFICERS

The officers of the United Daughters of the Confederacy shall be a President who shall preside at all meetings.

A Vice President, who shall preside in the absence of the President.

A Recording Secretary.

A Corresponding Secretary.

A Treasurer.

All these shall be elected to serve for one year, or until their successors shall be elected and qualified. In case of a tie, the President has power to cast the deciding vote.

ARTICLE VII.—FINANCE

A Committee on Finance shall be composed of five members, to whom shall be referred all matters of receipts and expenditures.

ARTICLE VIII.—CERTIFICATES OF MEMBERSHIP

Certificates of membership shall be furnished by each Chapter to all members in good standing. Such certificates shall be supplied by the United Daughters of the Confederacy with their seal attached. These Certificates must be signed by the President of the United Daughters of the Confederacy, the President of the State Division and the President and Secretary of the local Chapter.

ARTICLE IX. —BADGES—INSIGNIA—SEALS

Section I. The badge to be worn by the Daughters of the Confederacy shall consist of a representation of the [First National] Confederate flag (stars and bars) in white, blue and scarlet enamel, surrounded by a laurel wreath with the monogram, D. C. under the flag, and dates 1861-1865 on the loops of the bow that ties the wreath. Divisions and Chapters may use in addition a badge of their own.

Sec II. The seal of the United Daughters of the Confederacy shall be a reproduction of the great seal of the Confederate States of America, with the addition of the inscription, Daughters of the Confederacy, on the outer rim.

Sec III. The seals for all State Divisions shall be of the same design with the addition of the name of the Division.

Sec IV. All official documents emanating from the United Daughters of the Confederacy shall bear the impress of its great seal.

Sec V. The use of the name, seal and badge of the United Daughters of the Confederacy for business purposes other than the business of this Association is expressly prohibited.

ARTICLE X. —AMENDMENT

This Constitution may be amended by a two thirds vote at any Convention of the United Daughters of the Confederacy, provided notice of such intention to amend be filed with the Secretary at least thirty days before the day fixed for the Convention. Upon the filing of such notice the Secretary shall forthwith extend the same to each of the officers of the United Daughters of the Confederacy, and to the representative of each Chapter in direct connection with the United Daughters of the Confederacy.

We, the Committee appointed March 30, 1895, to revise the Constitution of the National Association of the Daughters of the Confederacy, and reappointed November 8, 1895, and empowered to put it with its amendments into proper shape for printing, hereby certify this paper to be in every clause a true copy of that passed on by the Convention of November 8, 1895, with the exception of a few grammatical and clerical corrections made necessary by the amendments.

Signed, Mrs. John. P. Hickman,
Mrs. Wm. M. Parsley,
Louisa McC. Smythe
Atlanta, November 9, 1895.[72]

APPENDIX B: EXCERPTS FROM THE 7TH ANNUAL MEETING, UDC

From *Minutes of the Seventh Annual Meeting of
The United Daughters of the Confederacy*

HELD IN MONTGOMERY, ALABAMA, NOVEMBER 14-17, 1900
MRS. EDWIN G. WEED, PRESIDENT
MRS. JOHN P. HICKMAN, SECRETARY

FIRST DAY

The United Daughters of the Confederacy met in their Seventh Annual Convention in the hall of the House of Representatives, where the first Confederate Congress met, in Montgomery, Ala.—the first capital of the Confederacy—on Wednesday, November 14, 1900. The Legislature of Alabama, being in session, adjourned that the United Daughters of the Confederacy might hold their first meeting in the State Capitol, which gave birth to the Confederate States. All the Daughters' hearts were filled with emotion as they approached the first Capitol of the Confederacy, and with reverence they each stopped and viewed the gold star inlaid in the stone in the balcony by the Sophia Bibb Chapter in commemoration of the spot where President Jefferson Davis delivered his inaugural address.

When the President, Mrs. E. G. Weed, called the assembly to order, the hall was filled with the representative men and women of the South, and proceedings were begun by Rev. Neal Anderson, of Montgomery, reading parts of two chapters from the Bible on which Jefferson Davis took the oath of office when he was inaugurated President of the Confederate States. The two chapters read from were Matt. 26:6-10 and Prov. 31:10-31. After the reading, he delivered a heartfelt prayer, in which he tenderly remembered Mrs. Jefferson Davis and Mrs. Stonewall Jackson, both of whom were too feeble to attend the Convention.

Mrs. Chappell Cory, President of the Cradle of the Confederacy Chapter, in behalf of the four Chapters of Montgomery, welcomed the Daughters to Montgomery in the following fluent and heartfelt, address:

ADDRESS OF WELCOME BY MRS. CHAPPELL CORY

"The wide gates of Montgomery never swung back to the sound of a gladder welcome than for you; the great heart of her people never throbbed with a finer joy or felt a tenderer thrill; for Montgomery is the typical city of the South, standing for the old and the new, ready with a smile for the eastern sun, but not yet forgetting the hallowed tear of memory for the sun that sunk so many years ago. So gladness and overflow of hospitality are here for you, while close on laughter treads the sad, sweet recollection of the cause you stand for and the days you keep green. There is warm clasping of the hand and prompt opening of every door and music and song and joy. There is also a deep wellspring of tenderness and solemn sympathy, full to the brim and overflowing, for all that you hold dear and which makes this hour of greeting and every hour of this great Convention a sacred treasure room in our hearts and lives.

"You have come from many places and from many States—some, from cities where the red glare of battle lit the skies; some, from old places over which the muse of history chants perpetually songs of other days; some, from where great heroes sleep in shrines that the faithful will guard always; some, from new-grown centers, and some have crossed the line from which later deeds of mutual help and daring have brushed the last traces of hostility; some, from the 'Lone Star State,' the new giant of the West, where so late a stricken city lay and thought on war's severest ruin as playhouse wrecks by contrast with the storm's rude fury, where heroism shone bright as ever in the front of battle, where the rush of sympathy proved, in spite of war and memories of wrong and suffering, there is still a universal brotherhood of man. From wheresoever you come—from farmhouse, hamlet, town, or city; from cherished landmark of the Confederacy, or where no steed of war's hard hoof was ever planted—we know your hearts are beating in a single time to a single hymn of love for the cause and for the men who died and for the great principles which will never die; and because you love and cherish these we know you love Montgomery and have come to see her loyal and generous people, and to go away loving them, too.

"The old, oaken doors in the hall below have opened to many an honored guest; the old dome above us has looked down on many a throng shouting welcome to the noble and the brave. Only a few days gone, and unnumbered thousands gathered here in hearty greeting to a young hero and an older one, whose names are forever linked into this new era of peace and brotherhood, and whose deeds are brighter for their part in robbing the past of bitterness and reconciling us all to that Providence which we long could only trust, not understanding its harsh decrees.

"Only a few years ago, so young in time as to seem but yesterday, a grand old man came to lay the first stone where stands the monument out yonder. Up the wide streets and over the wide grounds and through the old building came a rushing throng as of mighty winds, and hearts were glad and hearts were sad, and tears of joy were frequent as its smile. Bearded men and little children, women whose hearts were asleep in unmarked graves, and the young and the fair united in one great outpouring of thankful welcome to see for one last time the luminous sun of a grand day ere it sunk for evermore—the same sun that rose on this selfsame spot and whose first beams were greeted in their splendor with, the applause of coming victory and grandeur. Such welcome was never given man since time began; for all can shout when the conqueror comes, but this was very love.

"And so is this welcome which we give to you. You cherish the noble deeds of a noble race. You stand before the world the living witness that the past is not dead, but all in it that was good and great and true still lives and has its worshipers. You do not scatter flowers in a victors path; you water violets on the graves of honor and of valor; and to you the selfsame welcome of the heart goes out as went that day to Jefferson Davis, the martyr chieftain of our sacred cause.

"If crowding thousands do not shout and drums are silent and no glittering bayonets marshal you to your seats of honor, know that the loyal daughters of Montgomery are here to put their arms around you, every one, and clasp you to their hearts and love you there and rest you there."

The address was greatly enjoyed, and appreciation was shown by frequent interruptions of applause.

In behalf of the Alabama State Division, Mrs. John A. Kirkpatrick, of Montgomery, its President, welcomed the Daughters in terms that reached the heart of every member of the Convention, as follows:

"Daughters of the Confederacy:

"I bid you welcome to Alabama, welcome to that grand old State which gave to our loved Confederacy so many brave men, who marched to death, willing to lay down their lives to preserve the principles of liberty and the God-given right of self-government [that is conservatism].

"From all parts of our Southland you have come, called hither by the same unswerving loyalty to the memories and traditions of the old South and devotion to the principles of the 'lost cause.' What a world of memories come trooping forth at the very mention of that 'lost cause'! What a feeling of sadness sweeps across the soul at the recollection of buried hopes, battles, triumphs, and unselfish suffering! That 'lost cause' and the heroic efforts made to sustain it will live in memory till the stars shall pale and fade away and history shall have recorded the last period of time. Never did a cause evoke so much of high heroism, of patient endurance, and of self-denying patriotism. To it were given the daring deeds of the youthful warrior, the mature counsel of the aged statesman, while it was rewarded by the smiles and ennobled by the tears and prayers of devoted women.

"The bonnie blue flag no longer waves over this dome; the armies which almost made a new nation among the people of the earth have long since disbanded. Peace has spread her snow-white pinions over our land, and Prosperity reigns where War was wont to devastate.

"The flight of years has brought no diminution in your faith in the justice of what was battled for in the stormy past, nor a disposition to hide amid the hustling progress of the present the glory and achievements of Southern prowess.

"More than a quarter of a century ago these old walls looked down upon a thrilling scene, the beginning of Confederate history. To-day they behold a strange spectacle; for here, in this very capitol, in which was born the storm-cradled nation that fell—that loved Confederacy so dear to our hearts—here, under the flag of the victor, we, true daughters of brave Southern sires, have assembled as an association whose avowed purpose is to commemorate the heroic deeds of our dead and hand down true history to our children. In all history there is no record of any such society as ours. In all the bygone years never have the women of any defeated people been banded together for the sublime purpose of proving the rightfulness of the cause for which their people fought and caring for the weak and afflicted among those who survived the conflict. In all the cycles of the past there exists no monument by the women of any land to secure the record of the truth in history about a lost, yet sacred, cause.

"We have met here now, united in our work for a common purpose, grand in its origin, patriotic in its undertaking, and beautiful in its ministrations. The bond between us is necessarily a strong one, and the prosecution of our work but unites us the more closely to each other. Therefore, in the name of the thousand Daughters of the Confederacy who compose the Division of Alabama, I bid you welcome; in the name of every Confederate Veteran within this Commonwealth. I bid you welcome; in the name of those Southern heroes who sleep their last sleep and whose kindred we are, I bid you welcome. Our hearts are yours, our homes are yours, and to us you must not and shall not be the stranger within our gates. Welcome, thrice welcome, to Alabama!"

Mrs. Edwin G. Weed, of Jacksonville, Fla., President of the United Daughters of the Confederacy, responded to these addresses of welcome for the Association, voicing the feeling of each Daughter present. Her address was as follows:

"In the name of the United Daughters of the Confederacy, her delegates and visiting members, I thank you, sisters of Alabama, for your words of loving welcome to this charming and historic city. When we accepted your invitation last November in Richmond, we fully realized all that invitation carried of loving courtesy. Alabama's 'present copies fair her past.' Since the day the Indian chieftain planted his staff in her sunlit sod and proclaimed his 'Alabama,' she has ever been first in deeds of gracious hospitality. In the dark days of 1861, when the seven Southern States had left their father's house, it was Alabama who opened wide her heart and her doors and invited them to come in.

"In response to her loving call the great men from all parts of the South assembled here, and in this beautiful city of Montgomery was born the Southern Confederacy. Within these walls her first Congress assembled, and here were elected the officers to whose care the young Confederacy was committed. Mississippi gave her peerless son, Jefferson Davis, in whose hands we gladly placed the reigns of government; Georgia placed [Alexander Hamilton] Stephens by his side. [Christopher Gustavus] Meminger, of South Carolina; [Stephen Russell] Mallory, of Florida; Leroy P. Walker, of Alabama; Judah P. Benjamin, of Louisiana; and John H. Reagan, of Texas, composed the first Cabinet of the Southern Confederacy. They have all left us now, save Reagan, of Texas. They have 'crossed the river' and rest from their labors. On the steps of this building, holding in his hands this very Bible, Jefferson Davis took his oath of office and pledged himself to the faithful performance of his duties as President of the Southern Confederacy.

"Truly, my friends, we stand on 'holy ground.' Forty years have elapsed since these stirring scenes were enacted, and to-day we, the women of the South, the United Daughters of the Confederacy, meet here to renew our vows of loyalty to the sacred memories of the past. Forty years is technically a generation, but to loyal, loving hearts time has no limit. The great four years of glorious deeds of valor and fortitude have gone from us; the bitter years of 'reconstruction,' as it was called, are over; 'eighteen hundred' is a thing of the past, and a new century is with us; but the hearts of Southern women are faithful and loyal. Time has no power to obliterate from our minds the memory of the deeds of heroism enacted during those four years of warfare and struggle or to take from our hearts the devotion and grateful love they hold for the heroes of the South, from the immortal Lee to the youngest private in her service. We experience no regret, we feel no shame, for 'glory sits beside our grief.'

"Standing here to-day, we realize all the great State of

Alabama has done for us. Though it was deemed necessary to remove the capital to Richmond, Montgomery will ever be dear to our hearts as the birthplace of the Southern Confederacy. And so, Alabamians, we thank you with grateful appreciation for your welcome of to-day. We love you for your hospitality in the past, and, in the realization of that past and present, we gladly trust you for the future, feeling confident that the fair fame of the land we love so dearly will ever be sacredly guarded by Alabama's sons and daughters, the descendants of the patriots of 1861."

  At the conclusion of Mrs. Weed's address Mrs. J. D. Beale, of Montgomery, introduced Mrs. Virginia Clay Clopton, of Huntsville, to the Convention. Mrs. Clopton told of her thrilling experience while in prison at Fortress Monroe with her husband and President Davis. She spoke of the time when a Yankee divided his coffee with her and permitted her to make a cup for President Davis.

  Mrs. L. G. Dawson, of Montgomery, presented to the United Daughters of the Confederacy a large bunch of red and white carnations, with a card attached, which contained these words: "May these sweet floral messengers express to you the loyal love and every good wish that Southern hearts can give."

  Mrs. C. M. Goodlett, Honorary President, was presented to the Convention, and in a few appropriate and well-chosen remarks told of her work and experience in the organization of the Association. The Convention then adjourned to meet at 3 P.M. in the Auditorium.

SECOND DAY
Thursday, November 15, 1900

  The Convention was called to order in the Court Street Methodist Church at 10 A.M. by the President, Mrs. Weed.

  Proceedings were opened by Rev. Mr. Lamar reading a chapter from Philippians and delivering a short prayer. The minutes of the preceding meeting were then read and approved.

  On motion of Mrs. E. H. O'Brien, of Virginia, the press was requested to give the United Daughters of the Confederacy its proper title, which is the "United Daughters of the Confederacy," and not the "National United Daughters of the Confederacy."

  The President outlined to the Convention the work she had been engaged in during the past year in a very clear and comprehensive manner, which was favorably received by the Convention. Her address is as follows:

ANNUAL ADDRESS
"To the United Daughters of the Confederacy:

  "In the twelve months that have passed since last we met so much has been, accomplished in our organization of splendid, faithful work that I feel sure you will be glad to look with me over the six years of our life as an association and realize all the comfort and encouragement that comes from work well and successfully done.

"On September 10, 1894, in the city of Nashville, Tenn., our first meeting was held. Three States—Georgia, Texas, and Tennessee—were represented. In Richmond, Va., in November, 1899, at our annual meeting, there were representatives from twenty States, three hundred and sixty-one Chapters, and nearly eighteen thousand members. Since then our membership has been greatly increased, and when our Recording Secretary reads her report you will, I am sure, find that we have over twenty thousand members. This is the result of earnest, faithful work by the women of the South. From every part of the country comes the same report of growth and progress. We have now Chapters in New York, Philadelphia, Indiana, and Indian Territory, and from the Pacific Coast come the loving greetings of four California Chapters.

"My dear sisters, do you realize what this growth means? It means love, gratitude, fidelity; it means the cause we love is as dear in her day of adversity as in the day of our brightest hopes and anticipations; it means that love rises in the hearts of Southern women superior to defeat; it means that Appomattox, with its broken ranks of half-starved, ragged soldiers, is as dear to our grateful hearts as the victorious armies of Bull Run and Manassas. It is also a pledge for the future, that as long as time endures Southern women will stand faithful in their devotion to the cause of the South. Therefore, United Daughters of the Confederacy, we may glory in the growth and success of our work.

"Our organization is a peculiar one. Born of sorrow and adversity, consecrated to the preservation of memories glorious, but heartbreaking, we seem scarcely a part of the busy present; but by the side of our graves we sit, and, looking far into the future, we see our land redeemed and glorified by the love of her faithful children.

"As your President, I have been in constant contact with the noble, great-hearted women who compose the United Daughters of the Confederacy. I have gone into their homes and looked into the earnest work they are doing in their different Chapters. Never have I found any feeling of despondency or fear of failure. In the past year I have visited ten States and have been charmingly entertained by them. I have also been present at three annual Division meetings and have rejoiced at the growth in each Division. I have had many letters of earnest, helpful words; many inquiries regarding the work of the United Daughters of the Confederacy, all of which I have faithfully striven to answer.

"My books record: Letters written, 1,323; certificates issued, 1,479; new charters received, signed, and returned to the

Recording Secretary, 82.

"I attended the reunion of the veterans in Louisville, Ky., in May, and my heart thrilled with pride as I heard the old soldiers, in their uniforms of gray, tell of hard-fought battles and deeds of valor, and saw the old flags, tattered and torn, made sacred by the scars and wounds of many a battlefield. All this has been permitted me, as your President, and I thank you for it.

"The work of the past year has been of the deepest interest. Your Committee on the Cross of Honor has had a hard year of arduous work. To secure a perfect plan and system to regulate the bestowal of the cross on hundreds of thousands means much work, as only those who have undertaken it can realize. Mrs. Gabbett was made Custodian of the cross, in Richmond. With a brave heart, but delicate health, she has struggled on, trying to respond to all the demands made upon her. But for the aid and assistance of the two splendid women who compose her committee—Mrs. Plane and Miss Rutherford—I am afraid the work would have been too much for her.

"The Jefferson Davis Monument Committee has accomplished much faithful work during the past year. Mrs. Norman Randolph, of Richmond, Va., is Chairman of the Central Committee. With an enthusiasm born of love and devotion, she has never failed or faltered in the work she has undertaken. Every appeal that an eloquent tongue or pen can make she has made. Earnest and faithful, believing strongly in the success of her work, she cannot, will not fail. We must remember, however, it is not her work alone. As Southern women and members of the United Daughters of the Confederacy we are, each one of us, responsible for the success of this great work. More than thirty-five years have passed since the war and the South has no national monument to our great chieftain and the cause he represents, no monument to Jefferson Davis and the Southern Confederacy.

"United Daughters of the Confederacy, arise to the work, and remove this reproach. Whenever the name of Jefferson Davis is heard, it represents the Southern Confederacy. He was our chieftain and our representative, and we point to him with pride and love—a soldier without cruelty, a statesman without reproach, a martyr without complaint. As a soldier and a statesman, he is entitled to our admiration; as the martyr who bore without complaint the degradation of imprisonment and of chains (to the everlasting shame of the nineteenth century and the United States Government! be it said), he claims our grateful love and veneration. This monument must be erected, and as soon as possible. The committee has worked faithfully, but we must help. I am sure you feel, as I do, that we must erect such a monument, that coming generations will regard it with pride and wonder.

"The educational part of our work engages our minds and hearts. We must educate our Southern boys and girls as true Southerners should be educated, in the full knowledge of our war and the causes that led to it; they must be taught why their fathers gave up everything, even life itself, and the principles that were involved; they must be taught the history of the war and the history of the great men who made our country the glorious country it was; and this we can only secure by regulating the books that are used in our schools. Never falter in this work; it means everything to us and to our children.

"And now I come to the saddest portion of our year. Our hearts are filled with tender sympathy for a dear sister State whose sorrow and overwhelming anguish we can scarcely realize. Texas—our great, big-hearted, generous sister, who has ever been the friend of all in trouble—has been visited by such a calamity as the world has never seen equaled. Thirty-six hours of storm and wind and tidal wave, have laid the beautiful city of Galveston in a heap of ruins, and beneath these ruins are entombed ten thousand lives. The whole world stands aghast at such disaster. We mourn with our sisters in this dreadful hour of sorrow and anguish, and assure them of our love and sympathy.

"Now, my dear sisters, I will bring my lengthy address to a close, as every moment of time is precious. I thank you for the honor you have conferred upon me, and I pray that success may crown your work, not only for the coming year, but for all time, and that the faithful work of the United Daughters of the Confederacy may promote the good of our entire Southland. God bless you all."

Miss Mary F. Meares, the Corresponding Secretary, then submitted her report, which was adopted, and is as follows:

"Madam President, and Daughters of the Confederacy:

"There are happy moments that come to us all sometimes, and this is one of mine. It is indeed a happiness to be in Montgomery, the first capital of the Confederacy, rich in historic memories dear to us all; to know so many of her women, famed for their beauty and grace; to meet so many of the friends made at similar gatherings, and to have the opportunity of making new ones; to once more be honored in standing before this noble body to make an annual report as your Corresponding Secretary.

"During the past year I wrote 183 letters and 23 postal cards. This increase in correspondence is greatly due to the tremendous amount of work necessarily following the task we have assumed of erecting a monument to Jefferson Davis. In this connection, I have sent 975 circulars.

"Our Association, with its nearly twenty thousand members, is attracting attention outside this fair Southland of ours. With such a flourishing Chapter in New York, two Chapters in Pennsylvania, one in Indiana, three in California, four in Indian Territory, and one in Oklahoma Territory, the magazines and newspapers are beginning to feel that some notice must be taken of our Association. I have received letters from several of the leading magazines and papers, asking for information about our organization. As I stand here at the close of this nineteenth century and see how, in six short years, this organization has grown from a little, weak body of scarcely more than two hundred members, scattered in three or four States, to an immense society of nearly twenty thousand members, spread throughout these United States, I feel that if we grow in the new century, just dawning before us, as we have done in the old century, we will be like the seed promised to Abraham—without number. We have fought a good fight, but the battle is not yet won; we have run a good race, but the goal is not yet reached; so let us keep on working and growing until we can make the world acknowledge that the cause for which we struggled was just and right.

"In conclusion, let me thank you for the honor you have bestowed on me in twice electing me an officer of this grand and glorious body of women. Believing in the rotation of office and feeling that I have served my turn, and that some one else should have the honor, I lay down my work as an officer only to take it up with renewed zeal in the cause as a private in the ranks.

"I ask your indulgence for any mistakes made, and to feel that they were from the head, and not from the heart; and now, for myself, I want to thank you personally.

"Respectfully submitted, Mary F. Meares, Corresponding Secretary."[73]

Jefferson Davis, President of the Confederate States of America.

Alexander Hamilton Stephens, Vice President of the Confederate States of America.

General Robert Edward Lee, commander of the Confederate Army of Northern Virginia.

"Husbands, love your wives, even as Christ also loved the church and gave Himself for her." - Ephesians 5:25

APPENDIX C: MODERN FEMALE SUPPORTERS OF THE CONFEDERACY

A SMALL REPRESENTATION OF WOMEN FROM AROUND THE WORLD, WHO TODAY CONTINUE TO CHAMPION THE SOUTHERN CONFEDERACY & THE PRINCIPLES FOR WHICH SHE FOUGHT - & FOR WHICH SHE STILL STANDS

Amy Vachon
Arlene Barnum
Becky Muska
Beth Gayhart Collier
Candy White
Cassidy Ravensdale
Cathy Cornett Villarreal
Debbie Sidle
Dinah H. Kirkland
Eve Davenport Holder
Gail Rebecca Jessee
Judy Stephens

Karen Cooper
Kuuleme Stephens
Lani Burnette Rinkel
Lisa Stooksbury Thomas
Melinda Bowles Tabor
Rebecca Phillips Dalrymple
Rhonda Arimathaia Thacker Barrow
Sammy Hynds Harrison
Susan Frise Hathaway
Susan McKenney
Teresa Roane
Theresa Toney Willson

As in the Victorian Era, today's female Confederate supporters come from every country, race, religion, and background. This courageous woman is Karen Cooper of the Virginia Flaggers, holding one of the author's books.

APPENDIX D: CONTACTING THE UDC & OCR

UNITED DAUGHTERS OF THE CONFEDERACY
UDC Memorial Building
328 North Boulevard
Richmond, VA 23220-4009
Telephone: 804-355-1636
Fax: 804-353-1396
udc@hqudc.org
www.hqudc.org

CHILDREN OF THE CONFEDERACY (VIA THE UDC)
www.hqudc.org/children-of-the-confederacy

ORDER OF CONFEDERATE ROSE
www.scocr.org

As they did in the late 1800s and early 1900s, today the UDC and the OCR continue to work closely with members of the SCV, like the men pictured here, from Richmond, Virginia, 1896.

NOTES

1. See Jones, TDMV, pp. 144, 200-201, 273.
2. See Seabrook, TAHSR, passim. See also Stephens, ACVOTLW, Vol. 1, pp. 10, 12, 148, 150-151, 157-158, 161, 170, 192, 206, 210, 215, 219, 221-222, 238-240, 258-260, 288, 355, 360, 370, 382-384, 516, 575-576, 583, 587; Vol. 2, pp. 28-30, 32-33, 88, 206, 258, 631, 648; Pollard, LC, p. 178; J. H. Franklin, pp. 101, 111, 130, 149; Nicolay and Hay, ALCW, Vol. 1, p. 627.
3. See e.g., Seabrook, TQJD, pp. 30, 38, 76.
4. See e.g., J. Davis, RFCG, Vol. 1, pp. 55, 422; Vol. 2, pp. 4, 161, 454, 610. Besides using the term "Civil War" himself, President Davis cites numerous other individuals who use it as well.
5. See e.g., Confederate Veteran, March 1912, Vol. 20, No. 3, p. 122.
6. For more on this topic, see Seabrook, C101, passim.
7. For more on this topic, see Seabrook, TAOC, passim.
8. Davis, Vol. 1, p. iii.
9. Confederate Veteran, January 1898, Vol. 6, No. 1, pp. 11-12.
10. Confederate Veteran, August 1912, Vol. 20, No. 8, p. 367.
11. Confederate Veteran, May 1912, Vol. 20, No. 5, p. 203.
12. Confederate Veteran, October 1894, Vol. 2, No. 10, p. 294.
13. Confederate Veteran, August 1895, Vol. 3, No. 8, pp. 246-247.
14. Confederate Veteran, July 1894, Vol. 2, No. 7, p. 217.
15. Confederate Veteran, September 1895, Vol. 3, No. 9, p. 275.
16. Confederate Veteran, October 1898, Vol. 6, No. 10, p. 454.
17. Confederate Veteran, March 1895, Vol. 3, No. 3, p. 72.
18. Confederate Veteran, March 1898, Vol. 6, No. 3, pp. 105-106.
19. Confederate Veteran, July 1912, Vol. 20, No. 7, p. 335.
20. Confederate Veteran, October 1894, Vol. 2, No. 10, p. 307.
21. Confederate Veteran, April 1909, Vol. 17, No. 4, p. 178.
22. Article courtesy Lani Burnette Rinkel.
23. Confederate Veteran, September 1918, Vol. 26, No. 9, p. 414.
24. Confederate Veteran, October 1898, Vol. 6, No. 10, p. 484.
25. Confederate Veteran, April 1907, Vol. 15, No. 4, p. 179.
26. Confederate Veteran, April 1909, Vol. 17, No. 4, pp. 161-162.
27. Confederate Veteran, April 1907, Vol. 15, No. 4, p. 180.
28. Confederate Veteran, April 1895, Vol. 3, No. 4, p. 100.
29. Confederate Veteran, May 1893, Vol. 1, No. 5, pp. 147-149.
30. Confederate Veteran, January 1898, Vol. 6, No. 1, p. 42.
31. Confederate Veteran, June 1898, Vol. 6, No. 6, p. 249.
32. Confederate Veteran, April 1895, Vol. 3, No. 4, pp. 100-101.
33. Confederate Veteran, April 1898, Vol. 6, No. 4, pp. 162-163.
34. Confederate Veteran, October 1895, Vol. 3, No. 10, p. 310.
35. Confederate Veteran, July 1894, Vol. 2, No. 7, p. 217.
36. Confederate Veteran, January 1912, Vol. 20, No. 1, p. 12.
37. Confederate Veteran, July 1895, Vol. 3, No. 7, pp. 218-219.
38. Confederate Veteran, November 1912, Vol. 20, No. 11, p. 539.
39. Confederate Veteran, April 1898, Vol. 6, No. 4, p. 183.
40. Confederate Veteran, January 1903, Vol. 11, No. 1, pp. 35-36.
41. Confederate Veteran, January 1903, Vol. 11, No. 1, p. 7.
42. Confederate Veteran, March 1895, Vol. 3, No. 3, p. 85.
43. Confederate Veteran, October 1898, Vol. 6, No. 10, p. 482.
44. Confederate Veteran, June 1896, Vol. 4, No. 6, pp. 193-194.

45. Confederate Veteran, November 1896, Vol. 4, No. 11, pp. 361-362.
46. Seabrook, TMOCP, pp. 282-284, 372-374.
47. Ridley, pp. 490-502.
48. Confederate Veteran, November 1898, Vol. 6, No. 11, pp. 510-511.
49. Seabrook, ARB, pp. 393-394. See also pp. 21-22.
50. Confederate Veteran, September 1903, Vol. 11, No. 9, p. 408.
51. Confederate Veteran, January 1898, Vol. 6, No. 1, p. 18.
52. Confederate Veteran, October 1898, Vol. 6, No. 10, p. 479.
53. Seabrook, EOTBOF, s.v. "Harding, Selene."
54. Confederate Veteran, April 1894, Vol. 2, No. 4, pp. 105-108.
55. Confederate Veteran, October 1912, Vol. 20, No. 10, pp. 487-488.
56. Seabrook, EOTBOF, s.v. "Carter, Sallie."
57. Confederate Veteran, October 1895, Vol. 3, No. 10, p. 307.
58. Confederate Veteran, August 1907, Vol. 15, No. 8, p. 342.
59. Confederate Veteran, June 1907, Vol. 15, No. 6, p. 283.
60. Confederate Veteran, July 1898, Vol. 6, No. 7, p. 322.
61. Confederate Veteran, January 1908, Vol. 16, No. 1, p. 72.
62. Confederate Veteran, May 1912, Vol. 20, No. 5, p. viii.
63. Confederate Veteran, October 1895, Vol. 3, No. 10, p. 307.
64. Confederate Veteran, December 1907, Vol. 15, No. 12, p. 563.
65. Confederate Veteran, May 1894, Vol. 2, No. 5, p. 141.
66. Confederate Veteran, May 1909, Vol. 17, No. 5, p. 207.
67. Confederate Veteran, May 1918, Vol. 26, No. 5, p. 201.
68. Confederate Veteran, December 1894, Vol. 2, No. 12, p. 351 (first page of issue).
69. Confederate Veteran, August 1909, Vol. 17, No. 8, pp. 419-420.
70. Confederate Veteran, November 1898, Vol. 6, No. 11, p. 538.
71. Ritual courtesy Lani Burnette Rinkel.
72. Confederate Veteran, December 1895, Vol. 3, No. 12, pp. 374-376.
73. Minutes Seventh Annual Convention, UDC, November 14-17, 1900, pp. 3-8, 38-41, 43.

BIBLIOGRAPHY

V I C I T A G N U S N O S T E R, E U M S E Q U A M U R

Boyd, Belle. *Belle Boyd, In Camp and Prison*. 2 vols. London, UK: Saunders, Otley, and Co., 1865.

Browder, Earl. *Lincoln and the Communists*. New York, NY: Workers Library Publishers, Inc., 1936.

Davis, Jefferson. *The Rise and Fall of the Confederate Government*. 2 vols. New York, NY: D. Appleton and Co., 1881.

Franklin, John Hope. *Reconstruction After the Civil War*. Chicago, IL: University of Chicago Press, 1961.

Harkin, E. F., and C. H. L. Johnston. *Little Pilgrimages Among the Women Who Have Written Famous Books*. Boston, MA: L. C. Page and Co., 1901.

Johnstone, Huger William. *Truth of War Conspiracy, 1861*. Idylwild, GA: H. W. Johnstone, 1921.

Jones, John William. *The Davis Memorial Volume; Or Our Dead President, Jefferson Davis and the World's Tribute to His Memory*. Richmond, VA: B. F. Johnson, 1889.

McCarty, Burke (ed.). *Little Sermons in Socialism by Abraham Lincoln*. Chicago, IL: The Chicago Daily Socialist, 1910.

Miller, Francis Trevelyan (ed.). *The Photographic History of the Civil War*. 10 vols. New York, NY: The Review of Reviews Co., 1911.

Montagu, Ashley. *The Natural Superiority of Women*. 1952. New York, NY: Collier, 1992 ed.

Nicolay, John George, and John Hay (eds.). *Abraham Lincoln: Complete Works*. 12 vols. New York, NY: The Century Co., 1907.

Pollard, Edward Alfred. *The Lost Cause*. New York, NY: E. B. Treat and Co., 1867.

Ridley, Bromfield Lewis. *Battles and Sketches of the Army of Tennessee*. Mexico, MO: Missouri Printing and Publishing Co., 1906.

Seabrook, Lochlainn. *Abraham Lincoln: The Southern View*. 2007. Franklin, TN: Sea Raven Press, 2013 ed.

——. *The McGavocks of Carnton Plantation: A Southern History*. 2008. Franklin, TN: Sea Raven Press, 2011 ed.

——. *A Rebel Born: A Defense of Nathan Bedford Forrest*. 2010. Franklin, TN: Sea Raven Press, 2011 ed.

——. *Everything You Were Taught About the Civil War is Wrong, Ask a Southerner!* 2010. Franklin, TN: Sea Raven Press, revised 2014 ed.

——. *The Quotable Jefferson Davis: Selections From the Writings and Speeches of the Confederacy's First President*. Franklin, TN: Sea Raven Press, 2011.

——. *Lincolnology: The Real Abraham Lincoln Revealed In His Own Words*. Franklin, TN: Sea Raven Press, 2011.

———. *The Unquotable Abraham Lincoln: The President's Quotes They Don't Want You To Know!* Franklin, TN: Sea Raven Press, 2011.

———. *Encyclopedia of the Battle of Franklin: A Comprehensive Guide to the Conflict That Changed the Civil War.* Franklin, TN: Sea Raven Press, 2012.

———. *The Alexander H. Stephens Reader: Excerpts From the Works of a Confederate Founding Father.* Franklin, TN: Sea Raven Press, 2013.

———. *The Articles of Confederation: A Clause-by-Clause Study of America's First Constitution.* Franklin, TN: Sea Raven Press, 2014.

———. *Everything You Were Taught About American Slavery War is Wrong, Ask a Southerner!* Franklin, TN: Sea Raven Press, 2015.

———. *Confederacy 101: Amazing Facts You Never Knew About America's Oldest Political Tradition.* Franklin, TN: Sea Raven Press, 2015.

———. *The Great Yankee Coverup: What the North Doesn't Want You to Know About Lincoln's War!* Franklin, TN: Sea Raven Press, 2015.

Smedes, Susan Dabney. *Memorials of a Southern Planter.* Baltimore, MD: Cushings and Bailey, 1887.

Wilcox, Ella Wheeler. *Men, Women, and Emotions.* Chicago, IL; W. B. Conkey Co., 1899.

———. *The Heart of New Thought.* Chicago, IL: The Psychic Research Co., 1902.

———. *New Thought Pastels.* Holyoke, MA: Elizabeth Towne, 1906.

"The most interesting study of womankind is man." —
Ella Wheeler Wilcox, 1899

INDEX

Abernathy, Sadie, 206
Abraham (Bible), 321
Acklen, Adelicia, 229, 295
Adair, Ellen, 47
Adair, John, 47
Adams, John Q., 47
Adams, Shelby L., 344
Adams, William W., 175
Addison, Dr., 267
Akers, Albert, 261
Akers, Alice P., 261
Akin, Mary, 52
Akin, Warren, 52
Alfonso, XIII, King, 86
Allison, Margaret, 285
Allison, Mrs. John P., 139
Anderson, Loni, 344
Anderson, Neal, 312
Armstrong, Omagh, 160
Armstrong, Virginia B., 159
Arnett, Mrs. Charles T, 35
Arnold, Matthew, 18
Arthur, King, 343
Ashberry, Betsey, 251
Atkins, Chet, 344
Austin, Hallie H., 153
Avery, Elizabeth, 129
Baird, Fannie, 164, 229
Baker, Alice S., 164
Baker, Hyde, 276
Baldwin, Col., 28
Ball, Mary, 256
Ballentine, Sadie, 206, 207
Banks, Mary M., 234
Barbee, Nannie, 72
Barney, Nannie S., 246
Barnhart, Hester H., 128
Barnum, Arlene, 323
Barrow, Rhonda A. T., 323
Baruch, Sadie W., 137

Baskerville, Maj., 196
Bass, William, 195
Bassett, Lieut., 196
Bates, Mrs. Wharton, 237
Beal, Mrs. William, 151
Beale, Delia, 245
Beale, Mrs. J. D., 317
Beall, H. D., 96
Beall, Louise H., 96
Beall, Mrs. Thomas B., 142
Bean, Jennie C., 75
Beatty, Dr., 47
Beatty, Ellen A., 47
Beaumont, Capt., 197
Beaumont, Lomie, 233
Beauregard, Pierre G. T., 93, 272, 344
Bedichek, F. A., 199
Bedichek, J. M., 199, 203
Bedichek, Mary, 199, 200
Behan, Katie W., 92, 93
Behan, Mrs. W. J., 297
Bell, Dr., 220
Bell, Tyree H., 164
Bellamy, Eliza M., 139
Benjamin, Judah P., 316
Bennett, Rose, 32
Bernstein, Leonard, 344
Bethel, Col., 221
Bibb, Sophia, 24, 312
Black, Annie C., 161
Black, Mrs. John W., 125
Bland, Anna, 188, 228
Blank, J. P., 267
Blood, Col., 183
Blythe, Mrs. Turner A., 152
Bocock, Mrs. Thomas S., 244
Bolling, Edith, 344
Bonaparte, Napoleon, 104
Bond, Mrs. A. L., 150

Bond, Mrs. J. B., 173
Bonetti, Seth, 305
Boone, Daniel, 344
Boone, Laura, 282
Boone, Pat, 344
Booth, Pearl, 205, 206
Boothe, Mrs. W. J., 257
Boswell, Thomas T., 254
Boswell, William N., 254
Bowen, Ellen T., 251
Box, Capt., 202
Boyd, Belle, 272
Boyd, Jovita, 68
Boyd, Maria Isabella, 272
Boyd, Mary, 197
Brackin, Mae B. G., 159
Braden, Bessie, 206
Bradford, Mary, 192
Brady, Mr., 60
Bragg, Braxton, 69, 123, 228
Bragg, Elise B., 69
Breckinridge, John C., 344
Brevard, Marie, 278
Brewer, Sarah E., 169
Brewster, Bessie, 149
Briggs, George L., 248
Briggs, Minnie L. H., 248
Bringhurst, Robert, 52
Broadfoot, Kate H., 141
Brooke, Edward W., 344
Brooks, Preston S., 344
Brown, Bessie, 51
Brown, John C., 224
Brown, John T., 60
Brown, Mrs. G. A., 151
Brown, Mrs. John C., 160, 308
Brown, Mrs. Ridgley, 277
Bruce, Mrs. H. W., 71
Buchanan, James, 80
Buchanan, Patrick J., 344
Buck, Alice T., 263
Buford, Abraham, 344
Buford, Lieut., 195
Buford, Miss, 199
Buist, J. R., 196

Burke, Julian T., 257
Burnett, Elizabeth S. G., 68
Burwell, Fannie, 134
Busby, Fannie, 150
Bush, Bettina R., 278
Butler, Andrew P., 344
Butler, Benjamin F., 88
Butler, Capt., 220
Butler, Effie, 206
Bynum, Mrs. G. W., 280
Cabell, W. L., 241, 242
Cage, Annie G., 118
Cage, Edward, 118
Camp, Mrs. James B., 71
Campbell, Joseph, 343
Campbell, Mrs. Samuel, 200
Campbell, William, 228
Cantrell, Mrs. Perry, 176
Cantwell, Kate T., 136
Cappleman, Josie F., 299
Carlin, C. C., 257
Carloss, Mrs. James G., 237
Carlton, H. H., 58
Carr, Mrs. O. A., 290
Carrington, Paul, 196
Carson, Martha, 344
Carter, Anne H., 256
Carter, J. D., 58
Carter, Joseph W., 227
Carter, Mrs. Robert, 56, 223
Carter, Theodrick, 231, 344
Carter, Virginia, 206
Carter, WIlliam E., 226
Cary, Edward A., 302
Cary, Hetty, 97
Cary, Jennie, 97
Cash, Johnny, 344
Casler, Lucille B., 149
Casler, Mary V., 150
Catchings, Marjorie, 26
Catherwood, John, 75
Cato, Helen P., 197
Caudill, Benjamin E., 343
Cave, Rev., 129
Chandler, Enola A., 276

Cheairs, Nathaniel F., 208, 344
Cheairs, Susan P., 208
Cheatham, Frank, 185, 220, 223
Chesnut, Mary, 344
Chestney, Kate P., 55
Chestnut, Helen, 126
Childress, A. C., 89
Chipley, Clara, 44
Chisolm, Eliza L., 22
Christian, Julia J., 244
Christy, Howard, 80
Clark, E. A., 167
Clark, L. W., 165
Clark, Mrs. E. A., 167
Clark, Mrs. Isabelle M., 308
Clark, William, 344
Clarke, Lizzie, 245, 282
Clarke, Mrs. Lottie P., 308
Cleburne, Patrick R., 223, 224
Clement, Mrs. W. R., 151
Cleopatra, 191
Clingman, Thomas L., 146
Clopton, Minnie, 107
Clopton, Mrs. Clement C., 23
Clopton, Virginia C., 317
Cobb, Leoma, 150
Cochran, Carrie T., 21, 282
Cockrell, Frances M., 199
Cockrill, Jim, 197
Coleman, Estelle, 108
Coleman, Miss Claude V., 25
Collier, Beth G., 323
Colquhoun, Alice E., 257
Colquitt, Alfred H., 146
Combs, Bertram T., 344
Compton, Loulie, 161
Conklin, Grace L., 130
Cook, Mrs. W. J., 100
Cook, V. Y., 32
Cook, Varina, 32
Cooley, Mrs. Roselle C., 45
Cooper, Karen, 323
Copass, Mrs. J. H., 151
Corday, Charlotte, 191, 199
Cory, Mrs. Chappell, 312

Cotchet, Nesfield, 133
Couts, Mr., 240
Cowan, George L., 190
Cowan, Harriet Y., 189
Cox, Albert, 59
Cox, John I., 161
Cox, Mary, 161
Cozby, Marthy, 234
Craige, Josie, 137
Cravens, Mrs. J. L., 35
Crawford, Blanche, 206
Crawford, Cindy, 344
Crawford, Harriet A., 168
Crawford, Kate T., 166
Crittenden, Thomas T., 202, 203
Crocker, Mrs. Frank L., 245
Crockett, Davy, 344
Cromwell, Elisha, 134
Cromwell, Oliver, 104
Cruise, Tom, 344
Crump, Dr., 196
Crump, Mrs. W. B., 151
Culbertson, Mrs. W. T., 151
Cumming, Alfred, 224
Cummings, Mrs. M. E., 162
Cunningham, Nancy, 176
Curlee, Mrs. M. B., 280
Currie, Kate C., 239, 240
Curtis, Betsey, 251
Cyrus, Billy R., 344
Cyrus, Miley, 344
Daffan, Katie, 242, 301
Dalrymple, Rebecca P., 323
Damon, H. C., 234
Dasher, Sarah A., 304
Dashiell, Mrs. W. H., 245
Davenport, Elizabeth, 251
David (Bible), 295
Davidson, Mary P., 153
Davis, Caroline P., 162
Davis, Elizabeth, 172
Davis, Jefferson, 9, 11, 15, 17, 43, 52, 58, 66, 93, 103-105, 109, 112, 116, 117, 123, 126, 130, 169, 199, 228,

246, 251, 254, 262, 267, 274, 275, 279, 282, 286, 294-298, 301, 308, 312, 314, 316, 317, 319, 321, 343, 344
Davis, Jefferson C., 295
Davis, Jefferson, III, 286
Davis, Jefferson, Jr., 286
Davis, John R., 162
Davis, Margaret H., 275, 286, 294, 296, 298
Davis, Miss C. M., 266
Davis, Mrs. T. D., 151
Davis, Sam, 94, 171, 172, 175, 177, 178, 192, 207
Davis, Varina A., 178, 246, 275, 295
Davis, Varina H., 105, 106, 109, 246, 275, 279, 286, 294, 297, 298, 312
Dawson, Mrs. L. G., 317
de la Contrie, Marquis de Charette, 195
De La Houssaque, Edna S., 90
De Rosset, A. L., 148
De Rosset, Annie B., 138
De Rosset, Louis H., 148
De Rosset, M. John, 147
De Rosset, Mrs. Armand J., 145-147
De Rosset, Thomas C., 148
De Rosset, William L., 147
De Staël, Madam, 86, 191
Deaderick, Adelaide E., 163
Deering, Rose, 170
Dick, F. A., 127
Dickenson, Rebecca, 67
Dinsmore, Stella P., 236
Dodge, Gen., 192
Dollis, Joe, 229
Dorrity, Col., 221
Dowling, Dick, 240
Dowling, John D., 50
Dozier, Tennie P., 169
Dudley, Louise, 276
Dudley, Mary E., 162
Dudley, R. H., 162

Duke, Basil W., 73
Duke, Henrietta M., 73
Duke, Mrs. L. Z., 132
Dulaney, Mary, 276
Duncan, Mrs. James M., Jr., 117
Duncan, Nellie, 174
Dunlap, Mrs. Samuel C., 42
Dupont, Margaret, 206
Durham, Mrs., 151
Duval, Mary V., 205, 207
Duvall, Robert, 344
Dyer, Virginia, 162
d'Arc, Joan, 191
Early, Annie, 55
Edward I, King, 343
Edwards, Mrs. J. Griff, 245, 253, 254
Eggleston, Mrs. E. S., 119
Elliott, Joe, 181
Ellis, Edith K., 238
Ellis, Hallie, 56
Ellis, Josephine E., 159
Ellis, Mrs., 151
Ellyson, J. Taylor, 308
Ely, Nellie, 168
Emerson, Elise, 142
Emmett, Daniel D., 158
Epperson, Lulu B., 52
Erskine, Dr., 223
Erskine, John, 223
Eugénie, Empress, 86
Evans, Clement A., 37, 59, 62
Evans, Sarah L., 53
Ewell, Benjamin S., 264
Ewell, Col., 264
Ewing, Alexander C., 226
Ewing, Alexander H., 227
Ezelle, Agnes, 206
Falconer, Kinloch, 195
Farmer, Mrs. M. C., 151
Farrell, Jennie, 101
Ferguson, Mrs. J. M., 90
Ferguson, Mrs. Wayne P., 270
Ferguson, Wayne P., 270
Ficklen, Benjamin, 251
Fitzpatrick, Camille, 169

Foote, Shelby, 343
Forbes, Christopher, 344
Forney, Mrs. C. A., 35
Forrest, Mary A., 291
Forrest, Nathan B., 11, 163, 166, 174, 180, 190, 192, 208, 211, 232, 275, 276, 278, 281, 291, 343, 344
Forrest, Nathan B., III, 172
Forsythe, John, 224
Foster, Sarah A., 165
Fowler, May S., 36
Froudle, Mrs. Theodore R., 68
Fulmore, Mrs. Z. T., 234
Funkerhauser, Col., 197
Gabbett, Mrs., 319
Gaither, Felix Z., 173
Gaither, Mrs. Nat, 173
Gale, William D., 187
Gano, Richard M., 242
Garland, Emma J., 302
Gatson, Walker, 153
Gaut, John W., 227
Gaut, Sarah E., 226
Gayheart, Rebecca, 344
George III, King, 10
George, Walter F., 262
Gibbon, John, 30
Gill, Mollie Y., 214
Gilmore, Mary, 88
Gist, States R., 344
Goode, Dr., 196
Goodlett, Caroline M., 83, 84, 308, 317
Goodlett, Michael C., 83
Gordon, Augustus, 220
Gordon, Chapman, 219
Gordon, Charles, 219
Gordon, George W., 220, 222, 344
Gordon, James B., 220
Gordon, John B., 220
Gordon, Linda, 62
Gordon, Loulie M., 62
Gordon, Lute, 62
Gordon, Nat, 219

Gordon, Walter S., 62
Gordon, Wyley J., 220
Gordon-Law, Sallie C., 219
Gorman, Gladys, 135
Graham, Janie, 69
Grant, Ulysses S., 129
Grant, William, 251
Graves, Elenora, 69, 282
Graves, Robert, 343
Green, Mrs. Will S., 107
Green, Tom, 234
Greenhow, Rose O., 98
Greer, Alma, 40
Grier, Feriba, 137
Griffith, Andy, 344
Grundy, Felix, 230
Guaraldi, Vince, 344
Guild, Jo C., 27
Guild, Lafayette, 27-30
Guild, Pattie, 27-30
Gunter, Larkin, 193
Gunter, Marina, 193, 196
Hagood, Johnson, 146
Haley, Mary T., 174
Halstead, Murat, 63
Hamill, Anne J., 21
Hancock, Caroline, 79
Hancock, Mrs. G. H., 151
Hardee, Anna, 222
Hardee, William J., 23, 123, 222, 223
Hardeman, Etta, 53
Harding, John, 217
Harding, Selene, 217
Harding, William G., 217, 344
Harl, Nannie, 42
Harlow, M. B., 257
Harn, Hattie, 233
Harril, Mrs. T. C., 151
Harris, Alexander, 287
Harris, Mrs. Joe, 193
Harris, Mrs. S. W., 245
Harrison, Carter, 195
Harrison, Constance C., 97, 281
Harrison, Daisy H., 289

Harrison, Ellanetta, 73
Harrison, Mildred K., 245
Harrison, Sammy H., 323
Harrison, Thomas, 55
Harrison, William H., 195
Hatcher, Florence P., 175
Hathaway, Susan F., 323
Hatton, Robert H., 197
Hayes, Jefferson Davis, 286
Hayes, Joel A., Jr., 228, 286, 295, 296, 298
Hayes, Joel A., Sr., 295
Hayes, Lucy W., 105, 296
Hayes, Margaret D., 43
Hayes, Margaret H., 275, 279
Hayes, Oliver B., 228, 295
Hayes, Varina H., 295, 296
Hayes, William "Billy", 296
Hayne, Adele, 282
Hayne, Della, 153
Hayne, Mary, 266-268
Heard, Ethel T., 26
Helm, Ben H., 70
Helm, Mrs. Ben H., 70
Henderson, Bessie B., 135, 282
Henry, Patrick, 90
Hepburn, Hiatt P., 80
Hepburn, Susan P., 77-79
Heyward, Duncan C., 306
Hickey, John M., 164, 229
Hickman, Mrs. John P., 166, 308, 311, 312
Higginson, Thomas W., 185
Hill, Ambrose P., 28, 248, 249
Hill, Frances A., 248
Hill, Geraldine, 34
Hill, Henry, Jr., 248
Hill, Henry, Sr., 248
Hill, Lucy L., 240
Hill, Mrs. Ambrose P., 28
Hindale, Ellen D., 282
Hindman, Thomas C., 223, 224
Hindsdale, Elizabeth C., 140
Hines, Elizabeth D., 276
Hoke, Frances B., 282

Hoke, Lily, 136
Hoke, Robert F., 136, 146
Holder, Eve D., 323
Hood, Ida R., 236
Hood, John B., 192, 208, 344
Hood, Odile M., 89
Horner, Mimi P., 33
Houston, Sam, 195
Hughes, Mrs. D. J., 176
Hunter, Dr., 196
Hunter, Mrs. C. W., 246
Hussey, Eleanore F., 210
Hymes, Mrs. Henry, 242
Irwin, Mrs. J. W., 176
Jackson, Alfred E., 163
Jackson, Andrew, 48, 62, 75, 159, 344
Jackson, Hancock L., 83
Jackson, Henry R., 344
Jackson, Julia, 144
Jackson, Meta O., 163
Jackson, Mrs. Stonewall, 144, 244, 312
Jackson, Stonewall, 73, 103, 199, 244, 248, 258, 272, 288, 344
Jackson, William H., 217, 220
Jacobs, Elizabeth, 266, 268
James, Emmie S., 154
James, Frank, 344
James, Jesse, 344
Jefferson, Thomas, 63, 344
Jennings, Carrie, 160
Jent, Elias, Sr., 344
Jessee, Gail R., 323
Jester, Mrs. L. L., 240
Jesus, 343
John, Dr., 224
John, Elton, 344
Johns, Maggie, 280
Johns, Mary B., 191
Johnson, Andrew, 267
Johnson, Annie B., 70
Johnson, Col., 222
Johnson, Mrs. Cone, 237

Johnson, Mrs. Joseph, 102
Johnson, Thomas, 70
Johnston, Albert S., 27, 68, 71, 80, 176
Johnston, J. Stoddard, 77
Johnston, Joseph E., 11, 222, 224, 288
Johnston, Mrs. Albert S., 42
Johnston, Mrs. Joseph E., 224
Johnston, Sue, 167
Jones, Convére S., 136
Jones, J. C., 246
Jones, J. W., 59
Jones, James A., 251
Jones, Mary A., 154, 282
Jones, Mrs. B. L., 151
Jones, Rebecca C., 251
Jones, Sallie, 22
Jones, Victoria M., 90
Joplin, James W., 76
Jordan, Texa, 271
Judd, Ashley, 344
Judd, Naomi, 344
Judd, Wynonna, 344
Keenan, Sarah, 139
Kell, John M., 51
Keller, Helen, 26
Kelley, Lida, 125
Kellogg, J., 40
Kelly, Mrs., 151
Kennady, Margaret, 276
Key, Idene, 23
Kidder, Edith, 36
Kimbrough, Mary C., 291
King, T. S. N., 122
Kinney, Belle, 179, 180
Kirkland, Dinah H., 323
Kirkland, William W., 146
Kirkpatrick, Mary, 25
Kirkpatrick, Mrs. John A., 314
Kline, Mrs. W. L., 104
Knickerbocker, Percy, 151
Knox, Julia, 55
Knox, Sue, 36
Kyle, Kate, 201

Lafayette, Marquis de, 195
LaGree, Dr., 223
Lamar, Mrs. Walter D., 49, 50, 262
Lamar, Rev., 317
Landis, Corinne, 126
Lane, Mrs. W. P., 237
Langhorn, Morris, 196
Lanier, Sidney, 55
Latané, William D., 255
Latham, Mrs. T. J., 170
Law, Sarah, 163
Lee, Anne C., 256
Lee, Fitzhugh, 196, 246, 249, 256, 344
Lee, J. C., 21
Lee, Mrs. Fitzhugh, 246
Lee, Robert E., 27-30, 58, 85, 103, 104, 116, 125, 155, 174, 196, 199, 234, 245, 246, 248, 249, 253, 256, 288, 290, 309, 316, 322, 344
Lee, Robert E., Jr., 95
Lee, Stephen D., 6, 155, 344
Lee, William H. F., 344
Leonard, Sallie, 214
Lester, Laura, 131
Lewis, Annie D., 271
Lewis, Maud, 233
Lewis, Meriwether, 344
Lewis, Willie, 233
Lincoln, Abraham, 9, 11, 12, 14, 50, 163, 172, 188, 266, 274
Lippman, Mrs. Phil P., 68
Logan, Rev., 120
Long, Emily A., 138
Longstreet, James, 11, 344
Louise, Queen, 123
Loveless, Patty, 344
Lumpkin, Grace, 31
Lyon, A. A., 180
Lyon, Adelaide E., 163
Lyon, Susan W., 180
Macaulay, Thomas B., 14
Magruder, John B., 264
Mallory, Cora, 44

Mallory, Stephen R., 316
Manigault, Arthur M., 344
Manigault, Joseph, 344
Margaret, Princess, of Bavaria, 294
Margarite, Princess, 195
Marion, Francis, 220
Marks, Albert S., 123
Marks, Martha V., 37
Marmelstein, A. F., 55
Marmelstein, Louise, 55
Marshall, Harriet, 167
Marshall, Sally G., 276
Martin, Flora, 235
Martin, Laura, 105
Martin, Mrs. Aldred, 147
Marvin, Lee, 344
Mason, Emily, 85, 86
Mason, Stevens T., 85
Mathis, J. Harvey, 106
Matthews, George B., 290
Matthews, Robert, 159
Maury, Abram P., 344
Maury, Dabney H., 152
Maxey, Ora S., 149
Maxwell, Clarence W., 101
Maxwell, D. E., 101
Maxwell, Rebecca E., 100
Maxwell, William M., 101
May, White, 167
McAdams, Ellen L., 209
McClain, Levisa L., 50
McClendon, John J., 62
McCulloch, Grace, 128
McDaniel, Pattie, 67
McDougald, Annie, 54, 282
McFall, Anna E., 67
McGavock, Caroline E., 186-189, 344
McGavock, David H., 344
McGavock, Elizabeth I., 217
McGavock, Emily, 344
McGavock, Francis, 344
McGavock, James R., 344
McGavock, John W., 186, 189, 230, 344
McGavock, Lysander, 344
McGavock, Randal, 217
McGavock, Randal W., 344
McGavock, Sallie, 227
McGee, Lillie, 33
McGibbon, Miss, 289
McGinnis, Ellen B., 301
McGowan, Anna M., 126
McGowan, R. J., 126
McGraw, Tim, 344
McGuire, John P., 251
McIntosh, Miss, 105
McKenney, Susan, 323
McKinney, Annie B., 171
McKissack, Susan P., 208
McLaws, Lafayette, 264, 265
McLure, Lewis S., 128
McLure, M. A. E., 128
McLure, Mrs. M. A. E., 127
McLure, William R., 128
McMurray, Adele, 164, 282
Meade, Mrs. Richard K., 28
Meares, Gaston, 147
Meares, Mary F., 320, 321
Meminger, Christopher G., 316
Meriwether, Elizabeth A., 344
Meriwether, Minor, 129, 344
Meriwether, Mrs. Minor, 129
Metcalfe, Mrs. J. M., 173
Milledge, John, 57
Milledge, Mrs. John, 57, 59, 60
Miller, Georgia, 55
Miller, J. R., 34
Miller, James H., 271
Miller, James R., 34
Miller, Jean, 271
Miller, Jefferson D., 55
Miller, Jessie, 55
Miller, Louise, 55
Miller, May, 49
Miller, Mrs. James R., 34
Milner, Mary C., 23
Milton, John, 203
Mitchell, Caroline, 51
Mitchell, Etta, 106, 282

Mitchell, Lizzie, 143
Mitchell, Lou, 276
Mitchell, Lucy B., 279
Mock, L. Byrd, 33
Monroe, James, 85
Monroe, Thomas D., 70
Montague, Lula, 96, 282
Montgomery, Mary A., 291
Moore, Ethel, 177
Moore, Eva, 206
Moore, Robert, 197
Moore, Tom, 215
Morgan, John H., 73, 126, 192, 197, 344
Morgan, William H., 107
Morris, Mary L., 185
Morrison, Mary A., 244
Morton, Albert S., 203
Morton, Gen., 29
Morton, John W., 344
Mosby, John S., 344
Moss, J. W., 81
Moss, Kate, 81
Moss, Miss Joe, 81
Moss, Thomas E., 81
Motes, Eva, 52
Mullen, Mr., 268
Mumford, Mrs. William B., 88
Mumford, William B., 88
Munday, Sue, 192, 193
Murphy, Jeannette R., 68
Muse, Katie C., 241
Musgrove, Mrs. E., 24
Muska, Becky, 323
Myers, Penelope B., 134
Napoleon III, 191
Nash, Lydia L., 135
Nash, Sophia, 245
Neeley, Elizabeth, 245
Neely, Janie, 245
Nelson, Ella, 21
Nelson, Evelyn, 56
Nelson, John, 254
Nelson, Martha, 254
Nelson, Thomas, 254

Nelson, William, 254
Newbill, Grace M., 168
Newsom, Ella K., 121-124
Newsom, Frank, 122
Newton, Mrs. Willoughby, 255
Nichols, J. H., 193
Nichols, Kate L. S., 211
Nightingale, Florence, 121, 123, 191
Nisbet, Blanche, 51
Norris, Mrs. Owen, 96
Northen, William J., 63
Norton, J. K. M., 257
Nugent, Ted, 344
Oakes, Florence, 206
Oaks, Col., 222
Obenchain, W. O., 82
Ochs, Mrs. Fannie Van Dyke, 170
Odem, Tennie J., 235
Odenheimer, Mrs. F. G., 96
Ogilvie, Mrs., 214
Ottley, Mrs. John K., 54
Ottley, Passie M., 53
Overman, Margie, 137
Overton, John, 167
Owen, Frank A., 64
Owen, Ruth, 64
Oxford, Josie, 22, 52
O'Brien, Mrs. E. H., 317
O'Bryan, J. B., 205
Pace, Eleanore D., 234
Page, George, 291
Page, Mary R., 251
Page, Susan, 291
Paine, Eleazer A., 212
Palmer, Joseph B., 123
Park, Fanny, 229
Parks, Mary, 276
Parsley, Mrs. William M., 308, 311
Parsley, Murdoch, 142
Parton, Dolly, 344
Pasco, Elizabeth, 44, 282
Patee, Annie, 126
Patterson, Kate, 192
Patterson, Mary B., 250
Payne, I. H., 151

Peay, Caroline P., 33
Pegram, John, 97
Pender, William D., 134
Pendleton, Mrs. E. C., 107
Penzel, Charles F., 34
Penzel, Hedwig, 34
Perry, Willie A., 276
Pettus, Edmund W., 344
Peyton, Carrie, 55
Philips, Martha W., 133
Phillips, Charles W., 175
Phillips, Robert, 197
Pickett, Anastasia, 285
Pickett, Mrs. W. S., 222
Pilcher, M. B., 73
Pilcher, Matt, 230
Pilcher, Mrs. M. B., 73
Pillow, Gideon J., 221, 222, 344
Pitcher, Molly, 191
Pitman, Mary I., 169
Plane, C. Helen, 54
Plane, Mrs. , 319
Polk, Andrew Jackson, 194
Polk, Antoinette, 194
Polk, Bessie, 233
Polk, Cad, 197
Polk, James K., 344
Polk, Leonidas, 174, 221, 344
Polk, Lucius E., 344
Polk, Mrs. James K., 48
Polk, Omi, 233
Polk, Thomas, 144
Pollard, Miss R. M., 25
Porter, Felicia G., 230
Porter, Sam, 150
Powell, Ella M., 52
Presley, Elvis, 344
Preston, Henrietta, 80
Preston, William, 79
Price, Daisy, 276
Price, Helen, 197
Price, Sterling, 126, 128, 184, 240, 242
Prichard, Mary G., 244
Pulliam, Nannie, 285

Quarles, William A., 188, 230
Quintard, Charles T., 197
Raines, Anna M. D., 268
Raines, Mrs. L. H., 52, 308
Rambo, Regina E., 51
Ramsay, G. W., 257
Ramseur, Dodson, 139
Ramsey, Margaret V., 37
Randle, Lucy P., 285
Randolph, Edmund J., 344
Randolph, George W., 344
Randolph, Mrs. Norman, 319
Rankin, Grace, 138
Rankin, Jennie M., 136
Rathbone, Jeannette F., 288
Ravensdale, Cassidy, 323
Ray, Alice C., 133
Ray, Willie E., 140
Reagan, John H., 242, 316
Reagan, Ronald, 344
Recamier, Juliette, 191
Reed, William G., 144
Reeves, Lillian C., 35
Reid, Charles M., 266-268
Reid, L. W., 257
Reid, Martha, 101
Reid, Mrs. L. W., 257
Renn, Reita, 245
Reynolds, Burt, 344
Reynolds, Mary, 206
Rhea, Louise, 206
Richard, J. Fraise, 121
Richardson, Belle, 65, 66
Richardson, J. J., 65
Richardson, Mrs. R. N., 226
Ridley, Bessie, 245
Ridley, Bromfield L., 191
Ridley, Julia F., 49
Ridley, Mrs. Robert, Jr., 245
Rinkel, Lani B., 284, 301, 305, 323
Rivers, Martha, 206
Roane, Teresa, 97, 301, 305, 323
Robbins, Hargus, 344
Robert the Bruce, King, 343
Roberts, Eugenia, 143

Robertson, Mrs., 240
Robinson, Edwin, 60
Robinson, Fanny C., 57, 60
Roddie, Reuben M., 151
Roden, B. F., 23
Roden, Lillian, 23
Rogers, R. L., 59
Roosevelt, Theodore, 85, 93
Rose, S. E. F., 105
Rosecrans, William S., 196, 228
Rosser, Thomas L., 96
Rounsaville, Hallie A., 54
Rucker, Edmund W., 344
Rutherford, Mildred L., 49, 268
Rutherford, Miss, 319
Sansom, Dr., 120
Sansom, Emma, 192, 281
Sanson, Mrs. R. H., 173
Saul (Bible), 295
Saunders, Fanny S., 106
Saunders, Olivia B., 142
Saunders, W. J., 106
Sawyer, Daisy M., 138
Scott, Birdie, 90
Scott, George C., 344
Scott, H., 267
Scott, Mary E., 74
Scruggs, Earl, 344
Seabrook, John L., 344
Seabrook, Lochlainn, 14-16, 155, 156, 176, 323, 343-345
Sebring, Mrs. W. H., 181
Seger, Bob, 344
Selden, Caroline, 259
Semmes, Elizabeth, 251
Semmes, Raphael, 28, 180
Semple, Letitia T., 263-265
Semple, Mary S., 70
Sentell, Nellie, 150
Sevier, Mrs. L. V., 176
Shelby, Gladys, 125
Shelby, Joseph O., 125
Sheridan, Philip H., 193
Sherman, William T., 183, 291
Shields, W. C., 264

Shweizer, J., 40
Sidle, Debbie, 323
Simmons, Debbie, 166
Sims, Boyd M., 227
Sims, Daisy, 140
Sims, Heloise, 285
Sims, J. M., 140
Skaggs, Ricky, 344
Sloan, J. B. E., 154
Sloan, Marguerite, 154
Sloan, Mrs. Homer F., 32
Smith, Alleen, 278
Smith, Baxter, 229
Smith, Churchill S. P., 251
Smith, Edmund K., 44, 63, 259
Smith, Emma F. L., 269
Smith, Gen., 183
Smith, Imogene, 262
Smith, Mary A., 275
Smith, Mrs. Edmund K., 259
Smith, Peter, 251
Smith, Preston, 223
Smoot, William A., 257
Smythe, James A., 306
Smythe, Louisa M., 311
Smythe, Mrs., 308
Snaden, Capt., 251
Snow, Adelaide B., 282
Snowden, Mary A., 156
Spivey, Eula, 32
Spurr, Julia H., 71
Stark, Clair, 276
Stedman, Charles M., 262
Stephens, Alexander H., 9, 11, 316, 322, 344
Stephens, Judy, 323
Stephens, Kuuleme, 289, 323
Sterrett, Cmdre., 267
Sterrett, Samuel, 267
Stewart, Alexander P., 187, 191, 195, 344
Stiles, Rev., 224
Stirling, Kittiebelle, 24
Stone, Cornelia B., 297
Stovall, Elizabeth, 67

Strauss, Henry, 257
Streight, Abel D., 192
Stuart, Douglas, 257
Stuart, Jeb, 96, 249, 255, 291, 344
Stuart, Katherine H., 257
Stuart, Sallie, 257
Stubbs, Annie T., 89
Sumpter, Thomas, 220
Sydnor, Seabrook W., 238
Tabb, Augusta, 251
Tabb, Juliette O., 288
Tabb, Mrs. Randolph, 251
Tabor, Melinda B., 323
Talliaferro, Edwin, 264
Tallien, Mesdames, 191
Tanner, Lassie, 149
Taylor, M. R., 148
Taylor, Margaret, 276
Taylor, Richard, 11, 344
Taylor, Robert, 196
Taylor, Sarah K., 344
Taylor, Zachary, 344
Tench, Mrs. John W., 44
Thedford, Old Mrs., 166
Thomas, George H., 192
Thomas, Jane, 197
Thomas, Lisa S., 323
Thomas, Mrs. J. Jefferson, 308
Thomson, Stella M., 133
Thornton, Blanche A., 135
Thornton, Harriet A. S., 168
Thrash, Mrs. T. W., 134, 142
Tinsley, Dr., 264
Tocqueville, Alexis de, 307
Todhunter, Emory, 125
Toland, Margaret T., 36
Tompkins, Christopher, 250
Tompkins, Sally L., 250, 251
Torrance, Kate, 137
Trader, Ella K., 124
Trader, W. H., 124
Trigg, Mary, 206
Trousdale, Felix G., 165
Trousdale, William H., 174
Tyler, C. W., 165

Tyler, Emmie, 165
Tyler, John, 63, 263
Tynes, Ellen B., 344
Underwood, Ellen, 141
Vachon, Amy, 323
Van Dyke, Fannie, 170
Van Hoose, Jennie, 22
Van Leer, Sam, 197
Van Wyck, Mrs. Sidney, 42
Van Zandt, Virginia, 281
Vance, Robert B., 344
Vance, Zebulon, 138, 344
Vanmeter, Charles J., 81
Vanmeter, Kate M., 81, 82
Vega, Manny, 302
Venable, Charles S., 344
Vernon, Mrs., 222
Villarreal, Cathy C., 323
Vinson, Ada, 282
Vinson, Annie, 164
Vinson, Ida H., 88
Vivian, Alice, 230
Volck, Adalbert J., 249
Walcott, Mrs. Arthur, 151
Walker, Leroy P., 316
Walker, Maud, 245
Walker, Mrs. Owen, 159
Walker, Pope, 264
Wall, W. H., 267
Wallis, J. D., 229
Walshe, Elizabeth Q., 89
Warfield, Edgar, 257
Waring, Margaret, 153
Washington, Elizabeth W., 95
Washington, George, 9, 45, 256
Washington, John A., 344
Washington, Mary B., 256, 257
Washington, Mrs. J. E., 257
Washington, Thornton A., 344
Waterman, Alice W., 273
Watt, Elizabeth R., 144
Watts, Ann C., 37
Waud, Alfred R., 247, 255
Wayne, Anthony, 194
Webb, Gerald B., 296, 298

Webb, Lieut., 267
Webb, Margaret V., 296, 298
Webb, Mrs. Gerald B., 279
Webb, Robina, 296, 298
Webb, Varina M., 279
Weed, Mrs. Edwin G., 312, 315, 317
Welch, Mrs. D. A., 176
Welford, Mrs. John S., 251
Welles, Gideon, 267
Wellington, Duke of, 104
West, Decca L., 235
Westmoreland, Willis, 264
Wheeler, Ella, 55
Wheeler, Joseph, 55, 178, 236
Wheeler, Joseph, Jr., 55
Whitaker, Bessie, 139
White, Candy, 302, 323
White, Florida, 47, 48
White, Joseph M., 47, 48
White, Julia A., 88
White, Modena, 64
White, Mrs. Alexander B., 160, 276
Whiteside, Harriet L., 172
Whiting, William H. C., 146
Wickham, Mrs. William C., 196
Wickham, William C., 249
Wilcox, Ella W., 94, 329
Wilkes, Florence, 206
Wilkes, Mary A., 168
Wilkins, Sadie, 245
Wilkins, Sallie, 224
Wilkinson, Margaret, 285
Williams, Emma, 245
Williams, Louise A., 56
Williams, Maribel, 25
Willingham, Mary, 275
Willis, Mrs., 240
Willson, Theresa T., 323
Wilson, Louise, 245
Wilson, Virginia, 173
Wilson, Woodrow, 344
Winder, Caroline E., 186, 188, 189
Winder, Charles S., 344
Winder, John H., 344
Winstead, Mrs. R. O., 171

Winston, Judith, 230
Wintersmith, Emma, 276
Wintersmith, Margaret F., 276
Witherspoon, Holly, 71
Witherspoon, Reese, 344
Womack, John B., 344
Womack, Lee Ann, 344
Woodruff, Robbie, 192, 195
Woodside, Mrs. H. E., 176
Woodward, Elizabeth, 139
Woodward, Emma, 139
Wooldridge, John H., 177
Wormeley, Mary E., 163
Wright, Agatha, 236
Wright, Mrs. E. D., 108
Yandel, Dr., 221
Zachary, Capt., 264
Zollicoffer, Ann M., 173
Zollicoffer, Felix K., 173, 344

MEET THE AUTHOR

"ASKING THE PATRIOTIC SOUTH TO STOP HONORING HER CONFEDERATE ANCESTORS
IS LIKE ASKING THE SUN NOT TO SHINE." — COLONEL LOCHLAINN SEABROOK

LOCHLAINN SEABROOK, a Kentucky Colonel and the winner of the prestigious Jefferson Davis Historical Gold Medal for his "masterpiece," *A Rebel Born: A Defense of Nathan Bedford Forrest*, is an unreconstructed Southern historian, award-winning author, Civil War scholar, Bible authority, and traditional Southern Agrarian of Scottish, English, Irish, Dutch, Welsh, German, and Italian extraction.

A child prodigy, Seabrook is today a true Renaissance Man, whose occupational titles also include encyclopedist, lexicographer, musician, artist, graphic designer, genealogist, photographer, and award-winning poet. Also a songwriter and a screenwriter, he has a 40 year background in historical nonfiction writing and is a member of the Sons of Confederate Veterans, the Civil War Trust, and the National Grange. Due to similarities in their writing styles, ideas, and literary works, Seabrook is often referred to as the "new Shelby Foote," the "Southern Joseph Campbell," and the "American Robert Graves" (his English cousin).

The grandson of an Appalachian coal-mining family, Seabrook is a seventh-generation Kentuckian, co-chair of the Jent/Gent Family Committee (Kentucky), founder and director of the Blakeney Family Tree Project, and a board member of the Friends of Colonel Benjamin E. Caudill.

Above, Colonel Lochlainn Seabrook, award-winning Civil War scholar and unreconstructed Southern historian. America's most popular and prolific pro-South author, his many books have introduced hundreds of thousands to the truth about the War for Southern Independence. He holds the world's record for writing the most books on Nathan Bedford Forrest: nine.

Seabrook's literary works have been endorsed by leading authorities, museum curators, award-winning historians, bestselling authors, celebrities, noted scientists, well respected educators, TV show hosts and producers, renowned military artists, esteemed Southern organizations, and distinguished academicians from around the world.

Seabrook has authored over 45 popular adult books on the American Civil War, American and international slavery, the U.S. Confederacy (1781), the Southern Confederacy (1861), religion, theology and thealogy, Jesus, the Bible, the Apocrypha, the Law of Attraction, alternative health, spirituality, ghost stories, the paranormal, ufology, social issues, and cross-cultural studies of the family and marriage. His Confederate biographies, pro-South studies, genealogical monographs, family histories, military encyclopedias, self-help guides, and etymological dictionaries have received wide acclaim.

Seabrook's eight children's books include a Southern guide to the Civil War, a biography of Nathan Bedford Forrest, a dictionary of religion and myth, a rewriting of the King Arthur legend (which reinstates the original pre-Christian motifs), two bedtime stories for preschoolers, a naturalist's guidebook to owls, a worldwide look at the family, and an examination of the Near-Death Experience.

Of blue-blooded Southern stock through his Kentucky, Tennessee, Virginia, West Virginia, and North Carolina ancestors, he is a direct descendant of European royalty via his 6th great-grandfather, the Earl of Oxford, after which London's famous Harley Street is named. Among his celebrated male Celtic ancestors is Robert the Bruce, King of Scotland, Seabrook's 22nd great-grandfather. The 21st great-grandson of Edward I "Longshanks" Plantagenet), King of England, Seabrook is a thirteenth-generation Southerner through his descent from the colonists of Jamestown, Virginia (1607).

The 2nd, 3rd, and 4th great-grandson of dozens of Confederate soldiers, one of his closest connections to Lincoln's War is through his 3rd great-grandfather, Elias Jent, Sr., who fought for the Confederacy in the Thirteenth Cavalry Kentucky under Seabrook's 2nd cousin, Colonel Benjamin E. Caudill. The Thirteenth, also known as "Caudill's Army," fought in numerous conflicts, including the Battles of Saltville, Gladsville, Mill Cliff, Poor Fork, Whitesburg, and Leatherwood.

Seabrook is a direct descendant of the families of Alexander H. Stephens, John Singleton Mosby, William Giles Harding, and Edmund Winchester Rucker, and is related to the following Confederates and other 18th- and 19th-Century luminaries: Robert E. Lee, Stephen Dill Lee, Stonewall Jackson, Nathan Bedford Forrest, James Longstreet, John Hunt Morgan, Jeb Stuart, Pierre G. T. Beauregard (approved the Confederate Battle Flag design), George W. Gordon, John Bell Hood, Alexander Peter Stewart, Arthur M. Manigault, Joseph Manigault, Charles Scott Venable, Thornton A. Washington, John A. Washington, Abraham Buford, Edmund W. Pettus, Theodrick "Tod" Carter, John B. Womack, John H. Winder, Gideon J. Pillow, States Rights Gist, Henry R. Jackson, John Lawton Seabrook, John C. Breckinridge, Leonidas Polk, Zachary Taylor, Sarah Knox Taylor (first wife of Jefferson Davis), Richard Taylor, Davy Crockett, Daniel Boone, Meriwether Lewis (of the Lewis and Clark Expedition) Andrew Jackson, James K. Polk, Abram Poindexter Maury (founder of Franklin, TN), Zebulon Vance, Thomas Jefferson, Edmund Jennings Randolph, George Wythe Randolph (grandson of Jefferson), Felix K. Zollicoffer, Fitzhugh Lee, Nathaniel F. Cheairs, Jesse James, Frank James, Robert Brank Vance, Charles Sidney Winder, John W. McGavock, Caroline E. (Winder) McGavock, David Harding McGavock, Lysander McGavock, James Randal McGavock, Randal William McGavock, Francis McGavock, Emily McGavock, William Henry F. Lee, Lucius E. Polk, Minor Meriwether (husband of noted pro-South author Elizabeth Avery Meriwether), Ellen Bourne Tynes (wife of Forrest's chief of artillery, Captain John W. Morton), South Carolina Senators Preston Smith Brooks and Andrew Pickens Butler, and famed South Carolina diarist Mary Chesnut.

Seabrook's modern day cousins include: Patrick J. Buchanan (conservative author), Cindy Crawford (model), Shelby Lee Adams (Letcher Co., Kentucky, photographer), Bertram Thomas Combs (Kentucky's 50th governor), Edith Bolling (wife of President Woodrow Wilson), and actors Andy Griffith, George C. Scott, Robert Duvall, Reese Witherspoon, Lee Marvin, Rebecca Gayheart, and Tom Cruise.

Seabrook's screenplay, *A Rebel Born*, based on his book of the same name, has been signed with acclaimed filmmaker Christopher Forbes (of Forbes Film). It is now in pre-production, and is set for release in 2017 as a full-length feature film. This will be the first movie ever made of Nathan Bedford Forrest's life story, and as a historically accurate project written from the Southern perspective, is destined to be one of the most talked about Civil War films of all time.

Born with music in his blood, Seabrook is an award-winning, multi-genre, BMI-Nashville songwriter and lyricist who has composed some 3,000 songs (250 albums), and whose original music has been heard in film (*A Rebel Born*, *Cowgirls 'n Angels*, *Confederate Cavalry*, *Billy the Kid: Showdown in Lincoln County*, *Vengeance Without Mercy*, *Last Step*, *County Line*, *The Mark*) and on TV and radio worldwide. A musician, producer, multi-instrumentalist, and renown performer—whose keyboard work has been variously compared to pianists from Hargus Robbins and Vince Guaraldi to Elton John and Leonard Bernstein—Seabrook has opened for groups such as the Earl Scruggs Review, Ted Nugent, and Bob Seger, and has performed privately for such public figures as President Ronald Reagan, Burt Reynolds, Loni Anderson, and Senator Edward W. Brooke. Seabrook's cousins in the music business include: Johnny Cash, Elvis Presley, Billy Ray and Miley Cyrus, Patty Loveless, Tim McGraw, Lee Ann Womack, Dolly Parton, Pat Boone, Naomi, Wynonna, and Ashley Judd, Ricky Skaggs, the Sunshine Sisters, Martha Carson, and Chet Atkins.

Seabrook, a libertarian, lives with his wife and family in historic Middle Tennessee, the heart of Forrest country and the Confederacy, where his conservative Southern ancestors fought valiantly against Liberal Lincoln and the progressive North in defense of Jeffersonianism, constitutional government, and personal liberty.

LochlainnSeabrook.com

If you enjoyed this book you will be interested in Colonel Seabrook's other popular related titles:

- EVERYTHING YOU WERE TAUGHT ABOUT THE CIVIL WAR IS WRONG, ASK A SOUTHERNER!
- EVERYTHING YOU WERE TAUGHT ABOUT AMERICAN SLAVERY IS WRONG, ASK A SOUTHERNER!
- CONFEDERATE FLAG FACTS: WHAT EVERY AMERICAN SHOULD KNOW ABOUT DIXIE'S SOUTHERN CROSS
- CONFEDERACY 101: AMAZING FACTS YOU NEVER KNEW ABOUT AMERICA'S OLDEST POLITICAL TRADITION

Available from Sea Raven Press and wherever fine books are sold

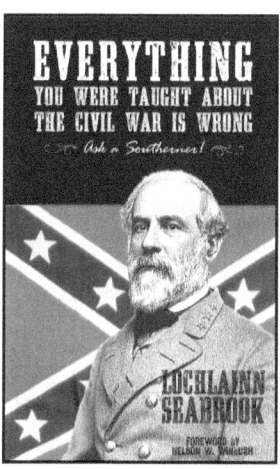

ALL OF OUR BOOK COVERS ARE AVAILABLE AS 11" X 17" POSTERS, SUITABLE FOR FRAMING.

SeaRavenPress.com • NathanBedfordForrestBooks.com

www.ingramcontent.com/pod-product-compliance
Lightning Source LLC
Chambersburg PA
CBHW020323170426
43200CB00006B/257